Henry B. Zimmer

The New
CANADIAN
REAL ESTATE
Investment Guide

Hurtig Publishers/Edmonton

Acknowledgements

This book is dedicated to the many real-estate investors, developers and their advisers who have attended my tax seminars over the years and have asked me to put it all down in writing.

I wish to thank my good friends Steve Katz of Vancouver and Leon Snider of Calgary—Steve for reviewing my material on U.S. real-estate investment and development activities for technical accuracy, and Leon for his valuable insights into real-estate investment alternatives.

A special thank you is reserved for my editor, Ingrid Philipp Cook, who polished my somewhat garbled prose not only for this book but also its predecessor, *The New Canadian Tax & Investment Guide*.

Above all, however, I would like to thank my wife, Shana, who is my greatest asset and mother of all my liabilities, for her encouragement and for typing this manuscript.

HBZ

Hurtig Publishers Ltd.
10560–105 Street
Edmonton, Alberta

Canadian Cataloguing in Publication Data

Zimmer, Henry B., 1943–
    The new Canadian real estate investment guide

ISBN 0-88830-211-8

    1. Real estate investment—Canada.   I. Title.
HD316.Z54   332.63'24'0971   C81-091334-8

Printed and bound in Canada by T.H. Best Printing Company Ltd.

Contents

CHAPTER ONE

Real Estate— A Hedge Against Inflation in the 1980s

In most places, the cost of rental properties has escalated dramatically over the last five years. At one time, a decision whether or not to make a real-estate investment was relatively simple. One hoped to break even or perhaps make a small profit on rents. Then, one could sit back and wait for capital appreciation. However, with inflation, concepts have changed. As prices go higher, there is significantly less emphasis on rental income and more importance is placed on the potential for capital growth. Even where a property fails to carry itself, the owner will very often tolerate this and subsidize his tenants in order to obtain appreciation.

Most investors tend to be persons in middle or upper income brackets. A fairly comprehensive understanding of tax implications is therefore extremely important before investment decisions can be made. This is because, out of each dollar of profit, many investors can expect to have at least 50% confiscated by the government. Conversely, if an investment generates a loss and the loss is deductible, the after-tax cost of incurring it is reduced to only one-half.

Today's high interest rates also contribute greatly to the fact that most investment properties generate negative cashflows (unless a large cash downpayment is made). Thus, an important aspect of *effective* ownership is to force the *government* to participate in subsidization. This is done by taking advantage of any write-offs that are available during the construction period (as described in Chapter Five), maximizing tax deductions during the ownership period and minimizing or postponing taxes resulting out of profits on sale.

This book will concentrate on tax aspects, although certainly the most important point is to research the actual rental market thoroughly before making an investment. If you don't have the expertise to do this, a good agent is mandatory. How do you know if any agent is in fact "good"? Certainly, he must be knowledgeable in the real-estate market and must be able to follow trends in prices. He should have many contacts among potential sellers *and* among local politicians to ensure a favourable response to requests for zoning approvals and construction permits.

A word of caution is in order. The tax planning concepts discussed in this book are based on laws in force as of June 30, 1981. Each year, the federal government brings down at least one Budget which makes modifications to the rules. Often, many of the changes are not of interest to the average person. In addition, the general framework of the Income Tax Act remains the same from year to year. However, keeping up with the tax rules is an ongoing process. For taxation concepts affecting your real-estate investments, this book may be only your starting point. Beyond checking out specific ideas with your own advisers, I strongly recommend that you keep up to date by reading digests of Budget proposals which appear in publications such as the *Financial Post* or the *Financial Times*. Your own accountants should be able to explain any relevant changes to you a few days after each Budget. As you will see in reading this book, you must always think in terms of after-tax dollars and discount additional investment income that you receive by the tax burden of earning it. Conversely, costs and expenses related to real-estate investment should be discounted by the appropriate tax bracket where these outlays are deductible.

The type of rental property which you choose to acquire is primarily a function of your own preferences. With respect to residential housing, there appears to be a continuing shortage of such accommodation in Canada. However, the spectre of rent controls may make this type of investment less attractive, although it is probably easier to enter the residential market in the first place. You could, for example, start with a single-family home or small duplex as a rental property.

Non-residential real estate might be somewhat more complex and more difficult to understand than a home or apartment investment. The basics of commercial real-estate are not, however, very different. Fortunately, non-residential investments are not endangered by politicians seeking votes from tenants. Thus, there are no rent controls. Returns also tend to be a little higher and, as leases become due, rents are generally increased.

The biggest problem with respect to non-residential investments is to find a good one—especially for the smaller investor without substantial cash. As you will see in the next chapter, you don't necessarily need substantial savings to get started. In many cases, you will be able to use your "borrowing power"—which is available because of excess earnings from your job, business or profession that you do not need to support your living requirements.

If you don't wish to invest by yourself, either because you do not have the expertise or the resources, you may consider two further alternatives. The first, is to pool your capital or borrowings with a few close friends or business associates in similar circumstances. The combined purchasing power of several persons is obviously greater than that of the sole investor. You must, however, consider that each member of the group will have to do a certain amount of work, absorb a degree of risk, and there is always the possibility of dissention and disagreement.

In most cases, especially if you are a new investor in a large, urban community, you will prefer to participate in a syndicate. You may perhaps sacrifice some liquidity, and yet, if the venture is profitable, you will certainly be ahead of the game. Investment units in a syndicate often cost as little as $10,000. If the investment is put together by a reputable organization, one of the major advantages is that your property will be managed for you. There may also be other benefits such as rental guarantees.

The Ideal Investment

Certainly, there is no such thing as an "ideal" investment. If an investor could have everything he wanted, he would consider the following characteristics:

1. No danger of losing one's initial investment.
2. Potential for capital appreciation.

3. The ability to liquidate the investment quickly, without effort and without excessive cost.
4. A high rate of return.
5. Certainty of cash flow.
6. Carefree management.
7. Availability of the property as easy collateral for loan purposes.
8. Income tax shelter.
9. Potential for effective leverage.
10. Pride of ownership.

Obviously, with any investment or potential investment, there are trade-offs. For example most real-estate investments cannot be sold at a moment's notice. The starting point is for *you* to determine both your primary and secondary objectives. I hope that this book will be of assistance to you in sorting out your own priorities.

As I have already mentioned, a major thesis of this book is that you do not necessarily need substantial savings to enter the real-estate market—as long as you have surplus "earning power". As you will see in the next chapter, the idea is to borrow money against your earnings potential and to use these funds as the downpayment for property. Today's high interest costs need not necessarily be too upsetting since, in Canada, interest expense is tax deductible as long as funds are borrowed for investment purposes. Therefore, for many people, the cost of borrowing will translate to only approximately one-half of the pre-tax rate. The name of the game is to strive for capital appreciation. This is especially advantageous because only one-half of your capital gain will be taxed on eventual sale.

I will show you that borrowing money for real-estate investment can become an executive's, professional's or business owner's "forced savings plan", and I will illustrate these concepts with case studies based on actual situations.

This book will also explain how real estate can operate as a tax shelter for Canadians. We will examine the uniquely Canadian rules pertaining to Multiple Unit Residential Buildings and the topic of "soft cost" or "first time" write-offs. You will see that these income tax concessions will apply to minimize your cash requirements for any particular real-estate construction project. In other words, part of your downpayment can easily be recovered through a reduction of income taxes otherwise payable.

I will explain the opportunities to minimize taxation on rental income by taking advantage of all legitimate expense claims during the period of property ownership, and you will see how to increase your profit on the sale of property through effective tax minimization or postponement. For most people, it will be not necessary to resort to a corporation or other complex arrangement as a vehicle for property ownership. Specifically, you will see that there are ample opportunities ranging from the use of income tax "reserves" for uncollected proceeds to income-averaging annuities which allow an *individual* to reduce or postpone taxes on profits arising from property sales. The Canadian reserve provisions are, for example, much more generous than those of the United States, while the United States has absolutely no provisions corresponding to the Canadian income-averaging annuity legislation.

For the more sophisticated investor, there is a chapter on real-estate holding companies which will explain when and how to use them. Often, a real-estate project will produce losses for tax purposes during the initial years of ownership. Many investors make the mistake of using a new corporation that has no other sources of income to buy property or build a project. In this way, they forgo the benefits of having *personal* tax losses which they could otherwise absorb against their other incomes. This book will provide detailed guidelines as to the correct method, which would be to hold property personally while there are deductible tax losses and only transfer the assets to a corporation once taxable income is generated. You will see that using a corporation at this *later* time will permit the owner to split his income with members of his family who are in lower tax brackets. A corporation can be used to minimize taxes on the eventual sale of property as well.

For the homeowner and potential homeowner, I will deal with the topic of principal residences. Our Canadian tax rules are extremely generous in that they provide that husband and wife can each own a principal residence where capital gains on eventual disposition are totally tax-free. This topic will be covered in two chapters, the first dealing with a primary home and the second dealing with recreational property. Like many advisers, I believe that a primary residence is generally a family's best investment. However, the interest costs incurred to finance a residence can be extremely harmful, especially since interest on money borrowed to acquire personal property is *not* deductible in Canada. I will therefore suggest that you make every attempt to pay down your residential mortgage as soon as possible in order to eliminate non-deductible carrying costs and then use your accumulated equity in your home as the base to *remortgage* for *investment* purposes.

The material on principal residences will also cover the Canadian Registered Home Ownership Savings Plan, special rules pertaining to the "change of use" of property (where rental property is transformed into a principal residence or vice versa), and the relatively new phenomenon of time-sharing. For many people, I feel that a timeshare may be a better alternative than a recreational property, since there is considerably less cost involved in tying up funds (where interest on borrowing is non-deductible) in a one or two week timeshare than in an expensive recreational cottage.

There is a chapter on effective tax reduction for real-estate developers and their advisers. The emphasis here is on sophisticated business planning. For example, I will present and explain a simple formula to evaluate Canadian capital-cost-allowance (tax depreciation) potentials and will deal with the tax and investment implications of demolishing a building before a property sale takes place. There are also legitimate opportunities, in some circumstances, to claim *double* the tax depreciation that is normally allowed within the Canadian income tax rules.

For the more knowledgeable and experienced reader, there will be two chapters on the subject of real-estate investment and development activities in the United States. This material highlights the implications of the new Canada–U.S. Tax Treaty, and presents an overview of the U.S. income tax rules for real estate owned by non-resident aliens and foreign corporations. If you are interested in this topic, you will see that there is a new Foreign Investment in Real Property Tax Act in the United States which has significant impact on

Canadians disposing of U.S. real-estate holdings. We will also examine alternative methods of structuring U.S. real-estate activities, ranging from direct investment through to the use of Canadian holding companies and U.S. corporations.

Finally, we will examine various general financial strategies to show you how real estate can be, perhaps, your most attractive investment option.

Unlike a popular novel, for many readers it will not be necessary to digest this book from cover to cover. Rather, I suggest that you concentrate on the topics that are relevant to your own situation—whether you are a homeowner (or potential homeowner), investor (or potential investor), developer, real-estate salesperson, or an adviser to any of these.

CHAPTER TWO

Using Your "Earning Power"—
The Key to Getting Started

There are two common misconceptions concerning real-estate investment. The first is that to enter the real-estate market, an investor needs at least $50,000 to $100,000 of savings for a downpayment on property. The second is that a real-estate investment is "no good" unless it carries itself with rental income sufficient to offset all operating expenses, including mortgage interest, property taxes, repairs, insurance, heating and electricity.

You don't really need a $50,000 stake for an initial investment as long as you have the personal "earning power" to carry a $50,000 loan. Also, a property doesn't necessarily have to carry itself—as long as the negative cash flow is more than offset by the potential for capital appreciation. Effective investing is largely a function of using the income tax system to help—by making the government a full partner in sharing losses and only a junior associate in splitting profits.

In Canada, we live with a tax system that makes saving very difficult. Anyone earning $30,000 a year will find himself paying away about half of all his *additional* earnings in income taxes. The pressures of inflation compound the difficulties of saving. There is a tremendous compulsion to spend. Today, a salesman is virtually guaranteed of making a sale any time he simply panics a potential customer by "confidentially" revealing details of the yet-unannounced 7% price increase slated for the first of the following month.

The same ingredients of high taxes and escalating inflation which characterize our Canadian society also promote real estate as an investment. This is because interest on money borrowed to make investments is *tax deductible*, and if a property operates at a negative cash flow, the shortfall is also largely absorbed by the government.

Canadian investment guidelines are somewhat different from those in the United States. The U.S. system takes a much more simple approach. Since all interest received by lenders is taxable, a borrower should, therefore, obtain an offsetting tax deduction. Any time an American borrows money, interest expense is *automatically* tax deductible—even if the funds are used for personal purposes. Thus, in the U.S., an individual is permitted to deduct interest expense on a mortgage to buy his home, as well as interest on money borrowed to acquire *personal property*, such as a car, or even interest paid on charge accounts.

In Canada, however, the deductibility test for interest expense is quite different. Here, interest is *only* deductible if borrowings are used for business or investment purposes. Books written on the subject of real-estate investment in the U.S. that are imported into Canada are, therefore, generally quite misleading and may be more harmful than beneficial.

Several years ago, Dr. Morton Shulman wrote a bestseller called *How to Invest Your Money & Profit from Inflation*. Dr. Shulman suggested that everyone should go and buy the most expensive home that the family could reasonably afford to carry. His thesis was that debt obligations would cost less and less each year because of continuing devaluation of the dollar, while the home would tend to appreciate as inflation forced replacement costs to spiral upwards.

Up to a point, I think Dr. Shulman gave sound advice. However, I really don't think he went far enough because, by targeting his book for *both* the Canadian and U.S. markets, he failed to distinguish between non-deductible and deductible interest. For a Canadian, it is expensive to borrow money at a first mortgage interest rate of 18% for the purchase of a home. Remember, that to *earn* investment income of 18% *after taxes* would require a pre-tax yield of 36% for anyone in a 50% personal income tax bracket.

Please don't misunderstand me. As you will see when you read Chapter Nine, I strongly believe in home ownership. This is because I, like everyone else, need a place to live. I much prefer to own my home even if this means paying non-deductible interest. After all, if I rented my home, my rent would *also* not be deductible. At least, with home ownership, *I* get the capital appreciation whereas, under a rental arrangement, the growth goes to the landlord and, at the end, the tenant has nothing.

My personal philosophy simply expands on that of Dr. Shulman. I also suggest that you should buy the biggest home that your family can afford to carry for the same reasons as mentioned by Dr. Shulman. This, in my opinion, is your best possible investment. I then feel, however, that your family should put maximum effort into paying for the residence over, say, an *eight*-year period instead of the normal term of twenty-five or even thirty years. The reason I pick eight years is because most mortgages will allow a borrower to pay down up to 10% of the principal balance each year on the anniversary date without penalties. Of course, the regular monthly payments will continue unchanged but, with a smaller principal balance outstanding, more and more of these payments will go to retire the debt itself. At the end of about eight years, your house will be paid for.

Like any other investment program, building the discipline to save is difficult. Four years ago, when my family and I moved to Calgary from Montreal, it was extremely disconcerting to buy a house and assume a first mortgage greater than the total selling price of our former home. Monthly payments were just over $1,000. Early the following January, I received my annual statement from the mortgage company allocating my payments between interest and principal. The principal balance had only been reduced by about $700. On the first anniversary, however, I then paid down 10% of my debt and was rewarded the *following* January to find that I had reduced my principal by an *additional* $1,200 over and above what I might have expected to be the normal debt reduction.

Once you pay off your mortgage, you then come to a very important crossroads in your life. If you want, you can breathe a sigh of relief, perhaps increase your spending level by the amount of monthly payments which you no longer have to make and rest comfortably. After all, if worse comes to worst and you lose your job, become disabled, or the great depression of the 1980s that some of the "gloom and doom" books talk about comes to pass, you will still be able to carry on with a roof over your head.

On the other hand, if you are adventurous and desire to accumulate *wealth*, there is no better place to start than with the equity which you would now have in your home. Once your house is paid for, if it is then remortgaged with the proceeds going for *investment* purposes, your interest expense now becomes *tax deductible*. If your income would otherwise allow you to carry only a $75,000 mortgage (where funds are borrowed to acquire a home in the first place) you are suddenly in a position where you could afford *twice* that debt load or $150,000.

While a first mortgage interest rate of, say, 18% is extremely expensive financing on a non-deductible basis, there is no cheaper source of funds available as long as the interest *is* deductible. After all, the after-tax cost of borrowing at 18% to an individual in a 50% tax bracket is only 9%. Can you do better than 9% with capital appreciation on an investment? I would hope so, given the inflation factor alone!

Actually, you don't even have to wait until your house is completely paid for if you wish to borrow for investment purposes. Each time your mortgage comes up for renewal, you can borrow up to your mortgage limit. To the extent that the new borrowings simply replace the amount still owing against the original purchase price of the house, your future interest expense will continue to be non-deductible. However, to the extent that the *increased* borrowings are used for *investment* purposes, the reverse will apply. Even though you may have only one loan outstanding, all you would have to do is prove that part of the borrowed funds were used for investment. This would produce the desired allocation of interest costs between non-deductible and deductible expenditures.

For example, if you are in a position to borrow $50,000 at 18% against your equity in your home, the monthly payments would be $730 based on a loan amortized over a period of twenty-five years. If these funds were used for investment and you are in a 50% tax bracket, your after-tax cost of borrowing would only be $365 each month. Can you afford to save $365 a month on your present earnings from your job, your business, or your profession? If you stop to think about it, you probably can. But do you? It is very difficult to save without a goal. To accumulate $50,000 at $365 a month (ignoring interest) would take 137 months of saving—almost twelve years. The frustration of knowing how long it takes to save a meaningful sum of money increases our natural inclination to spend our surplus earning power rather than adopting a savings program.

My point is that, if you *borrow* the $50,000 *now* and pay for that privilege at $365 a month, you will be in a position *today* to make a substantial investment. In fact, you could probably purchase about $150,000 of real estate with a $50,000 downpayment—*as long as the remaining financing of $100,000 is covered by rentals generated from that property*. You would then be buying the right to capital appreciation on $150,000 of property at a minimal monthly after-tax cost of $365.

Note that $50,000 is not a "magic number" which would be a realistic investment for everyone reading this book. Each one of us has what I call a personal "comfort level". This represents the maximum debt load with which you, the individual, are comfortable. Certainly, if your borrowing exceeds this comfort level, serious psychological disadvantages can result. It is certainly not my intention to suggest that you become so overloaded with debt that you become irritable, edgy or even suicidal.

Not everyone is comfortable owing money—even in small amounts. Many of us have grown up with parents telling us time and time again: "Neither a borrower nor a lender be." Last winter, I gave a series of tax planning seminars in Calgary to the employees of Dome Petroleum Ltd. and their spouses. At one session, where there were over one hundred participants, I had just finished talking about the idea of borrowing downpayments for real-estate investments when a young fellow raised his hand to ask a question. Actually, his question was more of a statement. He suggested that if each and every individual in the room were to borrow $50,000 for real-estate investment, the combined activity of that group alone would probably be enough to significantly inflate the overall price of property in Calgary. I laughed, and agreed with his conclusion! I pointed out, however, that I was confident that this result would *not* materialize because I was sure that very few people would take my advice. (Even devout missionaries can't convert everyone.) It is a fact that not many people can accept large debt loads. If you are not comfortable borrowing money, accumulate your $50,000 stake the hard way—$365 a month for 137 months. Remember, even if you invest $365 each month at a 15% yield, your interest *income* would be *taxable*—and your real interest factor is therefore only 7½%!

On occasion, I have heard the term millionaire defined as an individual who *owes* a million dollars. While this definition might be somewhat facetious, it does have merit. Presumably, if someone owes a million dollars, that same person has a million dollars of assets. Over time, the assets may double in value while the debt shrinks with inflation and is often paid off out of revenues generated from the assets themselves. Thus, eventually the borrower does become a bona fide millionaire!

In other words, my "executive forced-savings plan" simply consists of borrowing money for an investment (within the personal comfort level of the individual) where the debt is carried by the individual's monthly earnings from his employment, profession or business (and not necessarily by the investment itself). The borrowed funds, in turn, are placed into property which—it is hoped—will appreciate in value. In this book, I have suggested that real estate may be a good investment for capital growth. I should point out, however, that the same concept of borrowing against earning power would be just as applicable if you are more comfortable with stock market investments. The leverage may not be quite as good unless your stocks pay dividends in the same way as a real estate investment pays rents. In other words, with a stake of $50,000 I don't think it would be possible to purchase $150,000 of stock market investments where the interest costs on the remaining $100,000 of debt is offset by a dividend yield.

If you bought gold, art or antiques, your maximum purchase at a monthly cost of $365 would be $50,000. This is because these investments provide no income yield during the period of ownership and could not be used to support a large debt load.

I think that many of us can benefit from a forced savings program. In the fall of 1980, my book *The New Canadian Tax & Investment Guide* was published. Before I even began to write that book, I had had discussions with my publisher and I explained that I wanted to deal with tax *planning* as opposed to tax-return preparation. He asked me to define my market and I suggested that the material would be of interest to people earning $25,000 a year or more. My reasoning was that unless an individual's (or family's) earnings exceeded this level, it would be quite difficult to find extra disposable "earning power" with which to tax plan. When the book was finally released, both the text itself and the advertising were heavily weighted towards the "plus $25,000" market.

In October 1980, I went on a cross-country publicity tour which involved radio, television and newspaper coverage. From the very first day, I found that I was repeatedly asked the same question by many of the media people who interviewed me: How can someone earning less than $25,000 do some effective tax planning? Fortunately, I was lucky and thought of an answer the first time the question was asked. I reasoned that anyone earning less than $25,000 probably doesn't have $7,000 sitting in a bank account, term deposit or in Canada Savings Bonds. The significance of this amount is that at current interest rates, it takes approximately $7,000 of capital to earn $1,000 of Canadian investment income each year. As most people know, the first $1,000 of annual Canadian investment income (any combination of interest, dividends, or taxable capital gains from Canadian securities) is essentially tax-free.

Any time you can earn income which is tax-free (so that the gross and net yields are the same), you can accept a modest return on your investment. If you are earning *more* than $1,000 a year of Canadian investment income, the excess amount is taxable and a 16% yield on a Canada Savings Bond becomes only 8% after taxes. This is considerably less than the current rate of inflation and, if you have such an investment, you are actually losing money! However, if your only investment consists of $7,000 of Canada Savings Bonds earning interest at 16%, your gross yield and net are (almost) the same and you are doing slightly better than inflation. (You would be taxable on only $120 out of a pre-tax return of $1,120.)

However, if one earns less than $25,000 a year, how does he accumulate enough capital to earn $1,000 of investment income each year? The answer is a "forced savings program."

The idea is to have the individual visit his bank or trust company and contract for the purchase of Canada Savings Bonds (or similar investments) on a "buy now—pay later" plan. The amount contracted for should be such that the debt can be discharged over, say, a one-year period. For example, if an individual is capable of saving $100 a month, he might consider buying $1,200 of Canada Savings Bonds at the time a new issue is released, taking a loan for this purpose with a twelve-month payout period. Then, automatically, his banker will charge his account with $100 a month on the same day each month. Preferably, the monthly payment date would coincide with the individual's pay schedule and a good time to undertake such a program would be when the individual has just received a raise in salary. In this way, he would not necessarily have to cut back on his previous spending. He could simply look upon his situation as if he had forgone one semi-annual or annual raise. After one year, the individual in my example would have $1,200 (which he probably would not otherwise have saved up) towards the target of accumulating $7,000 of investment capital. The cycle is then repeated in the following year.

This is what I call a "junior forced-savings program". An executive forced-savings program simply involves larger numbers, more risk and requires a more sophisticated emotional outlook.

As we will see from the examples in the next chapter, an investment in property can be viable even if it involves a negative cash flow—as long as the investor can afford to subsidize his shortfall out of other income and as long as there is a good potential for capital appreciation. Remember *that if an investment fails to carry itself, the government will absorb approximately half the loss* (depending on the owner's tax bracket) *through reductions in income taxes otherwise payable.*

In January 1981, Joseph Granville, an American stock market analyst, predicted that the U.S. stock market would crash. Mr. Granville, who publishes an investment newsletter, recommended to his clients that they quickly withdraw their funds. Apparently, Mr. Granville was well-respected because the subsequent withdrawal of capital by his followers caused the market averages to plummet drastically. Mr. Granville's effect was, however, short-lived. The market did not actually crash and, in fact, within a few short weeks, it recovered all of the ground that it had so quickly lost.

My wife, who is certainly well aware that I am somewhat bullish on real-estate investments, has often cautioned me in the last year not to be a "Granville in reverse". If every reader of this book were to suddenly rush out to acquire property without thorough research and analysis, the results could end up to be not only highly inflationary, but also disastrous in the long run.

Chapter Three will present a simple approach towards evaluating real-estate investments by comparing negative cash flows to potentials for capital appreciation. Then, in Chapter Four, you will discover how construction and development activities can be used as a tax shelter, so that a substantial portion of your initial investment may be recovered almost immediately through reductions in income taxes otherwise payable.

Nevertheless, there is only so much material that you will be able to absorb from a book. In reality, you will need to cultivate at least one knowledgeable real-estate agent (if not several) and make liberal use of your own accountants and lawyers. I have several close friends who have made substantial fortunes in real estate over the past few years. Almost invariably, they tell me that for each property that they buy, they reject as many as ten others. Caution and common sense are, therefore, very much in order.

CHAPTER THREE

Negative Cash-Flow vs. Capital Appreciation

This chapter presents two case studies, based on actual experiences, both of which taught me a great deal about evaluating real-estate investments. The first of these examples is one previously dealt with in Chapter Five of *The New Canadian Tax & Investment Guide*. I will further discuss that example here because I can honestly say that I learned more from that one situation than from any other single case that I have ever been involved in over the last fifteen years as a Chartered Accountant. While the numbers in this example and the relevant interest rates may be somewhat obsolete, the method of analysis is still valid.

In October 1978, a group of four friends came to me and asked if I wished to join in a small real-estate venture. The concept which they advanced was that each of us would put up $10,000 or $15,000 and that we would try to find a property that would carry itself out of rental revenues with a minimum downpayment. One of the parties was a lawyer who promised to do all the legal work associated with this venture at no cost to the group. A second was involved on a full-time basis as a construction estimator and he agreed to analyse any potential property investment from a structural standpoint. The two others were both executives with large corporations who undertook to split the functions of looking after minor repairs, advertising for tenants, and rent collection. I, in turn, was asked if I would prepare a financial analysis before any investment was made and whether I would do the accounting. In theory, the idea was very appealing and I agreed to participate.

Several weeks later, a real estate agent brought me a listing describing a small apartment building which was for sale in one of the nicer sections of Calgary. My friends had inspected this property and were impressed by its excellent condition and the fact that it was fully rented. I was asked to review the figures. The first thing I did was to prepare the schedule which appears below.

What I wanted to do was to determine the probable cash flow from the property before mortgage repayments. In my projections I allowed for a vacancy rate of 3%. Of course, a vacancy factor varies from time to time and place to place and the 3% is for illustration only and should not be assumed to be reasonable in all cases.

ANALYSIS OF REAL ESTATE INVESTMENT

Gross rents projected		$70,000
Less: 3% vacancy factor		2,100
		67,900
Expenses:		
Taxes	$5,000	
Insurance	800	
Heating	2,200	
Light and power	1,500	
Garbage collection	700	
Janitor	2,200	
Management fee	3,400	
Supplies	300	
Maintenance	2,100	18,200
Cash flow before mortgage		$49,700

My next step was to calculate how much financing the property could carry. There was an existing first mortgage of $282,000 which had recently been placed on the building at 10¾%. I determined the cash flow after the required first mortgage payments to be as follows:

Cash flow before mortgage	$49,700
First mortgage $282,000 at 10¾%— annual payments from amortization tables	32,400
Cash flow after first mortgage	$17,300

At this point, I reasoned that either my friends and I had investment capital or we did not have the funds necessary to acquire the property. At that time, if we had cash, we could have invested in second mortgages at a 13% rate of return. Alternatively, we could have pooled our borrowing power to obtain a second mortgage at that same 13% rate. In either event, my conclusion was that money was "worth" 13%. The next question I asked myself was how much capital could one invest in this property so that the cash flow of $17,300 a year (after first mortgage payments) would cover this financing?

I consulted my mortgage tables and I determined that a cash flow of $17,300 would provide a 13% yield on an investment of approximately $130,000. In other words, if we invested our own funds, $17,300 would provide a 13% rate of return to *us* while, on the other hand, if we borrowed $130,000 instead, the property could absorb this debt and still break even. I therefore evaluated the property at $412,000 which was the sum of the first and second mortgage financing ($282,000 + $130,000).

The asking price for the building was $589,000 and I told my friends to disregard this property as an investment since it was greatly overpriced. Several weeks later, however, I was informed that the property had, in fact, been sold for $567,000. My friends were somewhat upset with the fact that I had passed up what somebody else obviously figured was a good investment opportunity.

I rechecked my figures and I found that I had made no arithmetic errors. Being somewhat curious as to the buyer's motives, I then went on to do some additional analysis. I first concluded that the buyer had overpaid $155,000 and I really couldn't understand why.

Actual selling price	$567,000
Break-even price	412,000
Excess cost	$155,000

I then reasoned that the purchaser must either have had funds of his own or substantial borrowing power. If he had capital, I concluded that he was willing to invest $155,000 at a zero rate of return instead of the 13% that he could otherwise have obtained in second mortgages. Conversely, if he borrowed the additional funds at 13%, my tables told me that the actual negative cash flow would be $20,500. My first inclination was then to doubt the sanity of the purchaser. He was either giving up $20,500 a year that he himself could otherwise have earned (this is called an *opportunity cost*), or he was willing to pay out the same amount each year to a lending institution.

However, I then decided to carry the calculations a little further. In the first years of ownership, whenever a rental property produces a cash-flow loss because of financing, most of that loss (as much as 99%) is as a result of interest expense. *Accordingly the loss is tax deductible.* This loss cannot be made larger by claiming depreciation write-offs (except where the property qualifies as a MURB—see Chapter Four), but in this case, the *after-tax* cash-flow loss would be considerably less than $20,500. In fact, if one assumes an investor in a 60% tax bracket (income level of about $70,000 in most provinces), the after-tax cash-flow loss is only $20,500 × 40%, or $8,200.

Against this loss, one would then have to balance a projected appreciation in value. Historically, real estate in Calgary had tended to appreciate by at least 8% per annum. Eight percent of $567,000 is $45,000. Even after subtracting (for simplicity) a 50% provision for real-estate commission costs and tax on the eventual gain on sale, there is still an anticipated after-tax appreciation at the end of only one year of $22,500. If you compare the after-tax cash-flow loss of $8,200 against $22,500 of probable appreciation, the investment starts to look more and more attractive.

After-tax cash-flow loss	
$20,500 × 40%	$ 8,200
Appreciation in value—projected	
$567,000 × 8%	$45,000
Less: 50% provision for tax on capital gains plus commission to sell	22,500
After-tax appreciation	$22,500

The only problem, however, is that in "real life" the cash-flow loss is *definite* while the appreciation in value is *speculative*. You should never pay too much for property unless you can accept the risk of a potential loss. Ironically, real-estate investments tend to favour those who have made money in the past. If you are wealthy, you can afford to subsidize a property that is losing money and still hang on until market conditions improve. As long as there is no sacrifice in your standard of living, then the investment might be worth the gamble. However, if you buy property subject to heavy debt and you are relying on immediate capital appreciation in order to quickly "bail out", then you are treading on dangerous ground.

And yet, as I showed you in Chapter Two, you don't necessarily have to be wealthy to acquire real-estate investments. In the previous example, if you can afford to subsidize a negative cash flow of $8,200 a year (after taxes) out of income from your business, your employment, or your profession, without suffering a decrease in your standard of living, then the worst that could happen (discounting a full-blown depression) is that a recession may keep you from realizing anticipated capital appreciation quickly. As long as you are prepared to hang on, you may realistically expect property values to move upwards with inflation. This is simply because construction costs tend to make new properties more expensive to build, thereby enhancing the resale values of properties which have already been built.

While it may be somewhat difficult for one individual to absorb a negative cash flow of $8,200 a year (after tax reductions), it certainly should not be that difficult for a group of three to five investors.

The important point about this case study is that it taught me that *a negative cash flow on a property does not necessarily mean the property is unattractive.* If my friends and I had each borrowed $31,000 apiece (or $155,000 in total), subsidizing the payments out of our personal incomes, we could have had a good investment. Today, real estate in Calgary tends to trade at somewhere between ten and eleven times gross rents (before expenses). This means that, even without considering rent increases after October 1978, today's resale price would be somewhere between $700,000 and $770,000. Taking normal rent escalations into account, a more realistic figure would be $900,000. Of course, hindsight is 20–20 vision!

I would be remiss if I didn't admit that this case study is probably somewhat oversimplified. Anyone with a degree of sophistication in real-estate analysis would not begin to chart a property over only a one-year term. Usually, five-year projections are made and the sophisticated analyst brings back all future cash flows or deficiencies (including after-tax profits on eventual sale) to a present value for purposes of his calculations.

If you are contemplating a specific real-estate investment, you should deal with advisers who are capable in assisting in the preparation of the more technical calculations that form part of a five-year projection. Naturally, you must keep in mind that the further you go from the present time in these projections, the more likelihood there is of significant errors entering into the picture.

Unless there are government-imposed rent controls, a cash-flow deficiency should decrease over time as rents are increased. This is especially true if a five-year mortgage is obtained in order to provide financing, and monthly payments are thereby fixed for a long term. As a rule of thumb, unless I can see a property carrying itself out of rentals within five years, I would not find the property attractive.

While the negative cash flow should decrease over time, the appreciation in value will generally tend to compound. (Of course, you may have to wait if there is a temporary recession in the area of the country in which your investment is situated.) So, I learned—the hard way—that it is not a criminal offense to subsidize the carrying costs of a property (in part) out of surplus earnings from other sources. However, it took another entirely different situation to teach me a very important fact about human nature—that one's debt load must never exceed the personal *comfort level* of the prospective borrower.

Investments and Appetites

Although I spend a fair portion of my time writing books and doing consulting work, my main activity centers around tax and investment seminars which I present in many cities in Canada. One of the benefits of what has turned out to be extensive travel, is that my wife (who handles all business arrangements) is often able to accompany me. Of course, much of the fun results from having our evenings free and, over the last few years, we have made friends in almost all major cities across the country. One of our favourite places (when it isn't raining) is Vancouver and we are there approximately twenty days each year.

It so happened that, in February 1980, we were invited to a friend's house for dinner for the first time. Before eating, my wife and I were given a tour of the home and I inquired as to its market value. Vancouver, at that time, was in the midst of an unprecedented real-estate boom and my friend figured that the value of his house was somewhere between $250,000 and $300,000. I asked him what his mortgage rate was and he proudly informed me that he owned the house with a clear title. He went on to explain that he had constructed the property about twelve years earlier at a cost of around $45,000 and that he had subsequently managed to pay off his financing.

Later, over dinner, as is so often the case, the conversation turned to the topics of investments and taxes. My friend started to complain bitterly that in spite of continuing raises in pay and bonuses, it was very difficult for him to save money. At that time, he was the sales manager for a large company based in British Columbia, and he was earning somewhere between $50,000 and $60,000 a year. While some of you may not sympathize with the monetary complaints of an individual at that income level, the inability to save is easily explained. At $60,000 of earnings, a resident of British Columbia is in a 55% income tax bracket. Accordingly, each time he gets a raise in pay, a bonus or any other employment-related benefit, the government takes away more than half off the top. Then, when one considers the expenses of supporting oneself, a dependent spouse and several children, the difficulty is saving substantial dollars becomes apparent. Also, as I mentioned in Chapter Two, it is very difficult to save *if one does not have a goal*. Even if one could put away several hundred dollars a month, it would still take a long time to amass significant capital—especially where the pressures of spiraling costs dictate that one should buy consumables now and not wait until future price increases make these more and more expensive.

After listening to my friend talk for a few moments, I interrupted and started to explain to him that his whole approach was wrong. I suggested that if he were a young business-owner, executive or professional with an income of between $50,000 and $60,000 a year, he could probably afford to borrow up to $100,000 if it were his intention to buy his *first* home. At that time, first mortgage rates were about 14% and to carry a mortgage of $100,000 would have required payments of around $1,200 a month. In other words, my thinking was that on a family income of $60,000 a year, it should be possible for my friend to pay out $1,200 a month (or $14,400 a year) without suffering a great reduction in his standard of living.

However, these numbers assume that the borrowing is incurred specifically for the purpose of buying a home in which to live, where the payments of $1,200 a month (almost completely consisting of interest in the early years) are *non-deductible*. Once there is an equity build-up in a house that is *already paid for* and one remortgages for investment purposes, the interest *becomes tax deductible*. The same person who could afford a personal debt load of $100,000 can now afford to carry $200,000 as long as he is in a tax bracket of 50% or higher! While the initial expense of borrowing would be $2,400 a month, upon filing an annual tax return, half the cost would be refunded by the government.

Having explained this to my friend and his wife, I suggested the following plan of action. I recommended that they remortgage their home to the extent of $200,000 and that they take the borrowed funds to buy an investment property at a cost of about $800,000. I suggested that they shop for an investment where the rental revenue on the $800,000 property would be sufficient to cover operating expenses *plus interest on the first mortgage financing of $600,000*. The remaining $200,000 of property cost could then be carried out of my friend's surplus earnings from his *job*. In the first year, the negative cash flow on the property would be approximately

$28,800 (being the payments required to amortize or pay off the borrowing of $200,000). On an after-tax basis, however, the negative cash flow would only be half, or $14,400.

However, against a potential loss of only $14,400, I told my friend that he could be reasonably assured (in a vibrant economy) of capital appreciation of, say, 10% on his total $800,000 investment. I went on to explain that, even after subtracting a provision for commissions and taxes arising from a future sale, the after-tax appreciation would probably be almost as much as he would earn *for a whole year from his job* (after taxes on his salary). These concepts are illustrated in the following schedule.

AFTER-TAX INVESTMENT COST

Purchase of property	$800,000
First mortgage (Covered out of property rents)	$600,000
Other financing (Covered out of cash flow from job—$1,200 per month after taxes)	200,000
	$800,000

After one year:

Potential capital appreciation (10% x $800,000)	$ 80,000
Less: Provision for commission to sell and taxes on eventual gain (50%)	40,000
	$ 40,000

vs.

After-tax cost of carrying the investment (50% x $28,800)	$ 14,400

By the time I had finished my little dissertation, my friend and his wife had turned a very sickly shade of grey. I had completely spoiled their excellent roast-beef dinner by hitting them right between the eyes with a concept that was totally alien to their thinking. For years, my friend had prided himself on living in a beautiful home almost rent-free, and now I was telling him to incur a debt load of $200,000! In retrospect, I did my friend a great disservice by failing to realize that every one of us has a different comfort level for borrowing.

In retrospect, I should have approached my friend with a more modest scenario. I should have asked him whether he felt that he could, at his current income level, afford to put away $300 a month if he had to. I am convinced that my question would have received an affirmative answer. I should then have suggested that he borrow $50,000 in order to acquire a real-estate investment worth, say, $150,000. Then, after one year, he could compare the potential appreciation on this property against the negative cash flow of $3,600 (12 X $300). (Again, an investment property would only be suitable if the rental income would cover the payments on the first mortgage financing of $100,000, even if the property itself couldn't carry the remaining $50,000.) Using these numbers, my friend might have appreciated what I was driving at.

The idea is simply to use your excess earning power for leverage in order to borrow money. If you are in a high tax bracket today and earn an adequate income from your job, business or profession, cash flow from investments is not necessarily important. What counts is the future appreciation that your investments can conceivably generate. Of course, your comfort level for debt might initially be small. Over time, however, if you are successful, you may find that your comfort level increases.

Actually, there is one further refinement to the concept of investing even where there is a negative cash flow. You should note that, in the first year, if you were to borrow $50,000 (at an interest rate of 18%) you would actually be required to pay out $730 a month to the mortgage company and not only $365. The cost of borrowing is only reduced to half *after* your tax return is submitted and a refund of taxes otherwise payable is later received. In order to make up for the difference, a sophisticated buyer will often borrow a little bit more than he actually requires for the actual investment. In the previous example, my friend could have borrowed say, $53,600 and not only $50,000. The $3,600 difference would then have been placed into a special bank account and would have been used over the first twelve months to make up the difference between the required monthly payments of $600 a month and the $300 a month which my friend could otherwise comfortably afford from his salary. Then, at the end of the year, when a tax refund was received, the special bank account could have been replenished by $3,600 and these funds would again have been available to subsidize the (hopefully decreasing) negative cash flow for the following year.

The technique of borrowing more than one's initial principal requirements is often used by real-estate speculators as well. A speculator is someone who plans to hold a property for only a short period of time. Where that is the case, the buyer does not usually worry about rental revenues and, if the speculative property consists of raw land, there generally is no revenue, in any event. However, in order to subsidize the cost of carrying his property, a speculator will often borrow not only the principal amount, which he needs to buy the property in the first place, but also an additional amount to cover short-term interest costs. Then, if the venture is successful, the property is resold at a price sufficient to recover the interest incurred during the holding period and also to provide a profit back to the speculator. Of course, speculation and investment are two different things but some of the financing concepts are certainly common to both.

Summary

In the last year, interest rates have skyrocketed in North America, making the cost of borrowing for real-estate investment very expensive—even after considering the deductibility of interest expense. Traditionally, rent increases tend to lag behind changes in interest rates by one or two years. In other words, landlords may not always be able to raise tenants' rents at the same time that their mortgages come up for renewal.

In most cases, a rental property won't carry itself out of rentals unless the owner puts up between 30% and 40% of the purchase price. If you invest a lesser amount (in order to acquire a larger property investment in the first place) a negative cash flow will result.

If you can accept the concept of a negative cash-flow subsidized by your other earning power, the next chapter of this book will show you how other tax write-offs from the property itself (especially during a construction period) will serve to minimize the amount of downpayment that you would otherwise need to buy into a project.

CHAPTER FOUR

Real Estate as a Tax Shelter for Canadians

A tax shelter may result when a tax-deductible loss from a particular source is offset against other income. In Canada, popular tax shelters include real-estate investments, motion picture films, oil and gas exploration ventures, and (to some extent) farming operations. With rising incomes, tax shelters have become increasingly popular in recent years.

Too many people place tax-shelter aspects ahead of investment considerations. They forget that a "tax shelter" is not the same thing as a "tax loss". A pure tax shelter only occurs when there are write-offs (such as depreciation) that produce losses for tax purposes, but where the value of an investment does not diminish and there is no loss of cash. Just because a loss is deductible, does not make it a tax shelter. Someone in a 60% bracket who actually lays out a dollar is still out of pocket a minimum of 40 cents—even if his expenditure is deductible. As I have explained in the last two chapters, the only time you should be willing to suffer a *negative cash flow* is in circumstances where the projected appreciation in the value of the property more than offsets your risk of subsidizing its cost through appropriations of other income sources.

In this chapter, we will examine how a real-estate tax shelter works. We will see how certain components of a construction project may be written off for income-tax purposes during the construction period. In addition, in certain cases, losses from the ownership of property may be increased through depreciation. The effect of claiming these income tax write-offs reduces income taxes otherwise payable and *decreases the amount of capital* that the investor himself has tied up in a particular construction project. The idea is to acquire as much property as one can reasonably handle with the least amount of personal capital.

In order to explain real-estate shelters, the best place to start is with a brief examination of the tax system that applied in Canada before the Tax Reform of 1972. We can then trace the evolution of the system until the present time.

Nostalgia

Before substantial changes in the Canadian tax laws were made in 1972, the acquisition of rental buildings was a popular tax deferral and avoidance technique. At that time, the Income Tax Regulations divided buildings into two "classes" for depreciation purposes. Class 3 (with a depreciation rate of 5%) included concrete and steel reinforced structures, while Class 6 (with a depreciation rate of 10%) contained wood frame, stucco on frame, and brick veneer buildings. In each case, capital cost allowance (tax depreciation) was claimed on the basis of the diminishing balance. Thus, if the cost of a Class 6 building was $100,000, the first year's depreciation was 10% of $100,000, the second year's depreciation was 10% of $90,000 ($100,000 minus $10,000) and the third year's depreciation was $8,100 (10% of $100,000 minus ($10,000 + $9,000)). For any acquisition of real estate, the tax rules required that land and building costs be segregated or apportioned. As is the case today, land costs were neither deductible nor depreciable. (To the extent that a real-estate acquisition also included furniture and fixtures, such as refrigerators and stoves, these appliances, were—and still are—depreciable at the rate of 20% per annum, also on a diminishing or declining balance basis. For purposes of the examples which follow, furniture costs are ignored.)

The tax shelter aspects of real-estate acquisitions resulted largely from a special provision of the tax depreciation rules. Before 1972, if a taxpayer bought a rental building late in a year, he was still permitted to claim a *full year's* capital cost allowance. This would produce a "property loss" deductible from other income. In other words, tax depreciation in the year of acquisition did not have to be calculated on a monthly basis in the same way as accounting depreciation. Thus, if one's downpayment was low enough, the first year's write-off often resulted in a tax saving that significantly reduced the actual cash investment. This is illustrated in Example 1.

EXAMPLE 1: A TYPICAL REAL ESTATE SHELTER BEFORE 1972
(The investor's marginal tax rate is assumed to be 60%)

Cost of Class 6 building—	
acquired at end of taxation year	
Land	$ 15,000
Building	100,000
	$115,000
Financing	
By way of mortgage (75%)	$ 86,250
Cash investment (25%)	28,750
	$115,000
Statement of rental income:	
Gross rents net of operating expenses	Nil
Less: Capital cost allowance	
(10% × $100,000)	10,000
	$ (10,000)
Tax saving on $10,000 rental loss	
(60% × $10,000)	$ 6,000
Cash investment (as above)	$ 28,750
Less: Income taxes recovered	(6,000)
Net cash invested in property	$ 22,750
Percentage cash investment (22,750 ÷ 115,000) =	19.8%

This simple case study illustrates the advantage of a tax depreciation write-off. The tax saving serves to reduce the owner's percentage of equity from 25% to just below 20%. This example meets the two basic requirements of a "pure" tax shelter:

1. There is no immediate loss of cash since the depreciation write-off does not involve any cash outflow, and
2. The property is presumably worth the same amount *after* the tax write-off as it was before. If the property had actually depreciated, the project would eventually end up losing cash.

In every year after the first, as long as the building carried itself from a cash-flow standpoint, further capital cost allowances could be claimed to produce for each year (before 1972) a tax loss deductible against other income. If the project was a good investment, it eventually ended up paying for itself. Under the pre-1972 tax system, there was no "day of reckoning" until the property was sold, and even then, proper planning could achieve a further postponement. To illustrate a typical situation, let's suppose the $100,000 building in the first example was then sold.

EXAMPLE 2: DEFERRAL OF RECAPTURED DEPRECIATION BEFORE 1972

Cost of building	$100,000
Less: Accumulated capital cost allowances (over several years)	45,000
Undepreciated capital cost (U.C.C.)	55,000
Less: Proceeds from eventual sale	(90,000)
Recaptured capital cost allowances	(35,000)
Purchase of other building in year of sale	150,000
New "base" for future capital cost allowances	$115,000
Recaptured capital cost allowances—revised	Nil

The second example assumes $45,000 of cumulative capital cost allowances for tax purposes. For an individual in a 60% bracket, this would have resulted in accumulated tax savings of $27,000 (60% x $45,000)—almost enough to have recovered the full original cash investment of $28,750. If the property were then sold for $90,000, it would become apparent that, in fact, the property had only depreciated by $10,000. The tax rules therefore provided that unwarranted depreciation was to be brought back into income, in the year of sale. In this case, the excess depreciation is $35,000.

However, whenever a rental building was sold before 1972, the tax on recaptured depreciation could be deferred if another property of the same class were acquired in the same year. (Example 2 assumes that a building costing $150,000 was purchased as a replacement.) The recaptured depreciation was thus eliminated and the only "penalty" was a smaller new base for *future* capital cost allowances (that is, $115,000). In addition, if the replacement building were acquired at the very end of the year (before any revenue could be generated), the taxpayer, instead of having recaptured depreciation as *income*, could then claim a tax write-off of 10% of $115,000 or $11,500.

Generally, buildings tended to appreciate and not depreciate in value. If the property in Example 2 were sold for $130,000, the maximum depreciation that could potentially be recaptured was limited to the depreciation claimed in the first place—that is, $45,000. The excess proceeds ($130,000 – $100,000) would have been considered as a capital gain—which was tax-free under the "old system"—and could also be used to pyramid one's tax-deferral structure. Over time, the shrewd investor was often able to build up a significant portfolio of real-estate holdings subsidized, to a large extent, by tax savings from capital cost allowances.

If one practised tax deferral by sheltering recaptured depreciation with other acquisitions throughout one's lifetime, the deferral became an absolute tax saving. Before 1972, death did not result in any disposition of property being deemed for tax purposes and there was no recaptured depreciation at that time. The fact that heirs were allowed to take over inherited depreciable property at *current fair market values*, and could begin to claim *their* capital cost allowances on that (inflated) amount, increased the advantages of having depreciable property in one's portfolio at the time of death.

The 1972 Tax Reform

Major changes to the rules were made in 1972. From that time on, the deduction of capital cost allowances on rental buildings and leasehold interests was limited to the net cash income from these properties after deducting operating expenses. Thus, in general, capital cost allowances can no longer either produce or increase rental losses. The reader should note that the limitation restricting the deductibility of capital-cost-allowance losses does not apply to corporations whose principal business is leasing land and buildings or property development. Such corporations may continue to offset rental losses created by capital cost allowances against miscellaneous other income. This is an extremely important point in tax planning for both real-estate developers and persons with substantial investments and will be dealt with in more detail in Chapter Eleven.

If one owns property and operating expenses such as mortgage interest, taxes, heating, insurance and repairs and maintenance exceed gross rental income, the *cash* rental loss continues to be deductible. However, this loss cannot be increased (or created in the first place) as a result of tax depreciation.

The opportunities that existed before 1972 to defer tax on recaptured depreciation were also blocked. A separate capital cost allowance class must be created for all rental buildings acquired or built after 1971 at a cost of $50,000 or more. Thus, a taxpayer may have many Class 3's or Class 6's, and when a property is disposed of, the negative balance in the capital cost allowance pool resulting from the sale cannot be offset against the costs of another rental property.

Furthermore, one can no longer avoid tax on recaptured depreciation by retaining rental property until death. The Income Tax Act now provides, at that time, a deemed disposition of land at fair market value, and buildings at a value halfway between undepreciated capital cost and fair market value—unless the property is bequeathed to one's spouse or to a "spousal trust". Even such a bequest only postpones the inevitable since the regular deemed-disposition rules would apply when the spouse, in turn, dies. Thus, on the death of an individual or his spouse, there will be at least a partial recapture of depreciation as well as exposure to capital gains. The estate would have to ensure that the taxes are paid before the property could be distributed without any encumbrances to the heirs. The rules are further designed so that any heir who acquires depreciable property on which there has not been a full recapture becomes ultimately liable for taxes when he himself makes a sale.

Multiple Unit Residential Buildings

After 1972, the federal government's attack on real estate as a tax shelter produced some rather interesting consequences. Investment capital quickly stopped flowing from the private sector to the construction industry. Many investors in upper tax brackets no longer maintained the same interest in real estate as they did in previous years, because they felt that the rewards would not be commensurate with the problems involved in having to administer property. The inability to claim depreciation losses greatly reduced an investor's potential leverage and increased the amount of cash that he personally was required to tie up within each property investment.

Almost immediately, the construction industry was clamouring for the reintroduction of tax concessions, and by 1974, there already was an acute shortage of residential housing in Canada. This, of course, resulted in higher rents being charged by landlords, with a corresponding increase in the rate of inflation. The complaints of the construction industry were quickly matched by those of potential renters.

Finally, in its November 1974 Budget, the federal government retreated somewhat. Two new classes of depreciable property were created—Classes 31 and 32—to contain the costs of multiple unit residential buildings for construction begun after November 18, 1974. A multiple unit residential building (MURB) is defined as a property where not less than 80% of the floor space is used for "self-contained domestic establishments" and related parking, recreation, service and storage areas. Class 31 parallels Class 3, both as to depreciation rate (5%) and also as to the type of construction (concrete and/or steel reinforced buildings). Class 32 was set up to parallel Class 6 (10% depreciation for wood frame or brick veneer construction). Capital cost allowance on these qualifying properties *is* allowed to create or increase a rental loss.

Since 1978, however, the government has started to phase out the rules allowing *any* building to be depreciated at 10%. Thus, any MURB where construction commenced after December 31, 1977, is automatically classified as a Class 31 property. Also, whenever a (pre-1978) Class 32 property is acquired by a new owner after the end of 1979, the depreciation rate to the buyer reverts to 5% only. Existing Class 32 properties are still depreciable at 10% to their current owners and to members of their family, if passed on. All other building acquisitions of wood frame or similar construction (such as office buildings, shopping centres, warehouses, or older apartment buildings) now automatically fall into a buyer's Class 3. It is also no longer possible to buy or build a Class 6 rental property, although the income tax regulations do permit a taxpayer to make an *addition* to an existing Class 6 property of up to $100,000 and still have that addition or extension depreciated at 10%. In addition, a wood frame building where there is only surface construction may still qualify for capital cost allowance at 10%. (In fact, with adventurous tax planning, Classes 6 and 32 *can* be maintained even if property is transferred in an arm's-length transaction. This will also be covered in Chapter Eleven.)

However, the rules pertaining to "separate classes" for all rental properties acquired after 1971 have not been amended or repealed. Thus, although capital cost allowance on a MURB may create a rental loss, such capital cost allowance is subject to ultimate recapture in the year of sale—without the relief that might otherwise be obtained if additional property is acquired (unless replacement properties cost less than $50,000).

The MURB rules were intended to stimulate new residential construction. The depreciation loss on an "end of the year" acquisition could then be offset against other income. This tax incentive has already been illustrated on page 30.

Soft Cost Write-Offs

As it turned out, the modest opportunity to shelter against taxes through MURB acquisitions only marked the beginning of the revival of the construction industry. For developers of real estate, in contrast to mere investors, a good deal more than just a capital-cost-allowance loss can be derived as a tax-shelter benefit. This is because there are several significant costs associated with real-estate construction which are capital in nature but which may be written off for tax purposes in the year or years incurred. These components are called "soft costs" and include:

1. Interest paid on borrowed money during the construction period.
2. Expenses of borrowing money (such as mortgage application and commitment fees and appraisal costs).

3. Landscaping of grounds.
4. Expenses of representation (for example, the costs of obtaining proper zoning approvals and building permits).
5. Costs of site investigation to determine suitability for a project.
6. Utilities service connections (such as the costs of obtaining power, telephone and water services).
7. Real estate taxes and insurance during the construction period.
8. General overhead expenses:
   (a) office expenses
   (b) off-site supervision during the construction period
   (c) advertising for tenants.

From an accounting standpoint, soft costs contribute to the total value of any project under construction. Also, one could not construct a replacement building without incurring these same costs. Thus, they are treated as long-term assets (capitalized) on financial statements, and are only written off through normal depreciation over the lifespan of a building. However, for tax purposes, soft costs are subject to an *immediate* write-off because of specific income tax legislation.

Originally, the term "soft costs" distinguished these particular components of a construction project from the "hard costs" of construction—the bricks, mortar and direct labour. There is another tax term with respect to these costs which in its own way, is just as descriptive. Soft costs are also known as "first-time write-offs", to indicate that these particular costs are incurred only *once*—during the construction period.

Soft Costs and Real Estate Developers

If one is in business as a developer constructing buildings for resale, these properties become *inventory* for tax purposes. In other words, a developer's project bears the same relationship to him as a dishwasher does to an appliance store or an automobile to a car dealer. For tax purposes, this means that a profit on sale is *fully taxable* as business income and is not a capital gain.

Assume, therefore, that a builder sells a construction project—land included—to an investor for $115,000. Assume also that the actual costs of the project are only $85,000, out of which $20,000 are categorized as soft costs. If a sale takes place in the year that the project was constructed, soft costs do not have any tax value to the developer. He must simply report as income the difference between his total costs of $85,000 and his selling price of $115,000.

Even if the sale takes place one year later, soft costs have, in this case, only *limited* value to the developer. In the first year, he may claim a $20,000 tax write-off for these expenditures but his inventory for tax purposes is then reduced to only $65,000 ($85,000 – $20,000 written off). Then, in the second year, when the building is sold to an investor for $115,000, a $50,000 profit would have to be recorded. This $50,000 would represent the actual profit of $30,000 plus a recapture of $20,000 of soft costs previously written off. In other words, soft costs are not of much use to a developer who is constructing a project for resale. They are only of value to someone who is building a project to *retain it* for rental purposes. Where this is the case, there is an immediate tax write-off, while the recognition of income can perhaps be deferred for many years until a sale is actually made. The effects of soft costs to a developer are illustrated in the table that appears on page 38.

About the time the MURB legislation was introduced, a number of developers came up with a rather interesting concept concerning soft costs. They decided to sign up their investors *before* beginning a construction project.

Under the new arrangements, the investors would themselves becomes the developers. The "real" developers would then become "subcontractors" or "project managers" who would supervise the actual construction activities. However, since the investors would be the owners of the project from the very outset, the project managers could break down their billings into both hard-cost and soft-cost components.

That is, instead of paying $115,000 for a completed project, the investor-developer would incur hard costs (including land costs) of, say, $95,000 and soft costs of $20,000. The soft costs of $20,000 could then be written off immediately,

	If Sale Takes Place in Year of Construction	If Sale Takes Place in Subsequent Year	
		Year 1	Year 2
Selling Price	$115,000		$115,000
Cost of project			
Land	15,000	15,000	
Hard Costs	50,000	50,000	
Soft Costs	20,000	20,000	
Total cost of project	$ 85,000	$ 85,000	
Soft cost write-off	$ (20,000)	$ (20,000)	
Inventory value for tax purposes ($ 85,000 – $20,000)	65,000	65,000	65,000
Profit on sale ($115,000 – $65,000)	$ 50,000		$ 50,000
Soft cost write-off "loss"	$ (20,000)	$ (20,000)	
Profit on sale of inventory	50,000		$ 50,000
Net profit (selling price minus total cost of project)	$ 30,000		$30,000

Therefore, if a project is built by a developer for resale, soft costs are of limited value.

---

and if the project qualified as a MURB, capital cost allowances could also be claimed on the remaining costs attributable to the building (but not land). The investor-developer would ordinarily be expected to retain his interest in such a project. He would thus benefit from an initial write-off, while any recapture could be postponed indefinitely until a sale took place.

A number of projects were marketed along these lines across Canada in the mid-1970s but the initial reaction of Revenue Canada was definitely not favourable. Revenue officials contended that a construction contract did not necessarily make somebody whose ordinary business was not related to that industry into a developer. Some claims have been disallowed by the various District Taxation Offices; however, no cases have yet come before the courts. In some instances, compromises have been made in the interest of expediency.

Investors' Soft Cost Write-Offs

Eventually, however, the conflict with Revenue *was* resolved. Of the tax rules pertaining to soft-cost write-offs, it has been established that only expenses of representation, site investigation costs, and utilities service hook-ups are restricted for tax purposes to taxpayers carrying on a *business*. It appears that soft costs are a valid deduction in all other cases—whether one is classified as a real-estate developer *or* one admits to being merely a passive investor—as long as the investor has an interest in a project "from the ground floor up". Again, the soft costs are also first-time write-offs—meaning that they are only valid deductions if the investor is an owner of the project during the construction period.

A comprehensive list of soft cost write-offs available to real-estate investors would include:

1. CMHC mortgage insurance fee: A fee paid to obtain a guarantee by the Canadian Mortgage and Housing Corporation of payments with respect to the first mortgage (usually 1.5% of the first mortgage).
2. Second mortgage guarantee fee: A fee paid to the project manager (usually the developer or general contractor) to guarantee payments of the investors on account of their second mortgages. This is sometimes a fee for providing a second mortgage at low interest (first mortgage) rates.
3. Legal fees re:
   • First and second mortgage documentation.
   • Construction and management agreements.
   • Tenants' leases.
4. Initial services fee (administration and supervision):
   • Charges for off-site administration and management of project.
   • Providing accounting services and reporting to investors.

- Guarantee of timely completion.
- Undertaking to pay net operating costs including maintenance, taxes and interest due to construction delays after scheduled date of completion.
5. Initial leasing and marketing fee:
    - Undertaking of the project manager to develop, prepare and review policies and procedures with respect to the marketing of rental units during the initial rent-up period, including advertising for tenants.
    - Commissions paid to rental agents.
6. Costs of obtaining financing:
    - Standby charges.
    - Appraisal costs.
    - Commitment fees.
    - Commissions paid to brokers to obtain financing (after November 16, 1978).
7. Insurance on the project during construction.
8. Cash-flow guarantee fee: A fee to compensate the project manager for undertaking to guarantee at least a break-even cash flow for a certain period (e.g., two years) after substantial completion of the project.
9. Landscaping costs (deductible when paid).
10. Real-estate taxes during construction.
11. Interest on mortgages (interim financing) during the construction period (at actual costs).

Deductibility of these soft-cost write-offs for real-estate investors has, in fact, been reviewed and accepted by Revenue Canada as long as the actual amounts are reasonable. As a general rule, most developers appear to be working with soft cost percentages of between 17% and 20%. In other words, the total soft costs tend to be between 17% and 20% of the costs of each particular project—including land, building and soft costs together. It should be noted, however, that as of the spring of 1981, with higher rates of interest being charged for interim financing, a reasonable soft-cost percentage may now be much greater than was previously the case.

There does appear to have been a recent tightening in the attitude of Revenue officials. It now appears that certain of the soft cost expenditures will not be deductible "up front" but will be required instead to be amortized over a reasonable length of time. For example, it is Revenue's view that the costs of advertising for tenants should only be written off over the length of the initial leases. Similarly, rental guarantee fees paid by an investor should be prorated over the guarantee period. The April 21, 1980 Budget introduced special legislation dealing with prepaid expenses, presumably to strengthen Revenue's position. This means that the full soft-cost tax shelter may not be obtainable immediately (as in the past), although essentially the same write-offs will be claimable over only a few years. This topic will be further discussed towards the end of this chapter.

The MURB legislation was originally intended to expire at the end of 1976. The Conservative government allowed the program to lapse for construction begun after December 31, 1979, although the Liberal government brought the program back for construction commencing October 29, 1980 to the end of 1981.

Whether or not the program will be extended into 1982 is not yet known at the time this chapter is being written. However, new MURB construction is not the only investment in real estate which can provide a tax shelter. The only significance of having a project qualify as a MURB is the 5% capital cost allowance which can be used to create or increase a rental loss. Since the repeal of the 10% depreciation factor for construction after 1977, one must make a very substantial investment in a project in order to have a worthwhile capital cost allowance to claim.

The important thing for investors to note is that soft costs are claimable on *all construction projects*—even if a project does not qualify as a MURB. None of the soft costs deductible by investors pertain specifically to residential property. In other words, one can have a perfectly viable tax shelter through *commercial* property construction. This would include office buildings, medical/dental (professional) buildings, warehouses, hotels, as well as duplexes, town houses and apartment buildings.

Furthermore, there are no restrictions which would require that a tax shelter project be situated in Canada. *Participation in a real-estate construction project outside Canada will give a Canadian investor the* same *soft-cost write-offs as a project in this country.* Since a Canadian is taxable on world income (less losses), a loss from foreign property is readily tax deductible against other income.

Usually, if a project is situated in a foreign country, the soft costs would be capitalized for foreign tax purposes as part of land and building. This would facilitate larger depreciation claims in the future which would offset taxable income generated for foreign tax purposes on that particular project. As with any other construction project, one would hope that the foreign property is a good investment and that it would begin to carry itself within a short period of time after construction was completed.

Such a project would not provide any Canadian tax shelter after the year of completion (since maximum capital cost allowances in subsequent years are restricted to those sufficient to bring the rental income down to zero). Therefore the investor must find further new projects in which to invest.

By acquiring an interest in one new construction project each year, many taxpayers can obtain an adequate tax shelter while they build up an impressive real-estate investment portfolio over time. These concepts are illustrated on page 43. The reader should note that the example assumes that a taxpayer invests in a project (in Canada or elsewhere) before actual construction begins and that the project is completed at the very end of the year without generating any rental income. However, so far no operating expenses are incurred either. The soft-cost write-offs of $20,000 produce a tax-deductible loss. The fact that capital cost allowance cannot be applied to make that loss bigger—unless the project qualifies as a MURB—does not really affect the viability of the project as a tax shelter to any great extent. If you compare the figures in Example 3 with those of the first example discussed in this chapter, it becomes evident that tax shelters are readily available even where a project is not a MURB. Ironically, the opportunity to claim soft costs could have been "discovered" many years ago. It appears coincidental that the existence of these tax advantages was only realized around the same time as the MURB program was introduced.

EXAMPLE 3: REAL ESTATE TAX SHELTER WITH SOFT COST WRITE-OFFS
(NOT A MURB)
(The investor's marginal tax rate is assumed to be 60%)

Land	$ 15,000
Cost of building materials, labour and contractor's mark-up (i.e., "hard costs")	80,000
Soft costs	20,000
	$115,000

Financing:	
By way of mortgage (75%)	$ 86,250
Cash investment (25%)	28,750
	$115,000

Statement of rental income:	
Gross rents net of operating expenses	Nil
Less: Soft cost write offs	$ 20,000
Capital cost allowances (not a MURB)	Nil
	$ 20,000
Rental loss	$ (20,000)
Tax saving on $20,000 rental loss in 60% tax bracket	$ 12,000
Cash investment (as above)	$ 28,750
Less: Income taxes recovered	(12,000)
Net Cash invested in property	$ 16,750
Percentage cash investment $16,750/$115,000 =	14.6%

The construction project in Example 3 is not a MURB. Example 4 makes the assumption that the project does so qualify. With the extra 5% tax write-off, the net cash investment is reduced from $16,750 to $14,350.

EXAMPLE 4: REAL ESTATE TAX SHELTER WITH SOFT COST WRITE-OFFS
(The investor's marginal tax rate is assumed to be 60%)

Land	$ 15,000
Cost of building materials, labour	
and contractor's mark-up (i.e., "hard costs")	80,000
Soft costs	20,000
	$115,000

Financing:	
By way of mortgage (75%)	$ 86,250
Cash investment (25%)	28,750
	$115,000

Statement of rental income:	
Gross rents net of operating expenses	Nil
Less: Soft cost write offs	$ 20,000
Capital cost allowances (5% x $80,000)	4,000
	$ 24,000
Rental loss	$ (24,000)
Tax saving on $24,000 rental loss in 60% tax bracket	$ 14,400

Cash investment (as above)	$ 28,750
Less: Income taxes recovered	(14,400)
Net cash invested in property	$ 14,350
Percentage cash investment	
14,350/115,000 =	12.5%

Commercial Construction—A Viable Tax Shelter

Almost ten years ago, the Department of National Revenue organized a special "Advance Rulings Section". The purpose of this undertaking was to allow taxpayers to bring *proposed* transactions before senior Revenue officials for a ruling as to the tax consequences which would result from these transactions if and when implemented. The protocol involves providing Revenue with a complete statement outlining the contemplated course of action along with a submission requesting that particular income tax results should apply. The taxpayer is permitted to present arguments in order to substantiate his position. The Advance Rulings Section will then review the taxpayer's request and if the examiner agrees with the conclusions, a favourable advance ruling would then be issued. Having a favourable ruling ensures that the transaction will not be adversely treated upon any subsequent Revenue audit. If the Rulings Division disagrees with the conclusions drawn by the taxpayer, a negative ruling would be issued. This would not prevent the taxpayer from doing whatever he intended in the first place, but would at least indicate to him that the transaction will likely be questioned.

During the mid-1970s, while the concept of soft-cost write-offs was becoming popular, many developers sought advance rulings in order to convince potential investors of the merit of their real-estate tax shelter projects. Today, since soft-cost write-offs seem to be ingrained within the tax system, it appears that there are relatively few requests now being made for Revenue's sanction. There are, however, several points worth noting. First, Revenue Canada is gradually tightening its administrative policy with respect to the timing of soft-cost write-offs. As mentioned previously, in some cases officials are suggesting that these costs should be written off over several accounting periods and not just during the construction phase. They feel that generally accepted accounting principles of matching costs against revenues over a period of time should be followed. Also, as I have indicated, the position of Revenue Canada has recently been strengthened by an Income Tax Act amendment. This change requires, for the first time, prepaid expenses to be deducted in the year or years to which these expenditures relate rather than at the time the outlays were made or the expenses were incurred.

Several years ago, I assisted one of my clients, a Calgary real-estate developer, in putting together a tax shelter based on a construction project consisting of a commercial (office) building. At that time, it was not completely clear as to whether Revenue Canada's administrative policy would permit soft-cost write-offs to extend beyond MURBS to non-residential construction as well. Accordingly, I recommended to my client that we approach Revenue Canada in Ottawa for an Advance Ruling. The client agreed and we subsequently found out that we were the first to approach Revenue Canada on a development involving commercial construction. The following figures summarize the cost allocations of this particular project. Note that the soft costs amounted to 18% of the total.

A COMMERCIAL CONSTRUCTION PROJECT AS A TAX SHELTER

First mortgage insurance fee	$ 30,000
Second mortgage guarantee fee	20,000
Legal fees re:	
Mortgages	12,000
Construction and management agreements	20,000
Tenants' leases	8,000
Initial services fee	135,000
Initial leasing and marketing fee	60,000
Cost of obtaining financing	20,000
Insurance	2,000
Cash-flow guarantee fee	60,000
Landscaping	3,000
Real-estate taxes during construction	5,000
Interest on interim financing	100,000
Subtotal (18%)	475,000
Land	400,000
Building	1,775,000
Total (100%)	$2,650,000

Revenue Canada agreed that there is no reason why part of a commercial construction project should not consist of soft-cost write-offs. However, their ruling was not entirely favourable. The schedule on page 47 summarizes the conclusions of the Advance Rulings Section.

In general, the only specific soft costs with which Revenue Canada had any quarrel was our claim for the initial services

EXAMPLE OF COMMERCIAL CONSTRUCTION PROJECT AS TAX SHELTER
SUMMARY OF RULING RECEIVED FROM REVENUE CANADA

First mortgage insurance fee	Deductible when withheld from mortgage draws
Second mortgage guarantee fee	*Amortize* over period of second mortgage
Legal fees re:	
Mortgages	Deductible
Construction and management agreements	Deductible
Tenants' leases	*Amortize* over length of leases
Initial services fee	Only services relating to lease-up are deductible. Supervision, accounting and timely completion bonuses are *capital*
Initial leasing and marketing fee	*Amortize* over term of leases
Costs of obtaining financing	Deductible
Insurance	Deductible. Payments for construction risks are capital
Cash-flow guarantee fee	*Amortize* over guarantee period
Landscaping	Deductible when paid
Real-estate taxes during construction	Deductible when incurred
Interest on interim financing	Deductible in year incurred

---

fee. They asked us to provide time records to substantiate our figures and, unfortunately, my client had not kept such records. In total, they suggested that our initial service fee of $135,000 should be reduced by approximately $50,000. Surprisingly, they suggested that accounting to investors is a capital expenditure and not a soft-cost write-off! This was actually the only point in the ruling with which I personally took serious exception.

With certain other components, such as the second mortgage guarantee charge and the cash-flow guarantee fee, Revenue suggested that these should be amortized. Since this project was an office building, and the leases were intended to be for five years, this meant that some of the expenditures would only be deductible over a medium-term period. In a residential project, leases generally tend to be on a year-to-year basis. If this is the case, the amortization factor becomes negligible.

However, notwithstanding the reduction in allowable initial-service fees of about $50,000 and the amortization requirement, the advance ruling did prove that commercial construction is a viable tax shelter for Canadians. I have never approached Revenue personally on the subject of *foreign* development projects and their Canadian tax shelter consequences, but I nevertheless feel that since there is no specific requirement that these expenditures be incurred in Canada, such a project would pass muster.

Timing of the Investor's Participation

As with almost any investment, one of the most crucial considerations is timing. The ruling which we obtained incorporated wording which I understand is common to all Revenue Canada rulings on soft costs:

> *Any costs incurred prior to an investor becoming an owner and paid by him to obtain his ownership interest in the project will be part of his cost of land and depreciable property, rather than deductible expenses.*

In other words, Revenue appears to be extremely strict in their interpretation that soft costs only belong to someone who is an owner before the particular expenditures are incurred or paid for. I cannot caution you strongly enough to stay away from the temptation to back-date documentation. Back-dating here would involve simply predating an agreement between the contractor and the investor who joins a project late to a point before the project began. Such practice constitutes tax fraud and the penalties are severe.

Several years ago, I happened to be at a conference where

Mr. James Gourlay spoke on the subject of back-dating. At that time, Mr. Gourlay was Chief of Special Investigations for Revenue Canada. Mr. Gourlay informed the participants at the conference that government authorities and scientists have co-operated to develop methods whereby a typewritten contract can be analysed to determine exactly when the contract was drawn. For example, if a contract was allegedly prepared as of a certain date but the typewriter used to type it was not manufactured until, say, six months later, this provides ample evidence of back-dating. Mr. Gourlay also told a story about a prestigious law firm which allegedly drafted a contract as of a certain date and sent it off to their clients with an enclosure letter. Unfortunately, the names of the partners on the letterhead did not correspond to the individuals who were members of the partnership at the time the contract was allegedly drafted!

As far as I am concerned, it is perfectly permissible to date a contract on, say, June 15, 1982 giving effect to a verbal agreement between the parties reached on, say, April 15, 1982 (provided there was such an agreement)—but don't back-date.

Partnership Arrangements

In some cases, it may be possible to circumvent the problem of passing on soft costs to an investor who is not an owner of a project from the outset by structuring the tax shelter project as a partnership.

Under the Canadian rules governing partnerships, profits and losses are allocated at the end of a partnership's fiscal period to the taxpayers who were members of the partnership at that time. Thus, if a partnership undertakes a construction project involving soft costs, these write-offs create a loss for income tax purposes. If the partnership adopts, for example, a calendar year-end, the losses are allocated to those persons who were partners on December 31. Thus, at least in theory, anyone who became a member of the partnership during the year (even in the last week of December) would be entitled to his share of the loss, even though the bulk of this loss may have been incurred before the taxpayer joined in the venture. In such manner, retroactive soft-cost expenses can, in fact, be passed on.

The use of such partnership arrangements to pass on soft costs to "late investors" is extremely tricky. It is possible that Revenue authorities could apply certain provisions of the Canadian Income Tax Act that would treat the admission of a new partner as the formation of a new partnership from that time on. Thus, prior soft costs could not be allocated to that particular partner. In addition, there are tax provisions negating attempts to share income or losses of a partnership in such a way so as to artificially reduce or postpone taxes otherwise payable.

I do undersand that in some cases Revenue Canada has, as a matter of expediency, issued favourable rulings whereby partners have been held to be entitled to their shares of profits or losses irrespective of when during the course of the (initial) year they became partners. Presumably, Revenue Canada recognizes that it is sometimes extremely important to commence construction of a project before all the investors are in place, and where a certain portion of the partnership units have already been sold, Revenue appears willing to sanction soft-cost allocations even to partners who join a little later on within that same fiscal year. However, because Revenue may be extending the limits of the law slightly in these circumstances, it is my recommendation that a ruling is required on a project-by-project basis. In other words, I would not recommend to a client of mine that he accept a developer's verbal assurance that (based on past experience or other rulings) soft costs may in fact be allocated even if the client invests in the project after the costs are incurred. I must stress that any ruling by Revenue is only binding for the particular project or situation to which the specific request for a ruling applies. Considerable caution is required in this area and persons seeking to invest into soft-cost projects through partnership arrangements should seek professional legal advice on these matters.

How to Structure Soft-Cost Write-Offs

From time to time, real-estate developers approach me for

assistance in calculating the soft-cost components in a construction project. Really, there is no "magic" in structuring a shelter—all that is required is a little bit of "creative accounting". My approach is to break down soft costs into two components: those that are "external" and those that are "internal".

The external soft costs are basically those cost components which are based on charges from parties unrelated to the developer. These costs include:

1. First mortgage insurance fee (generally 1.5% of the first mortgage).
2. Legal fees, based on a quotation obtained from the developer's attorneys with respect to mortgage fees, construction and management agreements and the costs of preparing tenants' leases.
3. The initial leasing and marketing costs, which include anticipated commissions to be paid to a realtor whose job it will be to find tenants. Often, this cost is a set percentage of projected rental revenues.
4. Costs of obtaining financing—including actual expected mortgage commitment fees, appraisal costs, and standby charges. (A standby charge is a cost which is imposed by a lender to ensure that each construction mortgage draw will be available as required.)
5. Insurance on the project during construction—where the calculation is based on a quotation from the developer's insurers.
6. Landscaping. This too can be determined objectively, by obtaining estimates from landscapers who are bidding on the contract.
7. Real-estate taxes during construction, which can be determined on the basis of property assessment values.
8. Interest on interim financing, calculated by estimating the length of time that each mortgage draw will be outstanding in relation to the entire construction project. Once the rate of financing is known, the rest is just simple arithmetic.

After the external soft costs are calculated, this leaves only a few others to be determined. These are the charges made directly by the project manager to the investors. The internal soft costs include:

1. The second mortgage guarantee fee
2. A cash-flow guarantee fee (if applicable)
3. The initial services fee

Essentially, these soft costs are simply the difference between the total acceptable figure of 17%–20% of the project and the external soft costs calculated previously. In other words, the figure is basically plugged! On most projects which I have seen, the initial services fee, which is the largest of the internal soft costs charges, is usually 5% of the entire project. The balance is allocated among the other two components. Usually, the initial services fee covers many things as described on pages 39-40. The more description one uses, the less chance there is that the total soft costs would be eroded significantly if Revenue Canada does take exception to some of the numbers. Thus, there really is no magic in determining the various numbers in a tax shelter project. All it takes is a little bit of creative accounting.

Accounting for Recaptured Soft Costs in the Year of Sale

One of the major problems with respect to real-estate investments in Canada involves the question of what happens for income tax purposes when a real-estate project is sold. Basically, the question is whether or not a profit will be treated as ordinary income or as a capital gain. Ordinary income is, of course, taxable in full while only one-half of a capital gain is taxed. This question will be dealt with fully in Chapter Six. For the time being, however, it is worth examining the position of someone who has claimed soft-cost write-offs and, at some future time, decides to sell his investment. If one has completely written off soft costs of, say, $20,000 as in the sample illustration on page 43, is it reasonable in the year of sale to treat only half of the soft cost recovery as a taxable capital gain? Of course, to write off $20,000 and recapture $10,000 is not logical. However, not all income tax provisions are logical. There is no specific requirement in the Income Tax Act which would require an investor to recapture his soft-cost write-offs.

The concept of recaptured depreciation only applies with reference to any amount originally added to the capital cost of a class or pool, that is to say, the "hard costs." In the example, the maximum recaptured depreciation would be with respect to capital cost allowances claimed from the (hard cost) base of $80,000 which was the only amount added to the pool or class in the first place. Thus, if the $80,000 of building costs were depreciated (over time) to, say, $72,000, the maximum recaptured depreciation would only be $8,000. Technically, proceeds over and above $80,000 (including soft costs previously written off) could be treated as a capital gain—only half of which would be taxable!

Surprisingly, the Income Tax Act has not been amended over the past few years to include a provision so that if soft costs are claimed, their recovery would automatically be deemed to give rise to ordinary income. In addition, no cases on this subject have come before the courts. Needless to say, however, Revenue Canada is not happy about having investors writing off soft costs in their entirety and then treating them as capital gains in the year of sale. The only valid attack that Revenue officials have to this point is, however, to deem the *entire profit* on the sale to be ordinary income—including all proceeds in excess of original cost.

In Chapter Six, we will examine the general criteria which have evolved in the Canadian courts to deal with the question of whether or not a profit gives rise to ordinary income or to a capital gain. In the meantime, I suggest that when you are confronted with a grey area, you have the right to adopt the reporting that produces the least amount of tax as long as such reporting is accepted by Revenue for assessment purposes. If you sell an investment and don't report your gain at all, this would be tax evasion. However, if you take advantage of the grey area and (at least) report your profit as a capital gain, you are complying with the letter of the law. Your worst exposure is that your tax return could be reassessed to reflect the entire gain on sale as (fully taxable) ordinary income. You are certainly no worse off (except for interest costs) than if you had reported the profit as regular income in the first place.

You should note, however, that the longer your holding period, the stronger your argument becomes for capital-gains treatment. As a general rule of thumb, I suggest that after, say, a five-year ownership, Revenue would be hard-pressed to assess your gains as ordinary income.

My general advice is that you report all real-estate gains as capital until reassessed by Revenue. However, when making your own private projections of internal rate of return on investment, I suggest that you calculate on the basis that your ultimate gain could be assessed as ordinary income. If the project is *still* viable from an investment standpoint, then by all means go ahead. On the other hand, if the success of a project is dependent primarily on tax advantages, then I recommend that you think twice before investing.

Types of Investment

In evaluating real-estate tax shelters, the next point to consider is the type of investment being contemplated. Are you getting a small percentage interest in a large project or do you obtain title to a specific unit? Certainly, a specific unit would be more readily saleable than a small percentage interest in a large project. However, what if that specific unit happens to be the only one which is vacant during a given year? The exposure to loss is certainly larger than an investment where the risk is shared. In some projects, you can maximize benefits if you obtain title to a specific unit while all the rents generated by the project are pooled together.

If we examine the alternatives of an investor with $50,000 of investment capital (which is either amassed or borrowed for the purpose of investment) there are basically three paths that can be followed. First, an investor in most regions in Canada (or perhaps even elsewhere) could acquire an investment in a duplex at a total cost of around $150,000. As discussed previously, this is viable as long as the rentals would subsidize a first mortgage of $100,000, which would be required over and above the $50,000 cash investment needed to purchase the property in the first place. A project of this type has its pros and cons. On the one hand, the investor becomes "his own boss" and may make his own decisions on how long to wait before selling, when and if to renovate, or when to raise rents. Of course, the investor also bears all the risk. What if the tenants "skip"? What happens if there is a surplus of rental units available, and the investor's unit remains vacant? How would you react to a telephone call in the middle of a dark winter night informing you that the water pipes had just burst? Of course, some of the nuisance factor of owning such a property can be alleviated by hiring a property administrator—at a cost.

The second possibility is that an investor with $50,000 of capital can pool his resources together with those of a small group of other people, preferably friends, relatives or business associates. It is helpful if the members of the group have different skills which complement one another. In this manner, the group can purchase a larger property—perhaps a small apartment building or a small strip shopping-centre or other commercial building. A group of this nature can divide the administrative responsibilities and join their efforts so that administration becomes much less of a burden. The major pitfall, however, is that often members of a small group do not see eye-to-eye, and if the particular investor is in a minority position, his wishes can be overruled by the majority. One of the problems of establishing such a group is to find other people with similar goals, objectives and income levels willing to pool their efforts. A good way to get started is probably to offer some kind of an incentive to a member of the group who actually uncovers investments which the group subsequently buys. If this is done, the individual members won't simply be sitting around waiting for someone else to unearth a viable investment project.

For those who do not feel comfortable either investing by themselves or within the framework of a small group, the third and last alternative appears to be participation in a large syndicate. Here, the investor sacrifices the pride of personal ownership and the opportunity to take an active role in administration for the security of professional management. Of course, where a developer has put together a large project, the investor's costs do include a factor for advertising and promotion of the project itself including prospectus costs, if applicable. This is often the equivalent of investing into a mutual fund with a "front end load". Nevertheless, the fact that these marketing and commission costs are built into the price of a unit does not necessarily mean that such an investment should be disregarded. You must attempt to assess the developer's reputation and you should try to develop some familiarity with real-estate values and growth potential in the area in which the project is being constructed. Remember also that real-estate shelters do not have to be restricted to residential construction or, for that matter, to Canadian projects—this gives you a tremendous flexibility in doing your shopping. Try to invest in those places where there is both political stability and a hot real-estate market. It is also important to consider what the developer or project manager is retaining for himself. In some cases, the developer may keep units at no cost to himself just for putting the project together. In other circumstances, the developer may not take an immediate percentage interest in the project but may provide to himself a bonus based on future profitability. Thus, if the project is well managed and produces a good rate of return over and above the cash flow required for debt repayments, the developer would then be entitled to a management fee on an ongoing basis. Similarly, if and when the project is ultimately sold, a certain percentage of the profit on sale would accrue to the project manager for his efforts in putting the entire deal together. Each syndicate has a tendency to be somewhat different.

How Much Shelter Do You Need?

You should also keep potential recaptured depreciation and exposure to capital gains in mind—especially in estate planning. Real estate is not a liquid investment. Therefore, you should make an overall attempt to balance your portfolio with holdings that could readily provide the dollars needed to pay taxes arising on death. As an alternative, you might consider sufficient life insurance to discharge your tax liabilities so that your heirs do not have to dispose of your real-estate holdings under forced-sale conditions.

Finally, beware of oversheltering. The table on page 57 lists the average marginal rates of tax for residents of Canada in 1981. A marginal rate of tax is the combined federal and provincial tax rate that would apply to the *next dollar* of taxable income earned by a taxpayer in a given year.

COMBINED FEDERAL AND PROVINCIAL INCOME TAX BRACKETS
FOR INDIVIDUALS IN 1981 (AVERAGE ACROSS CANADA)

On taxable income between	Approximate Marginal Tax Bracket
$17,800 – $ 21,800	37%
21,800 – 25,900	41%
25,900 – 27,800	44%
27,800 – 47,600	47%
47,600 – 77,300	53%
77,300 – 119,000	57%
Over 119,000	62%

People often ask me whether I, who profess to be knowledgeable on the subject of income taxes and "know all the loopholes", pay any income taxes. Actually, I do. I see nothing wrong with reporting a taxable income of somewhere in the $25,000 to $28,000 range. In 1981, at a taxable income of $27,800, my total tax would be approximately $8,000 to $9,000 depending on where in Canada I happen to live. The effective tax (actual tax as a percentage of taxable income) is less than 30%. If I were to shelter myself with real estate or other tax write-offs down to a taxable income of zero, the most I could save is, therefore, $8,000 or $9,000.

Always remember that the bigger your loss, the *smaller* your tax advantage becomes as the marginal tax bracket decreases. On the other hand, if the shelter proves to be a good investment and generates income upon its sale, taxes are always levied at *increasing* marginal rates. There is not much point in sheltering my tax payable of $8,000 or $9,000 to save 30 cents on the dollar today if a few years from now, I would have to pay 62 cents on the dollar, because of the income I had realized from the sale of the property.

On the other hand, I certainly believe that it is to my advantage to reduce my taxable income *down* to about $27,800. As my taxable income falls from say, $47,600 to $27,800, I have the advantage of saving 47 cents on each dollar sheltered. Even if the exposure is that I might have to pay 62% later on, at least I am saving (relatively) high taxes in today's money while my additional tax exposure is in dollars that presumably will be worth less because of inflation. These thoughts are summarized in table form on the next page.

EFFECT OF POTENTIAL "OVER-SHELTERING"

Taxable Income	Federal and Provincial Potential Tax Payable	Tax Shelter % if Taxes are Eliminated	Maximum Tax Exposure on Future Sale
First $27,800	$ 8,500	30%	62%
Next $19,800	9,300	47%	62%
Next $29,700	15,700	53%	62%

As a general guideline, I try to keep my clients from sheltering below $27,800 of taxable income (in 1981). As long as one saves at least 47 cents on the dollar today, he should be willing to accept the possibility of higher taxes later on. I must admit, however, that these last comments are personal and, therefore, somewhat subjective. From time to time, I have encountered people who have been extremely successful in eliminating their taxes completely through real estate and other shelters. These people take the attitude that, as long as they don't have to pay *any* taxes today, they refuse to worry about potential liability down the road. Some of these people have been extremely fortunate in being able to build impressive investment portfolios using funds that would otherwise have been confiscated by the Government of Canada. Some of their success is undoubtedly due to astute investment policies, while the remainder is a by-product of inflation and the fact that, in general, real-estate values have tended to rise over the last few years. Personally, I take a slightly less aggressive viewpoint since I don't think it is a criminal offense to pay some taxes. Naturally, you must establish your own philosophy on this subject and consult with your own advisers before deciding on how aggressive you wish to become.

Summary

The major advantage of real-estate shelters is that the tax saving from soft-cost write-offs may be used to reduce the cash otherwise required by an investor to acquire an interest in property. While the net downpayment may be small, the potential appreciation would apply to the entire investment.

CHAPTER FIVE

Minimizing Taxes and Optimizing Returns on Rental Property

Whenever you make an investment, one of the most important factors to consider is the tax consequences of holding that particular investment. Rental income from real estate is somewhat unique because of the varied and numerous legitimate expense claims which may be made during the period of property ownership.

In most cases, a taxpayer in Canada must report income on the basis of a calendar year. However, if a landlord provides services that are normally beyond those of simply furnishing space—for example, recreational facilities, maid services, office cleaning, or protective services, he may then be entitled to report income on a fiscal-year basis. This means choosing a year end which may differ from the calendar year, but which once chosen, cannot be changed in subsequent years without express written permission from Revenue Canada.

If one does have substantial rental income (after expenses) and it can be shown that the rental operations are really of a business nature, choosing a fiscal period other than the calendar year may be advantageous. Suppose, for example, that an individual inherits a substantial sum of money and decides to purchase a small motel with perhaps only a small amount of financing. Clearly, if there is little or no interest expense to pay, the net rental income for tax purposes can be significant. However, since the motel owner can now establish that he is carrying on a business (as opposed to receiving passive rental income) he may decide to report his income from the property using, say, a January 31 year-end. Thus, all profits for the period from February 1, 1982 to January 31, 1983 would only be reported on the 1983 tax return, which wouldn't have to be filed until April 1984.

Prior to the end of 1979, it was possible to artificially

reduce rental income by prepaying expenses such as insurance premiums or property taxes and deducting these expenditures in the year that they were made, rather than over the period of time to which they pertained. This practice is no longer possible because of changes in the Income Tax Act, which were discussed in the last chapter. However, where a landlord collects prepaid rentals, the law does not require that these amounts be reported as income until the time to which these rents apply. Therefore, if a landlord can arrange to collect the last month's rent on a five-year lease in advance, he has the use of a tenant's funds for fifty-nine months before he is required to report this amount as part of his income.

Allowable Expenses

The following is a check-list of available tax deductions to which an owner of real estate is entitled. You should always make sure that you are getting all possible legitimate tax write-offs.

1. Carrying charges, including interest expense on mortgages, vendor take-backs, and other financing.

2. Commissions paid to obtain financing (but not commissions in conjunction with the purchase or sale of the property itself).

3. Property taxes.

4. Utilities—heat, light and power.

5. Expenses of advertising for tenants, including commissions paid to rental agents. (If the lease is for several years, commissions may have to be prorated over the length of the leases for income tax purposes.)

6. Legal expenses incurred in conjunction with day-to-day operations. These would include expenses incurred to prepare leases as well as legal fees to collect rents and settle disputes with tenants or tradesmen, etc. Legal expenses incurred initially to acquire property form part of the cost of land and building. To the extent that the building cost is increased by these fees, they may be gradually written off as part of the

annual claim for capital cost allowances. Legal fees incurred in conjunction with the sale of property decrease the proceeds for income tax purposes and will result in a smaller taxable profit.

7. Landscaping of grounds around the property. Although landscaping is normally done for a long-term benefit, specific income tax legislation allows the cost to be written off in the year that it is *paid*. As mentioned in Chapter Four, landscaping forms one of the allowable "soft costs" for construction projects. Note that landscaping is one of the few expenditures where the Income Tax Act requires payment before permitting tax deductibility. In most other cases, expenses are deductible when they are incurred even if the actual payment does not take place until the subsequent fiscal period.

8. Accounting fees. Generally, Revenue authorities will not quibble with a taxpayer claiming the costs of having an income tax return prepared as an allowable expense against rental income.

9. Payments to a tenant in order to permit the landlord to cancel a lease prematurely.

10. Subscriptions and periodicals. Generally, the cost of literature relating to investments and potential investments are tax deductible. This would include not only pure real-estate material, but would also cover periodicals such as the *Financial Post* or the *Financial Times*. I hope that your deductible expenditures would also include the cost of this book!

11. Insurance premiums. Property insurance premiums will be dealt with in more detail later on in this chapter. It may, however, be possible in certain circumstances to also deduct the cost of *life insurance* premiums. Ordinarily, life insurance premiums are not deductible, and benefits when received are not taxable. However, expenses of borrowing money *are* tax deductible where the funds are used for investment purposes. From time to time, a lending institution will insist upon a term life insurance policy on the life of a borrower to secure a loan. Thus, if you borrow money for a real-estate investment and the lender does not take back a mortgage against the property itself, it may be possible to deduct the cost of term life

insurance if such coverage is required specifically by the lender to secure the loan. If the borrower happens to die, the insurance proceeds would go directly to the lender. However, with the debt now extinguished, the heirs would find themselves with an increased equity in the inherited property. The idea of making certain life insurance premiums deductible (by taking advantage of the general tax rule permitting a write-off for the costs of obtaining financing) is extremely technical. There is certainly scope for creative planning in this area, and you should definitely consult your own tax adviser on this matter.

12. Safety deposit box fees. The cost of a safety deposit box is generally deductible against any investment income that a taxpayer in Canada may have. Presumably, if the only investments are in real estate, the safety deposit box should actually be used to contain important related documents such as deeds, mortgage documentation, insurance policies, and so forth.

13. Repairs and maintenance. Generally, a deduction for repairs and maintenance expenses is restricted to minor repairs only. If an expenditure is so large that it involves a replacement of a major component part of a rental building, it may be treated as the purchase of a depreciable capital asset rather than as a current expense. This is especially so if a replacement upgrades the particular property. An example of a capital expenditure might be the installation of new copper piping or electrical system throughout a building. However, if a single defective pipe is replaced with a new one, this expense will be fully deductible in the year that it is incurred.

There is no clear-cut distinction between repairs and maintenance and capital expenditures. Generally, *a repair* is an expense incurred to ensure that a property will last over the time period that it is intended to be functional. On the other hand, *a capital expenditure* is one which will *extend* the useful life span of a property beyond what would otherwise normally be expected. Thus, a new boiler system or electrical system would probably be classified as capital. On the other hand, it may be possible to write off the expense of a new roof, especially if the property is situated in an area prone to major rain or wind storms. When in doubt, you may have your own accountant research the particular expenditure with specific reference to tax cases that have already been dealt with by the courts.

14. Salaries to superintendents and fees to property managers. The use of property managers will be dealt with later in this chapter. However, it is interesting to note that a superintendent or property manager does *not* necessarily have to be someone with an arm's-length relationship to the owner of property. In other words, it is perfectly permissible for you to employ your spouse or even a dependent child in connection with property administration, rent collection, or repairs and maintenance. In addition, your spouse or child could keep your books and records, which would also warrant the payment of a (tax deductible) salary.

The ideal situation arises where one's spouse or children are in lower tax brackets than the taxpayer who owns the property. For example, a child eighteen years of age or over will provide an exemption of $1,090 (in 1981) to a supporting individual as long as the child does not have a net income in excess of $2,180. (Of course, a property owner must have substantial rental operations to justify that much as a salary to a child.) If one is supporting a spouse with no other income whatsoever, that spouse may receive a salary of up to $490 (in 1981) without affecting the supporting spouse's exemption. Certainly, it shouldn't be too difficult to justify this amount for basic bookkeeping and record keeping. Naturally, if a salary is to be paid to a family member, you should be prepared to have your affairs subjected to the scrutiny of Revenue Canada officials. The key is the reasonableness of each expenditure.

15. Travel expenses in conjunction with property investment including reasonable automobile expenses. Perhaps one of the most contentious areas when it comes to allowable expenses is that of travel and automobile expenditures. In most cases, such expenses are only partially attributable to one's investment activities. Usually, you will probably use your car for personal purposes as well as investment-related activities. Personal expenses cannot be deducted and you would have to

apportion travel and automobile expenses between personal and business/investment use. If you do actually use an automobile for property inspection, rent collection, or in conjunction with repairs and maintenance that you yourself carry out, then your allowable expenses will include gasoline and oil, repairs, insurance, parking, car washes, and capital cost allowance.

You should calculate your entire expenses for the year and then claim a certain percentage as being property-related. Of course, the distinction between personal and non-personal use is not well-defined. Usually, you would want as big a tax write-off as possible, although the larger your claim, the more likely it is that Revenue Canada will take exception. Common sense should be your guide. Your expenses must be reasonable in relation to both your rental revenue and the type of properties that you have. If your properties require minimal personal attention and the gross rent is but a few thousand dollars, only a small amount of travel and car expenses becomes deductible. However, if your properties require personal supervision and your rental operations are extensive, it may be possible to substantiate (in rare cases) as much as 100% of automobile expenses as being legitimately deductible.

My rule of thumb is that travel and related expenses—even if your property is situated in a city other than the one in which you live—should not exceed the amount that you would otherwise have to pay to an independent property manager to carry out the functions that you yourself perform. This is especially true for a category of expenses which we might label "property inspection costs". If the building is located in your city or within a few hundred miles, you might have little resistance if your claim is audited. On the other hand, if your investment is situated in Florida or Hawaii, the tax authorities will probably take exception if you try to take any tax deduction whatsoever. (After all, Revenue assessors are human too.)

There is certainly no restriction against mixing business and pleasure. If you live in Vancouver and own an apartment building in Winnipeg, there is no reason that your annual inspection visit cannot coincide with a family wedding. This is, of course, provided that your expense would not be out of line in relation to your rental revenue. Many expenses are disallowed simply because taxpayers either do not have vouchers to substantiate them or because they can't actually prove that the expenses were related to a business or investment. I suggest that you keep receipts for everything.

16. Capital cost allowance. Capital cost allowance may also be claimed as an allowable expense against rental income. Usually, the tax depreciation rate on a building will be 5% on a diminishing or declining balance basis. Furniture and fixtures is subject to a 20% depreciation rate, while an automobile would qualify for depreciation at 30%. For other depreciation rates, you should consult with an accountant.

Vacant Land

If you invest in vacant land, your major expenses will usually be interest and property taxes. Unfortunately, the general rule is that the deductions for these expenses are not allowed to exceed the gross revenue (if any) from the land minus other deductible expenses. In other words, you cannot use property taxes and mortgage interest to create a (tax deductible) loss. Where interest and property taxes are disallowed, they are usually added to the cost of the property itself. This would reduce the taxable profit when the land is, in turn, sold.

There are, however, two significant exceptions. The first arises where vacant land is used in the course of carrying on a business in the year. Thus, if your business consists of land development for resale, you can use the interest and property tax write-offs to shelter profits from other parcels of land which you have developed and/or resold. In addition, property taxes and mortgage interest can create a loss on vacant land if the prime reason for holding the property is to gain income from the land itself. This would apply, for example, to a parking lot operation.

The restrictions against deducting interest and taxes on vacant land cease to apply once a taxpayer commences construction on the property. From that time on, these expenses become allowable soft costs (as was previously discussed).

Vacant land can also provide a significant tax shelter if the property is used for a farming operation. The tax definition of farming includes not only the more strenuous activities of growing a wheat crop or maintaining cattle, but also breeding race horses, tree and sod farming, and even bee-keeping. Moreover, there is *no* requirement that the owner of the property must necessarily carry out farming activities *personally*.

Tax Advantages of a Farming Operation

There are many tax write-offs to which a farm operation lends itself. First, the restriction against creating a loss from property taxes and mortgage interest does not apply. Second, a farming business is entitled to report its income on a cash basis. This means that expenses are deductible when paid while revenues will only be taxable when received. For example, one would get an immediate tax write-off for inventory, so if you were to buy cattle, hogs, or even some fruit trees, the costs of these could be deducted immediately even if there are no sales of livestock or fruit for many years. In addition, you can obtain an immediate write-off for amounts paid to clear and level land, dig or drill wells, lay drainage tiles, or construct unpaved roads.

Naturally, you must be able to prove that you are actually carrying on a business with a reasonable expectation of profit before your expense claims will be accepted if you are audited. You should be able to produce a budget showing specific financial plans for the future, and any money spent on the construction of a silo, the purchase of a threshing machine, or other farming utensils will greatly strengthen your position. Some actual sales of produce or farm livestock in the first few years can be extremely helpful and a little agricultural know-how will also be useful. A few years ago, I was able to assist a professional hockey player in claiming his farm losses for income tax purposes by stressing (in discussions with Revenue Canada) the courses that he took during the off-season at a local agricultural college.

Farm Loss Limits

Unfortunately, the opportunity to use farming as a tax shelter is not unlimited. In most cases, no matter how large your losses are, your yearly write-off will be automatically restricted to the first $2,500 of farming losses plus one-half of the excess loss over $2,500, to a total maximum of $5,000 in any given year. Excess losses can be carried back one year and then forward up to five years, but only if there is a profit from farming in the carry-over period. However, any losses that cannot be deducted during the carry-over years (to the extent that they represent property taxes or interest on farm land) may be applied to reduce an eventual capital gain on the sale of the farm.

In order to deduct the full amount of a farm loss (in excess of the $5,000 limit) against other sources of income, the taxpayer must not only show that he has a viable farming operation but also that farming is one of his chief sources of income—either alone or together with some other source. However, even if full-time farming is not feasible, there are other advantages besides tax write-offs. For example, where there is a transfer of "capital" or growth property from parents to children, usually the transfer is subject to capital gains tax. However, where property used in a Canadian farming business is transferred from parents to children, grandchildren or great-grandchildren (including in-laws), the transfer is free from tax provided that the recipient is a Canadian resident. The opportunity to effect such transfers is available not only in one's lifetime but also at the time of death. There is no forgiveness of tax—only a postponement. The tax consequences that ordinarily would have arisen will be passed on to the child to be contended with if the farm is subsequently sold to someone other than a family member.

These rules can be particularly advantageous if the farm happens to consist of prime land on the outskirts of a large city. In addition, if the property has been used in farming, it is more likely that the profit on the sale of undeveloped land will be treated as a capital gain as opposed to ordinary income. (See Chapter Six.)

Naturally, if you plan to engage in farming, the tax shelter consequences should be second to the question of whether or not the property itself is a good investment. Mortgage interest, property taxes, and most farm-related expenses are actually *outlays of cash*. Unless the farm property itself appreciates by more than the after-tax expenses of maintaining it, the investor may lose out in the long run.

Optimizing Returns on Rental Property Investments

In order to maximize one's return on an investment, there is much more involved than simply tax minimization. Specifically, other important factors include:

1. Selecting a competent property manager (if necessary),
2. Finding "good" tenants,
3. Maintaining adequate property insurance, and
4. Property renovation considerations.

The remainder of this chapter will discuss each of these important—but unrelated—topics.

Property Managers

Whether or not a property manager is required depends on the size and type of your investment and the amount of time that you yourself have available to devote to it. For residential investments, large property-management companies often won't consider fewer than fifty units. In some cases, however, small firms will handle residential buildings with as few as twenty units, and even less in the case of condominiums.

The management fee will generally range from 5% to 7% of the gross income collected. The more units, the lower the percentage. Sometimes, a management firm will quote a straight dollar fee. Alternatively, or in addition, a management company may also take a portion of rentals on new leases—say, the first month's rent. The functions of a property manager will vary. These will include keeping books, renting units, collecting rents, making regular inspections of the property, handling emergency repair calls, and preparing budgets. Often, a property manager will hire a superintendent and arrange for repairs to be made either by the manager's own staff or by outside tradesmen. As well, the property manager might handle the landlord's mortgage, tax and other payments. For commercial properties, a property manager will usually calculate and collect charges for maintaining common areas, and any automatic rent or cost increases.

In choosing a property management company, you should look for several things:

1. The length of time it has been in business,
2. References from existing customers,
3. Samples of the financial reporting package to be provided, and
4. Professional accreditation.

You might want to visit some of the properties that the management company is currently managing.

Choosing Good Tenants

If you go into a long-term rental investment, tenants are a major ingredient for success. The type of tenants that you will get depends largely on the property and its location. Obviously, a building with many bachelor apartments will attract single people and this may mean high turnover.

Last year, I did some personal shopping for tax shelter property with soft-cost write-offs. I had a choice of either buying three-bedroom units without garage facilities or two-bedroom units with garages—both for the same price. Most people, I think, would have selected the three-bedroom units because they were bigger. However, the more bedrooms you have, the more likely it is that you will get families with children; and the more children, the greater the potential for damages. (I know; I have four of them!)

In selecting tenants, there is no requirement that you accept the first applicants. Of course, discrimination on grounds of race, religion or nationality will run counter to human rights legislation. Ideally, you should require every applicant to fill out a written application. This alone may eliminate many undesirable prospective tenants. Once they realize that you will check, they may lose interest in renting. The form should include current and prior addresses, previous landlord and rents paid, length of former tenancies, name of current employer (prior employers also if the applicant has been with the current employer for less than two years), current income and function, credit references (including banks, credit cards and personal references), outstanding loans and monthly payments.

Once the application is filled out, you should verify at least part of the information. The most important thing is income. If the tenant's employer won't confirm the present income, try asking him whether, in his opinion, it is large enough to support the rent that you want to charge.

At the same time you receive the application, you should get "an offer to lease" and a cheque for the first and last month's rent. Be sure to cash the cheque. Obviously, if it bounces, the prospective tenant is not worthwhile.

The lease should be drafted by your solicitor and should be written in clear, understandable language. Basic landlord requirements include a covenant to provide tenants with quiet enjoyment of the premises and to look after major structural repairs.

Although a written lease is not required by law, you should still have one. Some important items that a lease should contain would include tenant responsibility for removal of snow and ice from sidewalks, prompt reporting of electrical or plumbing failures, clogged toilets or drains, and lawn maintenance. You should also forbid any painting or decorating without written permission. It is not only a question of tastes, but more importantly, you must try to circumvent *future work* that could otherwise arise in removing wallpaper or trying to paint over dark colours. You must also decide whether to permit your tenants to keep animals.

There are other points that you should also consider. Instead of painting for new tenants, try providing them with sufficient paint to do their own work. The lease should also be drafted so that tenants pay for all utilities. Either install separate meters or apportion your charges. Try to inspect your property from time to time in an informal way, and be sure that the right to inspect is written in the lease. As house prices continue to rise, fewer people can afford to buy their own homes. The landlord very often has the upper hand since vacancies are very low in most cities and tenants have few rental alternatives. However, remember that if a tenant renews a lease, this saves you the cost and nuisance of re-leasing.

Insurance on Property

As the owner of investment property, you should obtain three types of coverage: property, liability and income. You may also require boiler insurance, lease-guarantee insurance, fidelity bonds and crime insurance.

Property insurance is supposed to cover damage to the building itself and to improvements and common facilities that might be caused by fire or other risks generally included in homeowner insurance policies. The most basic insurance covers fire damage only. However, most policies include "all risk" or "broad form" coverage, which covers collapse of the building, damage caused by falling objects, or water damage. Usually, a standard policy will exclude damage to trees, shrubs or lawns as well as damage caused by floods or earthquakes.

Two special types of coverage that may be of interest are earthquake and flood insurance. In practice, earthquake insurance is common in British Columbia or California. Flood insurance may be expensive and difficult to obtain.

In purchasing insurance for investment properties, you must remember that there are certain risks that you normally wouldn't encounter in your own home. These include damage from fire sprinklers or the release of dangerous chemicals within a factory. Where your tenant installs his own improvements, these are generally excluded from your coverage. However, you may wish to extend your own insurance and then re-invoice the extended coverage back to the tenant on a cost-sharing basis. In general, I recommend that insurance policies should be structured on a "replacement cost" basis. The coverage must also be updated each year to keep pace with rising construction costs.

Third Party Liability Insurance. Public liability coverage insures you against injury to persons or property caused on or by your premises. You must insure for damages that may be caused by your own employees, such as a superintendent or security guard. You would probably require at least $1,000,000 of personal injury coverage for each occurrence. Such insurance is not expensive and is very important if you wish to protect your other assets from potential claims.

Income Insurance. Income insurance, or business interruption insurance, guarantees that you will receive rent and other income during the time rented property is unusable because of damage or destruction. In the case of a shopping centre, the policy should ideally cover both regular rentals as well as rents based on a percentage of sales under the terms of your leases. With this insurance, you will continue to be able to meet mortgage and real-estate tax payments even if revenues are temporarily suspended.

Lease Guarantee Insurance. Although not commonly advertised, lease guarantee insurance is also available. Under such a policy, the insurer agrees to guarantee the fixed rental income on leased premises, such as a shopping centre, for up to perhaps fifteen years. Should any tenant default on his rent, the insurer would continue to provide the rental income as long as the landlord makes all reasonable efforts to minimize his losses. Brokerage fees to re-lease the premises would also be reimbursed. This type of insurance can be written on industrial office or warehouse space. A retail store can also qualify.

Crime insurance may be an important component of your coverage, especially if you have extensive rental operations and own expensive cleaning equipment or other goods. *Fidelity insurance* is also available. It covers people working for you who might commit fraudulent or criminal acts. This would include property managers, for example, who collect rent. If bonded employees are handling cheques only (as opposed to cash), your cost for such coverage should not be too expensive.

Renovating Prior to Sale

In 1979, the Toronto Real Estate Board surveyed 101 of its member brokers for their views on the specific effects of different renovations. In order to improve the marketability and saleability of residential housing, most brokers suggested the following:

1. Modernizing or installing additional bathrooms
2. A modernized kitchen
3. Skylights, sliding patio doors and enlarged windows
4. Fireplaces
5. Adding a garage or carport for parking
6. Adding on an extra bedroom to a two-bedroom home.

The opinion of the brokers was somewhat divided with respect to other improvements. Central air-conditioning may be a valuable sales feature if one is trying to sell a home during the summer months, but is not generally considered by a prospective purchaser in the heart of winter. Similarly, an in-ground swimming pool may be viewed by many as an expensive nuisance and even as an insurance risk. The general consensus was that renovations should be concentrated on the interior of a house rather than the exterior.

With respect to commercial real-estate, spaciousness, light, and cleanliness appear to be the most important ingredients to ensure saleability.

The next two chapters will examine the tax consequences of selling property with a view towards maximizing one's ultimate yield from an investment.

Summary

To make money in real estate, it is not only important to locate a property that is priced fairly in the first place and shows potential for future appreciation. Maintaining the investment while you own it is just as vital. Bad tenants may cause the property to depreciate, while inadequate insurance may convert a bonanza into a disaster. You must either be prepared to devote time and attention or pay someone else to represent you. If you spend too much on renovations, you may never recover these costs. Remember, you must accept the risks if you hope to gain the rewards.

CHAPTER SIX

Minimizing or Postponing Taxes on the Sale of Property Without Incorporating

Capital Gains vs. Ordinary Income

Before even considering how taxes can be minimized on the sale of property, you should ask the question "Why sell at all?" You may be able to realize substantial funds without a disposition. Generally, I would not recommend that property be sold unless you feel that the particular property will no longer appreciate greatly in value—especially in relation to other investment alternatives. Even if the reason a sale is contemplated is to raise funds to invest in other assets, it may pay to refinance your holdings instead.

In 1980, a university professor who was approximately three years away from retirement came to me for tax advice. He had purchased a piece of recreational land in British Columbia sixteen years earlier for $500. The market value at the time of our meeting was in the neighbourhood of $80,000. During our discussions, he asked me what the tax implications of a sale would be. In his case, given the long-term holding period, I was fairly confident that he would obtain capital gains treatment. Even though his cost for tax purposes would be increased from $500 to the value of the property at the start of 1972 (the time at which capital gains became part of the Canadian income tax legislation) the gain would have been quite substantial. Since he was already in a fairly high income-tax bracket because of his university salary, taxes would have eroded as much as 25% to 30% of his profit.

The first recommendation I made was that, if he were to sell at all, his best choice would be to wait several years until after retirement, when his other income would be lower. In this way, the impact of tax on capital gains would not be that severe. However, I thought we should discuss the matter even further. I asked my client whether or not he felt that the area in which his property was situated had peaked in value or whether he anticipated additional future growth. The client told me that he saw no reason why the property shouldn't continue to appreciate in value. I therefore suggested that he might want to refinance the property instead of selling it and use the borrowed funds to make *other* investments. Even though the refinancing would produce an interest expense, this cost would be *deductible* as long as the funds were used for investment purposes. Even if a further investment in raw land were made, I pointed out to my client that he could afford to subsidize his (non-deductible) carrying costs out of excess earnings from his employment.

The moral of my story is that you should try to postpone a sale of property (especially if your tax bracket will be lower in future years) and borrow instead against increases in value. Even if a prospective purchaser is involved, it may still be possible to avoid a taxable sale. You can, for example, enter into a long-term lease. Under such an arrangement, tax will only become due as payments are received on that lease. If you require additional funds, you can mortgage the leased property. The rental income would offset the debt service charges against the loan. The net effect is to realize the cash value of a property now, while paying only minimal tax for many years. The concept of long-term leases will be explored in more detail in Chapter Ten, which deals with timesharing arrangements.

What happens if you decide to sell in any event, disregarding the potential benefits of retaining your property and refinancing it? When you sell depreciable property, such as a building, there is first potential exposure to "recaptured depreciation", which is fully taxable. This means that capital cost allowance deductions of prior years may be added to your other taxable income. In some cases, recaptured depreciation can be reduced or avoided if you purchase a new depreciable asset of the same class before the end of the year in which you disposed of the former property. However, as was described on page 33, there are restrictions on the ability to do this when rental properties costing $50,000 or more are involved. Proceeds over and above the original cost of land and building may be *either* fully taxable as ordinary income or may qualify

75

for capital gains treatment. Unfortunately, in Canada the distinction between capital gains and ordinary income is not clear-cut.

In Canada, the tax definition of *business income* includes not only the profits from a full-time business, but also income from "an adventure or concern in the nature of trade". The concept of "an adventure in the nature of trade" means that even isolated transactions can give rise to ordinary business income which is fully taxable even if the transactions are not part of a regular business. For example, assume that you approach me one evening at a dinner party and, in the course of conversation, you happen to mention that your television had just expired and that you were looking around for a new one to replace it. Perhaps your first choice is a Panatachi Model 007, which is listed in the stores for $1,000. You tell me that you are inclined to buy this particular TV but are a bit unhappy with the thought of paying so much money. Then, I happen to mention that I have good connections with a distributor and can get that identical television set for you at a wholesale price. In fact, if the store price is $1,000, I tell you that I can pick up that same television, brand new, for only $800. At this point, you tell me to go ahead and agree to pay me $800 on delivery.

Of course, being a good accountant and a bit of an entrepreneur, I am really able to buy that particular model for only $600. Assume that I follow through with a purchase at $600 and then sell the TV to you for $800. What happens to my profit of $200 for income tax purposes? Technically, it is income from an adventure in the nature of trade. Even though this may be the only time in my life that I ever make a profit on the purchase and sale of a television set, this is an example of a transaction where something is bought *specifically for the purpose of reselling it for more than its cost*. For tax purposes, I have income which is fully taxable.

Naturally, in a case where a one-time isolated profit of $200 is involved, I would have to be scrupulously honest (or perhaps even insane) to bother reporting this transaction on my tax return. However, what if I buy a piece of vacant land for $10,000 and, within three weeks, resell it for $50,000? In this case, I would *be forced* to report my profit—if for no other reason than I am deathly afraid of the consequences if I don't comply with the law. Fear of potential monetary penalties and even criminal action is perhaps the greatest deterrent to tax evasion!

Conceptually, there is very little difference between a one-time purchase and sale of a television set and a similar transaction involving a "quick flip" of a piece of real estate. Therefore, a gain on the disposition of real estate is often treated by the Revenue authorities as giving rise to ordinary income from an adventure in the nature of trade—especially if the holding period is short.

On the other hand, what are the tax consequences if land and building are purchased together, or if land is purchased and a building is constructed? The improved property is then held for, say, a ten-year period during which time the property returns rental revenues, and, at the end of this time, the property is sold at a profit. Given this scenario, I feel confident that the profit will be assessed as a capital gain.

In dealing with tax cases involving income versus capital gains, the courts have held that a capital property is one which is technically capable of producing income *during* the period of ownership and not only at the time that the property is sold. Thus, land and building together (from which rental income is received) will usually be treated as capital property for income tax purposes. On the other hand, a gain on sale of unimproved land will often be assessed as ordinary income. This will be the case even if buying and selling land is *not* a full-time business of the taxpayer.

The problem of distinguishing ordinary income from capital gains is somewhat unique to Canada—especially if one compares our laws with those of the United States. The U.S. structure differentiates between "long-term" and "short-term" profits, with a cut-off after a one-year holding period. Short-term gains are essentially treated in the same way as any ordinary income and this would even include profits on stocks and bonds where these properties are held for less than one year. On the other hand, where even speculative property is held for more than a year, a profit will be treated as a (long-term) capital gain, unless the taxpayer is clearly a trader in that type of property. In the U.S., only 40% of long-term capital gains are presently included in income.

In Canada, the length of a holding period is not the

deciding factor in dealing with the question of ordinary income and capital gains. In my opinion, it seems a shame that we do not have legislation similar to that of the United States. I don't mean to suggest that there is anything sacred or holy about a one-year holding period, but it would be nice to have a degree of certainty when dealing with the problem. I think it would also be in the interest of the government to set specific guidelines. If all short-term (however that expression may be defined) profits were assessed as ordinary income, this might cut down on part of the inflationary spiral in real-estate values caused by speculators.

Even in Canada, the problem of differentiating between ordinary income and capital gains is rather unique to real-estate transactions. When it comes to stock market trades, Revenue authorities take a lenient approach. In most cases, unless you are a broker or dealer in securities, gains and losses (even on speculative stocks) will be treated as capital. Technically, this is because even a penny mining-share could conceivably begin to pay dividends and an investor can argue that he acquired a particular security in anticipation of receiving dividends.

Although the administrative practice of Revenue authorities has always been to treat stock-market transactions as being capital in nature, the Income Tax Act was amended a few years ago for greater certainty and to clear up ambiguities. Specifically, the amendments provide for a "guaranteed capital gains election" which is a lifetime option to treat all gains and losses on Canadian marketable securities as being on account of capital. (This election is not, however, available to stockbrokers, confessed traders in securities, or most financial institutions.) Ordinarily, an individual would not even bother making the guaranteed capital-gains election since stock market profits will usually be treated as giving rise to capital gains in any event. However, if there is a one-time profit which is unusually large on a speculative transaction, it might be worthwhile to consider the election as a hedge against the possibility of an adverse reassessment.

When it comes to commodity trades (wheat futures, soya beans or pork bellies) or transactions involving gold, silver and other precious metals, the Canadian tax authorities take a rather lenient view. In general, they will allow a taxpayer to treat his gains or losses as being either capital or income as long as the taxpayer is consistent. This is so even though a commodity itself is very much like raw land, in that a profit can only be made at the time of sale and not during the period of ownership. (The opportunity to choose either income or capital-gains treatment is not, however, available if the particular commodity is closely related to the taxpayer's ordinary day-to-day endeavours. Thus, for example, a jeweller would have to report his gains and losses on precious metals as being on account of ordinary income, while the president of a chocolate bar manufacturing company would be required to adopt the same treatment if he speculates in cocoa or sugar futures.) It is therefore only with real estate that there is major confusion in Canada with respect to the question of what type of profit does a sale create—capital gain or business income?

Capital Gains Criteria

The distinction between capital gains and business income is not a problem created by the Tax Reform of 1972. In fact, before 1972, distinguishing between the two was even more important because, in those days, capital gains weren't taxed at all!

Over the years, many cases have come before the courts on this subject, and a number of criteria have evolved in order to deal with this contentious issue. These include:

1. The taxpayer's intention and course of conduct
2. Secondary intention
3. The relationship of real-estate transactions to the ordinary (earned income) activities of the taxpayer
4. The number and frequency of transactions
5. The declared objectives of a corporation pursuant to its letters patent or memorandum of association.

It is certainly worthwhile to review each of these criteria independently with a view towards a practical application. As you read the next few pages, I think it will become evident that in many cases, it is possible to build up some convincing evidence in order to substantiate a capital-gains position should you be faced with a dispute in this area.

The Taxpayer's Intention and Course of Conduct

At one extreme, if you were to purchase a piece of vacant land, construct a shopping centre on the property, hold it for a ten-year period and then sell at a profit, I am sure that you would be assessed as having made a capital gain. Given a ten-year holding period for land and building together, it seems clear that you could prove that your intention was to earn rental income on a long-term basis. However, what if you were to buy this same piece of vacant land, hold it for only a short period of time and then sell it without any improvements at all? Could you then successfully defend a capital gains position? The tax courts have held that one does not necessarily have to construct a building and hold it for many years in order to realize a capital gain on eventual sale. As long as the taxpayer's *intention* was to "create" a capital asset, and as long as he can prove that he had attempted to accomplish this objective, even a sale of unimproved land can result in the preferred tax consequences. Judges have often recognized that sometimes it is not possible to realize one's intentions. However, the taxpayer must at least show proof that he has actually tried to get proper zoning approvals, has requisitioned preliminary architects' drawings with respect to a proposed shopping centre project, has communicated with lending institutions in order to determine the availability of financing and has contacted proposed tenants (especially large chain-stores). Then, if something goes wrong and it is impossible to follow through with the project, the proof of intent alone could be sufficient to sway a Revenue official or a judge to allow the profit on sale to be assessed as a capital gain.

After all, many things can thwart one's attempt to "create" a capital asset. Perhaps the municipality refuses to allow the required zoning. Maybe it is impossible to raise the necessary financing. Someone else may have started a similar project within a radius of only one or two miles and it now becomes evident that the specific area cannot support two similar projects. Alternatively, the developer may encounter personal problems. Perhaps he takes ill and is advised by his physician not to enter into any strenuous long-term deals. There may be a divorce which requires that the property be sold in order to realize proceeds for a lump-sum settlement. Perhaps rising interest rates cause the project to lose its viability or there is a downturn in the local economy. For one reason or another, the owner feels obliged to sell and does so—at a profit. As long as the vendor can show that he actually *tried* to create a long-term asset, a capital gain could be the income-tax result—subject, of course, to the other criteria as discussed in the following sections.

Secondary Intention

Unfortunately, one also has to contend with the doctrine of secondary intention. The courts will often address the question of whether or not the taxpayer harboured a secondary intention to sell (at a profit) in the future—even when the primary intention may have been to earn rental revenue.

Secondary intention is an extremely difficult criterion to refute. No one can stand up in a courtroom and argue that his secondary intention was really to sell at a loss! Fortunately, however, in most cases a judge will only look at secondary intention if the facts dictate that this is warranted.

Let us return to the previous example of a piece of land allegedly purchased for the construction of a shopping centre but resold at a profit before any construction took place. Remember that there is usually quite a time-lag between the occurrence of a transaction and the point at which it is later examined by the Department of National Revenue, eventually resulting in an income tax dispute. Let us suppose that, in the intervening period, a new highway has been constructed adjacent to the subject property. It may be that an enterprising attorney with the Department of Justice (representing Revenue Canada in this particular action) discovers that the taxpayer's brother is the Provincial Minister in charge of roads and highways. What does this prove? Presumably, this indicates that the taxpayer in question had "inside" information, so that his property investment couldn't possibly fail to increase in value. In other words, even if the taxpayer was unsuccessful in realizing on his primary intention to build a shopping centre, there is nevertheless a well-defined secondary intention to turn a speculative profit. In this case, the criterion of secondary intention would probably override all the wonderful evidence that the taxpayer had assembled in order to prove his primary goals.

Intention is a question of fact; and it is always important to collect your evidence at the time transactions take place rather than two or three years later when they are audited. Several years ago, one of my clients, a real-estate developer by profession, purchased a building as a head office for his construction company. It was his intention to move his business into half the building and rent out the other half. However, three weeks after the purchase took place but before the developer actually moved in, the building burned to the ground. Fortunately, it was insured for about $300,000 in excess of the developer's cost. My client called me immediately, because he recognized that the tax authorities could conceivably try to treat his windfall profit as ordinary income rather than a capital gain. We sat down in an effort to assemble proof of his actual intention to use the property for both business and rental purposes. After a short time, my client remembered that he had already given instructions to the telephone company to have phones installed under the company's name at the new premises. Naturally, the order had been cancelled shortly after the fire took place. In addition, the client recalled that he had asked his printer to print new stationery with the new address as the company's office. That order, of course, had also been cancelled. We then immediately secured letters from both the telephone company and the printer certifying that these orders had, in fact, been placed. These letters were kept on file and came in very useful two years later when, in fact, the developer was audited and Revenue officials examined the particular transaction. My client was able to establish his position without even having to resort to a courtroom battle.

The Number and Frequency of Transactions

It is not likely that anyone can buy and sell raw land, or even land and buildings, on a recurring basis without eventually being assessed as a trader. This is so no matter how impressive a taxpayer's portfolio of evidence may be to show that he was "forced" each time to sell his property at a profit after short-term holding periods.

The number and frequency of transactions is the one standard that Revenue Canada will generally use to classify real-estate properties as inventory and not capital property—even where the assets consist of land and building together. Thus, notwithstanding the fact that these properties may produce rental income, a profit on sale could still end up being fully taxable.

Generally, on a first (or even second or third) transaction involving land and buildings, it should be possible to get capital-gains treatment—even if the holding period is very short. There are all kinds of things that can "go wrong" which common sense would require the taxpayer to liquidate his "investment". For example, there may be problems with tenants. Alternatively, the property may not be rented in the first place, or certain costs that weren't previously budgeted may make holding that particular property uneconomical. There can also be personal pressures to sell, such as ill health, family disputes, and so on. However, at some point, after a certain number of transactions, the taxpayer may suddenly find himself deemed a trader. Certainly "number and frequency" go together. For example, three transactions by itself means nothing especially if these transactions take place over, say, twenty years. Three transactions in one year, on the other hand, sounds suspiciously like the properties are inventory or trading assets to their owner. You may, however, always look for an angle to support a capital-gains position.

One of my favourite stories dates back about ten years, to when I was a tax manager with a large national accounting firm in eastern Canada. Our firm had a client, whom I will call Mr. Smith. In addition to practising another profession, Mr. Smith was also a substantial developer of real estate. Mr. Smith's activities were not in the nature of trading transactions, but consisted of construction for long-term holding. The projects with which he was involved were large commercial and residential buildings. Around 1970, Mr. Smith reached the age of seventy and he decided that he wanted to liquidate most of his assets in order to make his estate that much simpler to administer and so that funds would be available to pay taxes arising on death. At that time, there was still a federal estate tax and provincial succession duties, and capital-gains legislation was known to be just around the corner. Mr. Smith proceeded to sell his properties, one at a time. The first two or three transactions were treated on his books as capital dispositions, which were of course, not taxable. Finally, he sold his fourth building, which happened to have been the last building that he had constructed. The profit on this transaction was over a million dollars. At this time, Revenue authorities stepped in and they decided to treat the gain as giving rise to ordinary income. It was an "all or nothing" situation. On behalf of our firm, I argued with the Revenue officials as best I could but I got nowhere. Although I advocate using the "no worse off principle" when dealing with a grey area, you should note that Revenue officials *also* use that principle for their own benefit. They felt they may as well assess the transaction as being fully taxable because the government, in this case, had everything to gain and nothing to lose. Finally, I gave up and informed my client that the matter would probably end up in a courtroom and I suggested that he engage the services of a tax lawyer. My client's choice in tax lawyers was most fortunate as he chose one of the foremost attorneys in Canada to represent him. Mr. Smith's lawyer set up a meeting with the senior Revenue officials on the case and I was invited to attend on behalf of my accounting firm.

At that meeting, the lawyer started to ask my client questions. He traced the client's activities in real-estate construction over a period of twenty or thirty years, establishing that very few sales had taken place before the previous two or three years. Our actual meeting took place sometime in 1973, about three years after the sale which was the subject of the dispute. (Keep in mind that the wheels of justice grind slowly.) The lawyer then started to examine my client as to his motives and Mr. Smith indicated that his major intention in selling was to make his estate more liquid. The lawyer then began to ask detailed questions with respect to the client's previous sales. Mr. Smith revealed that most of his projects were large enough so that each building had its own specific name. In fact, being a staunch nationalist, Mr. Smith had given his properties such names as the "Canada Building" or "Confederation Place".

However, it appeared that the subject property was simply known as the "Smith Building" and the lawyer asked why he had departed from his normal method of picking names. Mr.

Smith appeared to be slightly embarrassed. He pointed out that construction on this particular project had begun when he himself had just reached the age of 65. At that time, his children (who were already grown up) came to him and suggested that he name this building after himself in recognition that this was probably his last major project. Mr. Smith admitted that he had bowed to the pressure exerted on him by his children. The lawyer then asked by what name the building was known at the present time, three years later. The client shrugged his shoulders and indicated that the building was still called the "Smith Building" and would probably retain that name throughout its existence. He went on to explain that the words "Smith Building" were engraved in the cement work over the front door and that there was also a bronze plaque bearing that name at the front of the property.

At this point, the lawyer turned very casually to the Chief Assessor from Revenue and asked whether *he* would have given his own name to a building he built if his intention was to resell it at a profit. The assessor immediately answered no and explained to the lawyer that this would be a very dangerous practice. The assessor acknowledged that once he had sold his hypothetical property, he would no longer have any control as to how that building would be maintained. The assessor went so far as to say that there was no way that he would possibly want a slum to bear *his* name. Suddenly he realized what he had said, proving that in 1965, Mr. Smith couldn't possibly have had the motive of constructing the building for resale. The case was dropped.

Of course, there were a few other arguments to support our position. For example, we had the architects certify that the property was built using much more expensive materials than those which would have been chosen had the property been erected for resale. There were three elevator banks when only two would have sufficed under the relevant building code, and as well, the windows were installed with double pane glass for better insulation when a single pane would have passed the necessary inspection.

I don't mean to suggest that you could buy or build a duplex, call the property the "Jones Building" and then attempt to achieve capital gains treatment if you sell it three days after the interior paint dries. The point of the story, however, is to always look for an angle to support your position.

The Relationship of Real Estate Transactions to the Ordinary Activities of the Taxpayer

If you are a real-estate broker by profession, it is likely that your profits will be assessed as giving rise to ordinary income even if you transact infrequently. Professional advisers, such as accountants and lawyers who have real-estate clients are also likely to be assessed as traders, at least after a few transactions. Furthermore, if you are *associated* in a real-estate transaction with a trader in such property, you will also run the risk of having your gains taxed as ordinary income.

I first ran into this particular problem of "association with a trader" almost fifteen years ago. At that time, I was a junior partner with a small accounting firm. One of our clients was an independent cab driver, and each year we prepared a financial statement for his taxi business along with his personal tax return. Our client had a wife with no income, whom he had claimed as a dependant for tax purposes for many years. At the time that this story starts, the cab driver's wife inherited approximately $10,000 from the estate of her parents. She was unsure as to how these funds could be best invested and a friend of the family approached her with a business proposition. It appeared that this particular individual was a real-estate speculator whose business involved putting together raw land syndicates. He would use both his own funds and also money collected from investors to buy raw land. The land would then be subdivided and resold as building lots. At that time, the real-estate developer was looking for "partners" and he offered the wife of the cab driver a percentage interest in his latest program in exchange for her $10,000 investment. The cab driver's wife trusted the real-estate speculator and agreed to participate. Initially, the story had a happy ending because roughly one year later, she received twice her capital back. She considered her profit as a capital gain and reported no income for tax purposes.

A year or so later, the tax authorities audited the real-estate speculator and reviewed the transactions for that particular syndicate. Being a trader by profession, the speculator had correctly reported his share of the profit as ordinary income. The tax authorities then went one step further. They obtained the names of all the partners and systematically assessed each one as being a trader in real estate. Our firm launched an objection to the assessment on behalf of the cab driver's wife. Unfortunately, we lost our case. The judge held that association in a transaction with a real-estate trader brands the participant as a trader as well.

I don't mean to imply that you should necessarily stay away from speculative real-estate transactions or deals involving real-estate traders. If you can see your way towards making a substantial profit, income tax considerations should generally not be your main concern. However, if you are one of those people who walk the tightrope between being classified as an investor or a trader, I don't think it pays for you to lose "investor status" unless the dollars are worthwhile.

For example, if you give me the opportunity to invest, say, $100,000 in a speculative raw-land deal "guaranteed" to yield a profit of $10,000 after only one month, I would probably turn down your offer to participate. This is because, for a $10,000 profit, I personally don't feel that I want to run the risk of being branded as a trader in real estate. On the other hand, if you offer me the opportunity to invest that same $100,000 for a surefire profit of $1,000,000 after only one month, you had better believe that I would sign on! We all have our price and the tax tail should never wag the economic dog.

Declared Objectives of a Corporation

In the past, the courts have sometimes examined the descriptive powers of a corporation as reflected in its letters patent or memorandum of association. If a corporation was formed specifically for the purpose of transacting in real estate, its profits were often assessed as giving rise to ordinary income. In recent years, however, this criterion has become of negligible importance. This is because most corporations today are formed with very broad charter powers and can do almost anything. Thus, it is not uncommon to see manufacturing companies or corporations that operate retail stores having as one of their powers the right to transact in real estate.

If you do wish to use a corporation to hold (passive) property investments, the only concrete suggestion that I can make is that you should not use the name John Doe Developments Ltd. You are better off with John Doe Investments Ltd. or John Doe Holdings Ltd. A corporate name including the word "developments" or "construction" denotes the activity of a trader. On the other hand, if your company is, in fact, a development or construction company, it then becomes most appropriate to use a proper description.

Postponing Taxes on the Sale of Real Estate by Acquiring Other Similar Properties

Normally, as we saw earlier, a disposition of real estate gives rise to recaptured depreciation and, if sold at a price higher than the original cost, either a capital gain or ordinary income. In certain circumstances, these profits can be deferred. For years, the Income Tax Act has permitted a deferral of gains when property is disposed of under "involuntary" circumstances. This would include proceeds received as a result of an expropriation by the government (federal, provincial or municipal), a fire, flood, or earthquake. If expropriation or insurance proceeds are received, the owner has up to two years from the end of the year in which the disposition takes place to acquire replacement property. As long as the taxpayer invests at least the same amount which he received as proceeds, he has the right to postpone the recognition of profits for tax purposes. All that happens is that the tax cost of the replacement property is decreased by the amount of the gains which have been deferred. If only part of the proceeds is reinvested, then a portion of the gain becomes recognized in the year of disposition.

In 1977, the Canadian government extended the concept of income postponement to *voluntary* dispositions of real estate used in carrying on a business *other* than the business of real estate ownership or development. If business real estate is sold, the taxpayer (individual or corporation) has up to one year from the end of the year in which the sale takes place to purchase a replacement property. Again, to the extent that the taxpayer reinvests at least the same amount which was received in the first place, the entire profit can be postponed (with a corresponding decrease in the tax cost of the replacement property).

These rules are extremely important if a business outgrows an existing facility. A company manufacturing shoes can, for example, dispose of its manufacturing plant on a tax-deferred basis as long as a replacement property is either purchased or built within the required period of time. In an Interpretation Bulletin, Revenue authorities even concede that a warehouse building can be used (on a tax-deferred basis) to replace a manufacturing plant. In addition, the replacement property is permitted to be of both a different size and in another location. Also, the wording of the Income Tax Act is broad enough so that it really doesn't matter what takes place first—the disposition of the former business property or the acquisition of the replacement. In drafting the legislation, the government recognized that, in certain cases, the new facility must be "in place" before the business can allow the former property to be sold.

The opportunity to "roll over" on a tax-deferred basis from a former business property to a replacement property is especially useful if the taxpayer operates a hotel or motel. The gain on a sale can be deferred if a similar property is reacquired.

The chance to replace real estate is also extremely important with respect to farming businesses. A farmer can postpone payment of tax on profits from the sale of his farm simply by acquiring a replacement within the statutory one-year period. When the relevant legislation first appeared in 1977, there was some question as to whether a farmer could replace a grain farm with a cattle ranch or whether it would be permitted to replace a dry-land operation with irrigated property. It appears, however, that Revenue officials take a rather broad viewpoint and will allow the "rollover" even if the replacement farm involves a different type of farming operation.

There is an interesting loophole in the legislation in that the replacement property does not necessarily have to be situated in Canada. For some inexplicable reason, the legislators appear to have forgotten to impose the requirement that the replacement be purchased in this country. I am personally aware of several farmers in southern Alberta who have sold their farms, retained Canadian residency, but have purchased replacement property in northern Montana where much more land was obtainable for the same money. However, these farmers are faced with a trade-off. In general, the tax rules in Canada permit a family farm to pass tax-free from generation to generation as long as someone within the immediate family is actively engaged in farming at the time the transfer takes place. However, this opportunity to transfer farms within a family only applies where the farm is situated in this country. Therefore, some of the heirs of the southern Alberta farmers may be somewhat upset to find that there are adverse tax consequences at the time their parents die.

If you wish to postpone taxes on a real-estate sale by acquiring replacement property, it is important to note that this option is not available where the property is used in a business of real-estate ownership or development. A few months ago, a client came to see me on this particular subject. It appears that the client owned a controlling interest in two separate corporations. The first operated a car dealership and the second owned the real estate on which the dealership was situated. The dealership corporation paid rent to the real-estate company. The only reason for the separate existence of the two companies was to facilitate a potential sale at some future time. Using two corporations, it was possible to structure matters so that the dealership could be sold and the real estate retained, or vice versa. The problem which was brought to me centered around the fact that the real estate had, over a period of time, become too valuable for its use as a car lot. The client wanted the real-estate company to sell its property, and his intention was to have it acquire a replacement lot a few miles away in an industrial park where significantly more land could be bought for the same money. He wanted to know what the tax consequences would be.

Technically, the existing structure created a potential problem. Unfortunately, the business of the real-estate company is property ownership and the "rollover" would not apply. I recommended to the client that he write to Revenue Canada in Ottawa for an advance ruling, asking that the business of the real-estate company be deemed to be that of operating a car lot, since use of the property itself was restricted to a related company. I explained to my client that if a favourable ruling were obtained, there would be no problem in carrying on with the existing structure. The real-estate company could simply sell its property and acquire a replacement. If an unfavourable ruling were received, I suggested that the two corporations be legally amalgamated. In this way, rental income in the real-estate company would disappear, as would rental expense within the dealership. The real estate itself would then comprise a business property and would be eligible for the tax rollover. Under both alternatives, there would be no tax payable. I recommended to my client that he discuss these suggestions with his own accountants and, unfortunately, never heard anything further. This case study suggests, however, that proper structuring is extremely important if one wants to achieve tax benefits. Fortunately, the client was intelligent enough to seek advice before actually entering into a transaction and not afterwards.

Minimizing Real-Estate Profits by Reinvesting in Construction Projects

In Chapter Four, we examined the use of soft-cost tax write-offs to create a shelter against other income. One of the best uses of these write-offs is to offset a non-recurring profit which arises in the year that a particular property is sold. There can be an excellent opportunity, for example, for a vendor of land to enter into a joint venture with a real-estate developer who is buying the landowner's property. The following case study will show how this can be done.

About three years ago, a Calgary developer approached me to assist him in carrying out a proposed real-estate project. The developer wanted to buy a vacant lot for $450,000 and construct a building on it which would be sold to investors for a total price of about $3,000,000. The project would involve soft-cost write-offs of approximately 20% of $3,000,000 or $600,000 in total. Thus, on completion, the project would appear on the books of the investors as follows:

Cost of land	$ 450,000
Cost of building construction (includes contractor's profit)	1,950,000
Soft costs (20% of total)	600,000
	$3,000,000

Unfortunately, the landowner was not too keen on selling. The land was actually held by an Alberta corporation and the controlling shareholder was somewhat upset that, with a cost for tax purposes of only $60,000, a sale at $450,000 would have created a tax liability of over $90,000, and a net cash-flow of just under $360,000.

Sale of Land	$450,000	(A)
Adjusted cost base	60,000	
Capital gain	$390,000	
Taxable capital gain	$195,000	
Corporate tax at 47%	$91,650	(B)
Net cash flow (A – B)	$358,350	

Fortunately, the landholder was willing to discuss his tax position with my client so that we could think about creating a structure which would be advantageous for both parties. My client told me that if he could put together the project at a selling price of $3,000,000, the investors could put up as little as a 15% down payment and the project would still carry itself out of rentals.

With that information and after several hours of juggling numbers, I suggested to my client that he offer an extra $90,000 ($540,000 in total) to the landholder, provided the latter would agree to reinvest into the construction project to the extent of a 40% interest. The numbers worked out beautifully. I calculated that with a 40% participation, the landholder corporation would wind up with 40% of the available soft-cost write-offs and that this amount would be sufficient to completely offset the entire taxable capital gain arising as a result of the sale of the land in the first place.

Moreover, if the landholder were to take his $540,000 proceeds and then reinvest a 15% downpayment for his 40%

interest, the cash required would only be $180,000. The landholder would thus wind up with the *same* $360,000 in his "pocket" that he would have retained had he sold his land outright for $450,000 *and* he would still retain 40% of his own property! Granted, there would be a mortgage payable with respect to his interest, although, as mentioned previously, the project was set up so that anticipated rental revenues would be sufficient to carry this debt. The entire plan is illustrated below.

Of course, a deal is only good if it is fair to all parties. From the developer's standpoint, it would be unfair to charge off the extra $90,000 paid for the land to the other investors who would be buying the remaining 60% of the project. In other words, the project would still have to be built at a total cost of $3,000,000, which would require the contractor to suffer the entire $90,000 additional cost as a reduction of his own profit. However, although the contractor's profit would initially be reduced by $90,000, we were able to structure the arrangement so that we paid for the land only upon *completion* of the

---

LANDHOLDER'S POSITION IN COMMERCIAL REAL-ESTATE
TAX-SHELTER PROJECT
(After sale—followed by 40% participation)

Sale of land (inflated)—deferred		
payment		$540,000
Adjusted cost base		60,000
Capital gain		$480,000
Taxable capital gain		$240,000
Less: Soft cost write-off		
40% × $600,000		(240,000)
Net taxable income		Nil
Net cash-flow:		
Sale of land		$540,000
Cost of investment property:		
(40% × $3,000,000)	$1,200,000	
Downpayment (15% × $1,200,000)		(180,000)
Net cash (Note: landholder also owns		
40% of project)		$360,000

project instead of at the outset. In order to provide security to the vendor, we used a chartered bank to guarantee payment at that time. The $3,000,000 project took approximately one year to build. Thus, although my client, the developer, lost $90,000 initially, he saved approximately $54,000 by paying for the land at the end rather than at the beginning at the then-current interest rate of 12%. The remaining $36,000 that was otherwise "lost" ($90,000 minus $54,000) was more than offset by the savings in commissions that would otherwise have had to be paid to someone in order to find alternate investors to buy 40% of the project. This is illustrated in the table below.

Unfortunately, not every deal can be structured so that the numbers work out as beautifully as this one did. The example does, however, show that a joint venture between a landowner and a real-estate developer can produce benefits for everyone.

Just to complete the example, it might be useful to show how an outside investor would have benefited from this particular project. Let us assume that an independent party acquired a 10% interest. His total cost would then be 10% of $3,000,000 or $300,000. As mentioned before, this project required a 15% downpayment in order to carry itself. Thus, an investor purchasing a 10% interest would require a $45,000

CONTRACTOR'S POSITION IN COMMERCIAL REAL-ESTATE
TAX-SHELTER PROJECT

Cost of land	$ 540,000
Cost of building construction (includes contractor's profit)	1,860,000
Soft costs (20% of total)	600,000
	$3,000,000
Contractor's mark-up is reduced by	$ 90,000
Less: Interest saved on payment for land upon completion* ($450,000 × 12%)	54,000
Net loss to contractor—offset by advantage of having pre-sold 40% of project	$ 36,000

*Use bank guarantee to landholder

downpayment (15% X $300,000). The investor would then obtain soft-cost write-offs of $60,000, being 10% of the total soft costs of $600,000. In a 60% tax bracket, the tax saving from write-offs would be $36,000. Thus, after taxes, the investor's *net* investment is a paltry $9,000 ($45,000 initial investment minus $36,000 income taxes recovered). To "carry" $300,000 worth of real estate with a $9,000 after-tax investment is super leverage!

To be realistic, I must confess that the previous example is now three or four years old. At that time, interest rates were considerably lower than they are today in 1981, and I suggest that it is now unlikely that you could find any real-estate project that would carry itself with only a 15% downpayment. Today, it would appear acceptable to put down 25% in the hope that the rents would cover the remaining 75% financing.

There are other aspects to the tax shelter game. For example, an ideal situation may arise where an individual is looking for tax shelter and the individual himself owns a business which needs premises out of which to operate. The idea here would be to combine the shelter needs of the individual with a lease back to his own company. You might also consider a long-term lease between the individual and his corporation with a prepayment of rent.

For example, the individual could provide his business with a ten-year lease at a fixed rent (plus escalations for taxes, heating, etc.) whereas normally a commercial lease is for only five years. In exchange, however, for a ten-year term, the corporation would be required to pay the tenth year's rent "up front". As long as the corporation does not try to claim a tax deduction until the tenth year, the individual would not be taxable until that time either. However, he would have the *use* of those funds from the very outset to provide his initial downpayment. Thus, the investor might end up with little or no cash at all tied up in his own project.

The concept of combining an individual's tax shelter with a lease back to his own business is fairly common in structuring medical-dental (professional) buildings. Here, a group of doctors or dentists get together and as individuals they contract for a building to be built. The developer which they choose allocates the soft cost write-offs among the participat-

EXAMPLE OF TAX SHELTER FROM MEDICAL-DENTAL BUILDING

Assumptions:

Undepreciated capital cost of interest in building	$80,000
Annual operating costs of interest in building (including mortgage interest, real-estate taxes, heating, etc.)	$12,000

ALTERNATIVE 1: Doctor/dentist charges his own practice a rental just high enough to meet operating costs.

Statement of Operations from Professional Practice

Rent expense	$12,000
Tax savings 60%	$ 7,200
Net rental expense	$4,800
Net cost of premises	$ 4,800

Statement of Rental Income

Rental income	$12,000
Operating expenses	(12,000)
Net rental income	Nil
Net cash flow to doctor/dentist	Nil

ALTERNATIVE 2: Doctor/dentist charges his own practice with a rental sufficient to cover both operating expenses and depreciation.
Note: C.C.A. is capital cost allowance.

Statement of Operations from Professional Practice

Rent expense	$16,000
Tax savings 60%	$ 9,600
Net rental expense	$ 6,400
Net cost of premises ($6,400 – $4,000)	$ 2,400

Statement of Rental Income

Rental income	$16,000
Operating expenses	(12,000)
C.C.A. (5%x$80,000)	(4,000)
Net rental income	Nil
Net cash flow to doctor/dentist	$ 4,000

ing doctors. The doctors as landlords then lease the premises at a slightly inflated amount to their own practices. The rent paid becomes a deductible expenditure on the income statement of the practices. Then, the rent received is used to pay the expenses of the property (including debt service charges) with *the extra rent paid being sheltered by capital cost allowance.* Thus, the professional is essentially able to extract funds from his own practice through his rental property on a tax-deferred basis. This is illustrated in the example on the previous page.

By charging an additional rent of $4,000, which is in turn, sheltered by capital cost allowance, the doctor in this example is able to reduce his net cost of occupancy by half—from $4,800 to $2,400. This is just another example of effective tax planning.

Summary

Making a profit on real-estate sales is only one of an investor's concerns. A major consideration is, of course, to *keep* as much of the gain as is humanly possible without having to share it (to a disproportionate extent) with the government. A key point, therefore, is to strive for capital gains treatment on profits. An understanding of the proper guidelines is therefore mandatory if you wish to "stack the deck" in your favour.

You can also postpone taxes in some cases by acquiring replacement properties or by investing in redevelopment projects to improve the quality of your property holdings. There are many angles as long as you keep an open mind.

CHAPTER SEVEN

Income Tax Reserves and Income-Averaging Annuity Contracts

Deferring a Capital Gain by Using a Tax Reserve

Whenever a sale of property is made, the tax rules provide that a reserve can be claimed against one's gain as long as at least some part of the proceeds is deferred. These rules apply to land and securities (public and private) as well as to any capital gain on a building. You should note, however, that there is no reserve for recaptured depreciation. Even under a deferred payment program, a vendor must contend with recaptured depreciation in the year of sale. For that reason, I strongly caution you to consult your own advisers if the concept of the deferred payment plan, as described below, appeals to you.

For our purposes, let us assume that we are dealing with a piece of vacant land, such as recreational property, which is personally owned and on which no depreciation has been (or can be) claimed. If a portion of the proceeds is not due before the end of the year of sale, the formula for the tax reserve is:

$$\frac{\text{Amount not received}}{\text{Total selling price}} \times \text{Original capital gain}$$

The capital gain is reduced by the reserve, and thus each dollar collected represents a partial recovery of the vendor's cost as well as an element of profit. If a reserve is claimed in the year of sale, this is deemed to be a capital gain in the immediately following year. Therefore, the gain is spread over the period of time in which payment is to be made.

Income tax reserves have two specific benefits for tax planning purposes. They are used in estate planning to effect an "estate freeze" and in order to split income among family members. In addition, a reserve can be used to defer income that would otherwise have to be recognized by a vendor when property is sold, especially late in a given year. The purchaser may still obtain title. We will now examine the use of tax reserves in both non-arm's length and arm's length transactions, respectively.

For example, assume that a father has a piece of property with a cost of $50,000 and a fair market value of $150,000. Perhaps Father is a wealthy person and would like to pass the future growth of this property to his child. If Father were simply to make a gift, this would result in a deemed sale at fair market value for tax purposes. Thus, Father's $100,000 capital gain would be triggered immediately and $50,000 would become taxable.

In order to prevent taxes from becoming immediately payable, Father could sell this property to his child in exchange for a non-interest-bearing note due "thirty days after demand". As long as no demand is made by Father before the end of the year, no part of the proceeds will become due or payable. Consequently, a full reserve against the gain may be claimed.

Cost to Father	$ 50,000	
Fair market value on date of sale (for a note due 30 days after demand)	$150,000	
Capital gain		$100,000
Less tax reserve: $\dfrac{\$150,000}{\$150,000} \times \$100,000$		(100,000)
Net Capital Gain		$ Nil

Under the Canadian income-tax rules, there is no requirement that interest be charged on any transaction between any two individuals. Presumably, if a father intends to pass on the benefits of growth to his child (or children), he would not want to earn interest from them either. If he therefore sold the property for a non-interest-bearing note due, say, in twenty years, Revenue officials could argue that Father did not sell at fair market value. They would apply present value techniques and deem this note to be almost worthless.

However, if the consideration for the sale is a note due thirty days after demand, Father can technically request payment at any time and receive his proceeds within one month. Thus, the fair market value of that note is approximately equal to its face amount. On the one hand, the note cannot be discounted and yet the reserve is still available as long as Father does not actually make any demands.

If Father retires and his tax bracket decreases, he can always demand payment over a long period, recognizing his capital gain slowly. No reserve is permitted by law in the year of death or in situations where a taxpayer becomes a non-resident of Canada. However, the capital gain can actually be postponed until both Father and Mother die. This is as long as the debt receivable is left by will from Father to Mother (on the assumption that he dies first).

This type of tax plan provides the best possible situation—an indefinite deferral of accrued capital gains at the present time, with future growth being passed on for the benefit of the next generation.

Estate Freezing

In general, direct transactions between individuals make for simpler tax planning than does forming holding companies or trusts. This is especially true when relatively finite assets are involved and family relationships are good. If the property discussed in the previous section were a recreational facility, such as summer cottage, it would not be unusual for the agreement to provide for a sale from parents to children in order to freeze the potential capital gain but at the same time providing that the parents would still have the opportunity to use the property in their lifetimes. This type of sale coupled with a note taken back is one of the simplest "estate freezes".

An estate freeze is a transaction which occurs when an asset with growth potential (such as real estate or shares) is *exchanged* for an asset whose value is fixed or frozen. In the previous case, the frozen asset is the note receivable, which can never be worth more than its face amount of $150,000.

In the last few years, tax advisers have been concerned that someday Revenue Canada officials may no longer sanction the use of a reserve in conjunction with a sale that is made for proceeds due "thirty days after demand". For example, in the previous transaction, Revenue could disallow the use of the reserve on the basis that Father *could have* demanded payment during the year, in which case the proceeds would have become due before the end of the year of sale. This particular matter has not as yet been dealt with before the courts.

There is, however, no problem if an alternative method is used which would essentially produce the same outcome. Instead of an interest-free note payable "thirty days after demand", we may substitute a non-interest-bearing note due "three hundred and seventy days after demand" but with interest payable from date of demand.

The fact that the principal amount is due three hundred and seventy days after demand means that, even if a demand were made (hypothetically) on January 1, no proceeds would actually be due before the end of the year. Moreover, since interest would start accruing from date of demand, Revenue officials would not be able to argue that such a note isn't worth an amount equal to its face value. In practice, I therefore recommend the slightly more sophisticated approach of the three-hundred-and-seventy-day note instead of the thirty-day note.

An Opportunity for Adventurous Planning

One of the major tax benefits of a direct transaction between individuals is the fact that for income tax purposes, the property is transferred at its fair market value. In the preceding example, the child would record a tax cost for his land of $150,000 even though his father's $100,000 capital gain is postponed. What happens if the land is then (immediately) resold to an outsider for $150,000? The child in the example would have no capital gain for income tax purposes! Ironically, there is no law that requires the child to repay his father at the time the property is sold. In other words, as a family unit, $150,000 of proceeds may be received while the capital-gains tax is deferred. Presumably, Father could tell his child where the money should be reinvested. The replacement property could then become collateral against the note which the child still owes to Father.

Of course, this approach of selling property on a reserve

basis to a family member who in turn resells the property to an outsider is tricky. First, it should be noted that this concept would *not* be applicable if the parties involved were a husband and wife. Under the income tax rules, as soon as the wife resold the property for cash, the capital gain would revert back to her husband. The government cannot prevent effective tax avoidance, however, when the taxpayers involved are anyone other than husband and wife. Actually, one would not normally want to transact with minor children, so for purposes of our discussions, assume that the child (or children) in question are already grown up.

You might ask whether or not Father could effectively control his child so that the latter would reinvest the proceeds where Father dictates. Legally, to the best of my knowledge, Father would have no control other than the right to demand payment against his note. This, of course, would attract the income taxes that he was trying to defer in the first place. However, from a practical standpoint, Father does have some control. He is the one who prepares his own will! If we assume, just to extend the scenario, that Father's total net worth is $1,500,000 and that the asset in question represents only one-tenth of his estate, it is presumably in the interest of the child to co-operate when asked to reinvest in a particular property. In most cases, however, unless the relationship between parents and children is good, one had best refrain from this type of planning.

Another factor to consider is that if the practice of selling property to a family member before selling it to an outsider becomes too popular, Revenue Canada may try to prevail on Finance to block the loophole. That is, restrictions on the use of income tax reserves could be imposed. For the time being, however, the opportunity to defer taxes on this basis is certainly wide open. In fact, as we will see towards the end of this chapter, with even more adventurous planning, we might be able to *eliminate* capital gains taxes entirely!

A Second Use for Tax Reserves

The tax-reserve provisions can also be used to defer income whenever property is sold and the seller does not wish to pay immediate taxes on his profits. With proper planning, a purchaser can obtain a clear title while still passing on tax advantages to the vendor. For example, in November 1978, a client came to me with what he thought was a complicated tax problem. He owned a piece of vacant land in downtown Calgary and had just received an excellent offer from a developer. However, he was somewhat concerned with his potential tax liability on such a substantial profit. The client indicated that it was too late in the year to find an acceptable tax shelter.

I suggested that he sell the property under an agreement for sale which would provide for payment to be deferred in full until January 1979. I explained that, as long as the proceeds are not *due* before December 31, a reserve could be claimed against his profit. Initially, the client's reaction was that this arrangement would not be feasible—the purchaser needed an immediate clear title so that he could start developing the property before the end of the year. Of course, my client was not prepared to release title without adequate security. My client also told me that the purchaser had sufficient cash for the full amount.

I then recommended that the purchaser simply take the available cash and place the funds into a term deposit due sometime in early January with his *own* bank. I also suggested that with this term deposit as collateral, the purchaser's bank could then guarantee the debt owing by the purchaser. An irrevocable guarantee from a Canadian chartered bank is just as valid as having the security of a mortgage against a piece of property. If the buyer were to default, my client would have immediate recourse for the full price from the purchaser's banker. There would also be no risk to the banker, since he would have the security of the purchaser's term deposit. The transaction took place as I suggested, and my client obtained the one-year tax deferral that he was looking for.

In theory, the preceding tax plan could be taken one step further. The transaction could have been structured so that the buyer's payment would not be due for ten years (instead of after only two months). The purchaser would again take his cash and buy a term deposit to serve as collateral for the bank guarantee. The agreement with the vendor would provide that the balance of sale would bear interest at the same rate that the purchaser would be getting on his term deposit. In this respect, the purchaser could not possibly be adversely affected. His interest income and expense would simply offset each other.

Again, with the term deposit as collateral, the chartered bank could promise to guarantee payment to the vendor at the end of ten years. However, since the note would not be due until the tenth year, the vendor would not have to take any of his gain into income *until that time*. If he wanted to, the vendor could receive interest income throughout the period on the full balance of the purchase price. This is substantially more than he would have had if he were simply to have collected his cash, paid taxes on his profit, and reinvested the difference. This can be illustrated using the following example.

Cost of property	$ 10,000
Anticipated selling price	100,000
Capital gain on disposal	90,000
Taxable capital gain	45,000
Taxes at 50%	22,500
Cash available to reinvest ($100,000 – $22,500)	77,500
Available pre-tax return at assumed rated of 15% (per annum)	11,625

Under the foregoing arrangement, the annual return on investment would only be $11,625 (before taxes) if the property were sold and the net profit were invested to yield 15%. As an alternative, if the vendor accepted a note for $100,000 due at the end of ten years, with interest at 15%, the annual before-tax investment income would be $15,000 each year. Thus, for a ten-year period, the vendor would be receiving investment income on dollars that otherwise would have been paid away immediately as income taxes. Because of the chartered bank's guarantee, the vendor is also assured of getting his purchase price at the end of ten years.

Let us now carry this arrangement one step further. What would happen if the vendor were not interested in receiving interest income only, and wanted, instead, to invest in other property with growth potential? Presumably, he could take his note receivable from the purchaser's bank and approach his own banker for a loan in an amount equal to the debt receivable. The vendor's banker might lend dollar for dollar on the security of the guarantee from another chartered bank. In this manner, the vendor would have the full use of all his capital in *any way* that he so desired with no taxes payable until the end of the tenth year! His interest income on the balance of sale owing by the purchaser would offset the interest expense on the bank loan taken out. Having the use of profits and postponing taxes is effective planning. Of course, with inflation, one shouldn't worry too much about the impact of a tax which is deferred for ten years.

I have discussed this arrangement with many tax accountants and lawyers over the past few years. Certainly, there is nothing fraudulent in planning one's affairs to reduce taxes otherwise payable. The Department of National Revenue is, of course, aware that this loophole exists. As it happens, this arrangement has already been tested in the courts and the Minister lost.

Esskay Farms Limited vs. Her Majesty The Queen

In this case, a company trading in real estate acquired a large parcel of land near Calgary in 1961 and subsequently sold the greater portion of it. Of the remaining 117 acres, 30 were usable for housing and the balance consisted of unstable river bank. The City then constructed a public utility adjacent to the company's property. In 1969, the City offered to buy the 117 acres for $247,000. The company agreed to sell but in order to obtain a deferral of tax, wanted payment of the purchase money to be deferred for eight years. The City was precluded by law from accepting these terms. By arrangement, therefore, the real-estate trading company sold the land to a trust company for the identical price offered by the City, subject to the condition that $100,000 would be payable in 1976 and the remaining $147,000 payable in 1977. Shortly afterwards, the trust company sold the property to the City for $247,000 but did not receive all the purchase money until 1970. The Minister assessed the taxpayer-company on the net proceeds on the sale of the land in the taxation years 1969 and 1970. The Minister's contention was that the trust company had simply acted as an agent of the taxpayer and that the whole transaction was a sham in order to postpone the recognition of income.

The Minister's appeal was, however, dismissed. The court held that the trust company had acted on its own behalf and therefore could not have been an agent of the taxpayer. The transactions were upheld since the parties had executed documents which created the legal rights and obligations intended. The fact that the trust company resold the land at its cost to the City did not prevent Esskay Farms from continuing to claim its reserve against profits.

The Use of Tax Reserves Within a Family—Revisited

Previously, the material in this chapter explained how the concept of an income-tax reserve could be used to postpone taxes when real estate is sold from a parent to a child. By accepting a note due sometime in the future, a transferor can postpone the recognition of his gain. However, the recipient of the property acquires it at a tax cost equal to its fair market value. On a subsequent resale, the family unit receives proceeds, but the tax is deferred.

These opportunities to take advantage of income tax reserves can even be extended beyond the framework of real-estate profits. For example, if a parent has marketable securities which have appreciated substantially and the intention is to sell them, he might consider an initial sale, using the reserve, to one or more of his children. The children would then immediately resell the securities and purchase other investments.

Similarly, public company shares could be sold to one's stock-broker, who would buy the securities on his own behalf and not as an agent. Of course, the broker would only purchase the securities if he had, in turn, a prospective purchaser. If your broker is a well-known and reputable firm, and you receive a commitment to pay you several years later with interest at appropriate rates, you could probably borrow dollar for dollar from a lending institution against your receivable debt. Again, you could have your "cake," you would be able to "eat it", but you would not have to pay taxes until the note from the broker fell due. Your broker could simply collect the cash which he receives from his other client (the one who in turn purchased your shares) and place these funds into a deposit certificate. The interest which is received by the broker would be used to pay interest to you, and if you in turn borrowed funds from a lending institution for investment, your interest expense would offset the interest income from the broker.

Income-Averaging Annuity Contracts

Another fertile opportunity for effective tax planning for individual investors in real-estate is the income-averaging annuity contract (IAAC). The income-averaging annuity rules were introduced in 1972 as a method of leveling the peaks and valleys created by the receipt of non-recurring incomes in certain years. There are actually nineteen different items which qualify for income-averaging annuity treatment. These include taxable capital gains and recaptured depreciation on the disposition of real-estate holdings. It should be noted that an income-averaging annuity is not available to corporations. Often, I am asked by clients whether I feel that their real-estate investments should be made personally or whether they should be held by a limited company. A full analysis of this topic is contained in Chapter Eight. However, for the time being, you should be aware that holding property through a corporation precludes the eventual use of an annuity to shelter profits on disposition.

If an individual realizes a taxable capital gain and/or recaptured depreciation, he is permitted to take his cash and purchase an offsetting, tax-deductible annuity. The annuity must start to pay a return within ten months after the purchase is made. Thus, the individual would receive annual payments of principal and interest over the term of the annuity. All amounts received under the income-averaging annuity contract would then be included in income in the years received. The advantage of the annuity is that instead of being taxed on a large lump sum in one year, the tax burden is spread over many years. This is illustrated by the schedule on page 108.

In this case, I assume that an individual has made a capital gain of $200,000. Of course, $100,000 is the "tax-free half" and can be reinvested wherever the taxpayer so desires. The taxable portion, however, is "rolled over" into a five-year

	Year of Taxable Capital Gain	Additional Taxable Income of Subsequent Year	
		1	2–5
Taxable capital gain	$100,000		
Purchase of five-year IAAC	80,000	$20,000	$20,000
Net special income	$ 20,000		

annuity to yield $20,000 a year (combined principal and interest). Instead of being taxed on $100,000 in one year, the taxes are, therefore, spread over a six-year period—the year the taxable gain is received and the subsequent five years.

An income-averaging annuity can be purchased for either a specific term (generally up to fifteen years) or for life. If a life annuity is chosen, there can be a maximum guaranteed period of fifteen years. This means that if the taxpayer dies before fifteen years have elapsed, payments will continue to his heirs until that guaranteed period has been reached.

There are two special rules worth noting. The first is that the maximum amount that can be invested into an income-averaging annuity in any given year is the special income that was received minus the equivalent of one year's annuity receipts (see the previous schedule). The second special rule (which was already mentioned) is that the annuity must begin within ten months following its purchase. The intention is to spread the special income over the year it is received as well as each subsequent year. Income-averaging annuities may be purchased in the year that the special income is received and up to sixty days thereafter. If a taxpayer so desires, he may therefore delay the acquisition of his income-averaging annuity until March 1 of the subsequent year in order to have payments commence January 1 of the year following. In this manner, it is possible to delay the recognition of annuity income for one year. In the example under discussion, the taxpayer could report only $20,000 of (net) income in the year he realizes his capital gain and not recognize any additional income until the second subsequent year. Although the previous example reflects a five-year payout, most people would opt for a ten- or fifteen-year annuity program.

The income-averaging annuity has its advantages and disadvantages. The first advantage, of course, is the fact that income taxes otherwise payable are deferred. Second, it gives the taxpayer the opportunity to reinvest dollars that have not been taxed. If the individual in the previous example were in the 50% tax bracket, only $50,000 could be reinvested out of a $100,000 taxable capital gain without the use of the annuity. With the IAAC, however, there is $80,000 reinvested in the annuity itself *as well as* $10,000 left over after taxes are paid on the $20,000 which was taxable in the year the gain was realized. In other words, a total of $90,000 is available for reinvestment instead of only $50,000.

There is a further advantage if the taxpayer will be in a lower tax bracket during the years in which the annuity is to be received than he was in the year in which the gain was first realized. There are also some unbelievably attractive income tax advantages if the beneficiary of an income-averaging annuity contract subsequently becomes a bona fide non-resident of Canada. Under the provisions of the Canadian Income Tax Act, if a taxpayer becomes a non-resident and then deregisters an income-averaging annuity, his worst exposure to Canadian income taxes is a flat-rate 25% withholding tax. When one considers that only half of a capital gain is taxable in the first place, this means an effective tax cost of as little as 12½% of the entire gain. In fact, where an individual is contemplating non-residency, it would be to his advantage to dispose of *all* capital assets *before* leaving Canada and purchase an income-averaging annuity to shelter his profits. Then, the annuity could be collapsed once the individual is no longer resident in Canada and, if the individual wanted to, he could then reacquire the property which was sold. In most cases, the foreign country would consider the collection of the income-averaging annuity as a non-taxable return of capital and the repurchase of the property would result in a higher cost for purposes of foreign capital gains tax. Thus, there can be a tremendous tax saving. You should note, however, that the Canadian authorities are not particularly pleased with this opportunity to effectively avoid taxes. You would have to be prepared to remain a non-resident of Canada for a minimum of two years after leaving. Otherwise, Revenue Canada will at least attempt to establish that you have never surrendered residency status in the first place. This does not mean that you could not visit friends and relatives from time to time during this period, but obviously, the longer you spend in Canada the less secure your tax position would become. If you own a home in Canada you would also be well advised to either sell it or rent it out on a long-term lease. Otherwise, the Minister could argue that you still are resident because you have a home in this country. Certainly, the topic of residency and non-residency is complex. Anyone who is contemplating a change of status would be well advised to seek professional advice first.

The major disadvantage of an income-averaging annuity is the fact that the purchase of the annuity involves the commitment of funds for a long-term period at a predetermined (inflexible) rate of interest. Once the yield is established, it does not fluctuate as do regular rates, and there is no provision to protect your cash flow from the ravages of inflation. A second disadvantage would arise in cases where an individual's tax bracket increases as the years go by. Therefore, in practice, I hesitate to recommend the unqualified purchase of an income-averaging annuity unless an individual is in a retirement position and is simply concerned with a cash flow to finance his income needs. However, with certain refinements, the income-averaging annuity does lend itself to some outstanding opportunities for planning.

Using an Income-Averaging Annuity as Collateral for a Loan

At the time this is being written, the Department of National Revenue allows an income-averaging annuity to be pledged as collateral for a loan. In addition, since an annuity will pay interest income, it is permissible to borrow in order to buy the annuity in the first place. The interest expense on the borrowing would be an allowable deduction offsetting the interest element of the annuity itself.

In the last couple of years, a number of qualified issuers of income-averaging annuities, such as trust and insurance companies, have evolved arrangements whereby individuals could take advantage of the law. The structure consists of a "back-to-back" loan in order to purchase an income-averaging annuity where *both* the loan and the annuity are created by the particular trust or insurance company. This arrangement is also referred to as a "wrap around" income-averaging annuity. The example on page 113 illustrates this concept. For purposes of our discussion, we'll assume that a taxpayer realizes a taxable capital gain of $100,000 on the disposition of real estate which he would like to spread over the following five years. At the same time, he wants the greater part of his proceeds available for *other real-estate investments* from the outset. The steps involved are as follows:

1. The taxpayer realizes a taxable gain of $100,000, out of which he appropriates $10,000 to pay taxes in the current year on his gain minus that portion which will be sheltered through the annuity. $90,000 is available for reinvestment in other property. (Note that this $90,000 is over and above the individual's tax-free half of his gain and the recovery of his original cost.)

2. Out of the $90,000, the taxpayer sets aside $5,000 in order to fund part of the purchase price of the income-averaging annuity as further described in the next step. $85,000 is then invested in property with capital growth potential.

Capital available for investment from outset:	
Taxable capital gain	$100,000
Less: tax on $20,000 at assumed rate of 50%	(10,000)
	90,000
Less: Trust company fee	(5,000)
	$ 85,000

3. The taxpayer then approaches a trust company which arranges to lend him $75,000 so that he may purchase an $80,000 income-averaging annuity. The difference of $5,000 represents the trust company's fee for providing this accommodation.

4. The documentation is drawn so that over the following five years, the annuity would pay $20,000 each year. The taxpayer

would not, however, receive *any* funds personally. Instead, the dollars would go directly back to the trust company in settlement of the $75,000 loan (principal and interest). At the end of five years, the annuity runs out but the loan is fully discharged. Since this is a "back-to-back" or "wrap around" situation, changes in interest rates over the five-year period are *not* relevant. The trust company has no exposure because it is simply paying off its loan receivable with its rights under the income-averaging annuity. The trust company does, however, receive its $5,000 fee for providing its services.

5. Over the five-year period in this illustration, the $20,000 received each year from the annuity is taxable income. However, the interest on the trust company loan repayments is deductible. As with any other loan arrangement, in the first few years, most of the payments are on account of interest. Thus, although the taxpayer would still receive a net income of $75,000 over five years, most of the tax would not have to be paid until years three to five. If the arrangement were over a fifteen-year period, the tax burden over the first five years would be negligible.

If the taxpayer's income increases during the period of the annuity, he can use the extra cash flow of those years to cover his tax liability. If this is not sufficient, he could always draw down against the original capital which was reinvested from the outset ($90,000 minus $5,000 of trust company fees). It becomes fairly obvious that the opportunity to defer taxes on $80,000 while keeping most of one's capital available for reinvestment would more than offset the trust company fee required to provide the accommodation. This is especially so because part of the $5,000 trust company *fee* is, in fact, tax deductible. Most trust companies would categorize part of the amount as a "high ratio loan fee", which becomes an expense of borrowing money. As we have already seen in Chapter Four, expenses of borrowing money are deductible.

More Adventurous Planning Using Life Insurance Annuities

With income-averaging annuities, it may be possible to virtually eliminate capital gains on the transfer of real estate and

EXAMPLE OF "WRAP AROUND" INCOME-AVERAGING ANNUITY CONTRACT

Year		1	2	3	4	5
Taxable capital gain on real estate	$100,000					
IAAC (5 years)	(80,000)	20,000	20,000	20,000	20,000	20,000
Net income	$ 20,000					
Trust company loan used to purchase IAAC	$ 75,000	(20,000)	(20,000)	(20,000)	(20,000)	(20,000)
Taxable income from IAAC		20,000	20,000	20,000	20,000	20,000
Less: Interest on loan		(9,000)	(7,000)	(4,500)	(2,500)	(2,000)
Net taxable income		11,000	13,000	15,500	17,500	18,000

113

other investments from a parent to a child. On pages 99–102 we examined the opportunity to *postpone* gains on dispositions by making sales to family members, rather than gifts. The transferor would sell his property in exchange for a note due sometime in the future and would then shelter the gain for tax purposes by claiming a reserve. In the example on page 99 the deferred capital gain was $100,000.

Let us now assume that Father is getting on in years and suddenly discovers that he has not got long to live. Under those circumstances, he might undertake to do the following:

1. He calls the note owing to him by his child. The child writes a cheque for the full purchase price and Father returns a gift of cash. Outside of the province of Quebec, the cash gift is not taxable. Alternatively, it should be noted that claiming a reserve is optional even if proceeds are not demanded. Thus, in anticipation of death, Father's tax return for the final year would be filed without taking into account the reserve. By calling the note or failing to claim the reserve a taxable capital gain of $50,000 is triggered.

2. Against that $50,000 taxable gain, Father borrows $44,000 and buys an income-averaging annuity from a life insurance company to yield $6,000 per annum for his lifetime but *without any guaranteed term*.

3. The family members then approach the same insurance company and purchase a life insurance policy on Father's life for $44,000.

4. Father then dies and the income-averaging annuity contract ceases. The insurance company thus "inherits" the $44,000 income-averaging annuity proceeds against which there is now no liability to make payments! Instead, the insurance company pays off the life policy. The insurance proceeds are then received by the heirs *tax free* and are used, in turn, to pay off the loan which Father incurred in the first place to purchase the annuity. In this manner, what would otherwise be taxable income from an annuity gets transformed into a tax-free life insurance receipt! The capital gain is not only deferred—it is eliminated. The children end up with the property at a tax cost equal to its fair market value on the date they acquired it.

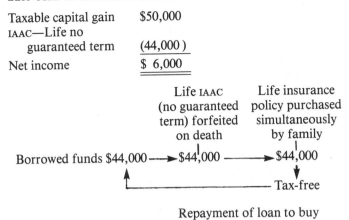

Taxable capital gain	$50,000
IAAC—Life no guaranteed term	(44,000)
Net income	$ 6,000

Life IAAC (no guaranteed term) forfeited on death

Life insurance policy purchased simultaneously by family

Borrowed funds $44,000 ⟶ $44,000 ⟶ $44,000 ⟶ Tax-free

Repayment of loan to buy (tax deductible) IAAC

Result—$44,000 out of a $50,000 taxable capital gain is not only deferred, but is eliminated. The children obtain the property at a tax cost equal to its fair market value at the date they acquired it.

You might ask the question, how can an insurance company issue a policy on someone's life if the individual is dying? Actually, to the best of my knowledge, there is no restriction on issuing such a policy. Normally, of course, an insurance company would not accept such a risk. However, since the income-averaging annuity ceases at the moment of death, any risk to the insurance company is nil! For an accommodation fee (similar to that charged by trust companies under "wrap around" situations) it is my understanding that such an arrangement can in fact be structured. Of course, if too many people begin to use this loophole, the government will block it. However, for the first few adventurous taxpayers a glorious opportunity does exist. Of course, one should exercise caution and consult one's own advisers.

While the last example uses some "gimickry" to subvert the system, there is also a much more legitimate opportunity to use income-averaging annuities to tax plan for senior citizens with substantial investment holdings.

To change the scenario slightly, assume that the father in the previous example is seventy years of age but is enjoying reasonably good health. He has, however, retired and perhaps he is in a slightly lower tax bracket. As described previously, Father sells property to his children, triggering a capital gain of $100,000. In the absence of a reserve, $50,000 is taxable. As reflected in the example on page 115, Father again borrows $44,000 to buy an income-averaging annuity for life with no guaranteed term. Simultaneously, the family purchases a *diminishing term-life insurance policy* on Father's life. Over the next few years, if Father continues to live, he will receive payments under the income-averaging annuity contract. At worst, the annuity will slowly trigger income over that period of time, with the proceeds being used to gradually repay the borrowed funds. The taxable portion of the annuity would be reduced by the interest expense on the borrowed monies. Under these circumstances, the value of the insurance policy will decline.

On the other hand, if the family is 'lucky'', Father will die soon after he purchases the annuity. Again, under those circumstances the balance of the annuity is forfeited on death and the insurance policy converts what would otherwise be taxable income into tax-free proceeds. The proceeds are then used (as described previously) to pay back the funds borrowed to buy the annuity in the first place.

Ordinarily, one would expect that an insurance policy taken out on the life of a senior citizen would be rather expensive. However, a close analysis of the situation will reveal that the insurance company is really not at risk. From its standpoint, it simply uses the proceeds of the income-averaging annuity contract to pay off its obligations under the life insurance policy. Such an arrangement can be structured at a reasonable cost to the taxpayer.

It should also be noted, in passing, that the opportunities to use income-averaging annuities apply not only to real estate profits but, as well, to other capital gains such as on the disposition of publicly and privately traded shares and other securities.

Capital Gains and Interest Income – a Deadly Combination

Before leaving the topic of property transactions that do not involve the use of real-estate holding companies, it would be worthwhile to examine the tax implications of a conventional instalment sale. Under such an arrangement, a taxpayer will often dispose of property under an agreement where the buyer will pay him his price over a period of time with interest at prevailing rates. Unless the dollars involved are very substantial, the opportunity to use the income tax reserve for uncollected proceeds will provide favourable tax treatment. This is especially the case where, for example, the taxpayer disposing of the property is a farmer with very little other income.

Take a situation where a farmer sells land with a cost of $250,000 for $750,000. Assume that the purchase price will be paid in eight equal instalments of $93,750 each with interest at 15%. The tax consequences of the capital gain itself are not too serious. If a taxable capital gain of $250,000 is spread over eight years, the annual taxable income is only $31,250. Assuming that the farmer in my example has little other income, the annual tax bite on this amount would probably not exceed $10,000 of combined federal and provincial taxes. This produces an effective burden of only about 33⅓% and certainly this is not a severe hardship. However, where a taxpayer starts with a taxable income of $31,250 (assuming that his other income simply offsets his personal exemptions), he is already into a 50% tax bracket in most provinces of Canada. This means that if one adds interest income *on top* of the taxable capital gain, the 15% yield becomes only 7½%. In other words, half of the interest receivable over the eight-year period will be confiscated by the government in the form of taxes. The cumulative interest, in this situation, would be well in excess of $300,000.

Without proper planning, the only opportunities that the farmer would have to reduce his tax burden would be to lend his *after-tax capital* each year (that is, the instalments of purchase price plus interest minus taxes payable) to his family or to a family corporation so that he would not be burdened with *compound* income on top of everything else.

However, with proper planning, much of tax impact can be softened. The first possibility is to structure the initial acquisition of property so that it is jointly held by a husband and wife. Then, when a sale takes place, the taxable income is split.

Joint Ownership of Property Between Husband and Wife

One of the many differences between the Canadian tax system and that of the United States is that Canada taxes a husband and wife separately, whereas the United States permits (and encourages) the filing of joint tax returns. Since Canada treats husbands and wives as separate taxpayers, the Income Tax Act is therefore somewhat concerned with the potential that might exist for income-splitting between spouses.

Thus, where a taxpayer transfers property to a spouse, or to a person who subsequently becomes a spouse, the income generated by the transferred property reverts back to the transferor. In addition, the rules go on to provide that if the transferee disposes of the property and substitutes something else, the income on the substituted property *also* reverts back to the transferor. These "income attribution rules" apply as long the the transferor is alive, is resident in Canada, and the transferee is his spouse.

Fortunately, however, income attribution only applies to "*transfers* of property", i.e. when a gift or sale is made. As a result of a much-celebrated tax case which came before the courts over twenty years ago, it is clear that the term "transfer" does *not* include a loan. Thus, where a husband lends money to his wife, the income generated from these funds is her income and not his. Moreover, there is no requirement in Canada that interest be charged on a loan from one individual to another.

Accordingly, for tax purposes, it is generally recommended that spouses split income between themselves by simply making loans of investment capital to one another. However, if taxpayers use this method, the documentation should be prepared evidencing each transaction as a loan. Usually, the loan would not be interest-bearing and would be repayable on demand.

Transfers of Capital Property Between Spouses

When one transfers capital property such as real estate to a spouse, the transfer is automatically deemed to have taken place at the transferor's tax cost. In other words, no matter what the current value of that property is, no capital gain or loss is recognized at that time. However, when the transferee

118

subsequently sells the property, the capital gain or loss reverts back to the transferor. The computation of this gain or loss is based on the transferor's original cost for income tax purposes. Thus, one accomplishes absolutely nothing in the way of reallocating capital gains or losses by making gifts or sales of capital properties between spouses.

Nevertheless, with proper planning the rules can be beaten. If a husband (for example) wishes to transfer both income and growth to his wife (in a lower bracket) he would first have to lend her the cash. The cash would then be taken by the wife and invested in the real-estate property in question. In this manner, the capital growth would accrue to her benefit for tax purposes. In addition, any income generated on the property during the ownership period would also be taxed in her hands.

If you want to take advantage of these tax planning provisions, it is important that no shortcuts be taken. It is insufficient to simply register the ownership of the property in whole or in part in the name of a spouse who is in a lower tax bracket. You would have to be able to show Revenue Canada that a loan was made in the first place and that these funds were used for the purpose of making the investment. Again beware of back-dating transactions, because creating documentation to evidence a loan after the fact is fraudulent and the penalties can be very severe. To summarize, make loans first and buy the property after.

Instalment Sales Revisited

Returning to the situation where a farmer sells land with a tax cost of $250,000 for $750,000 (page 117), it is obvious that the tax implications of both capital gains and interest income could be alleviated substantially if the property were owned jointly by husband and wife. At the time of purchase, the farmer could have loaned part of the funds for a downpayment to his wife, and she in turn, could have purchased a half-interest in the property. This eventually would have resulted in a splitting of both capital gains and interest on a subsequent sale.

Often, I am asked by clients to suggest a proper structure for the acquisition of property. Assuming for the time being, that a real-estate holding company is not feasible, when is it best to have real estate owned by husband and wife jointly? Of course, each case is different. If husband and wife are both in approximately the same income tax bracket at the time of acquisition, and it is anticipated that their incomes will remain relatively equal, it is usually advantageous to acquire property together. If there are profits, the profits can be split, while losses during the ownership period can also be allocated equally. However, what if one of the two is in a higher tax bracket than the other? If the property is going to generate profits from the outset, it is usually better to have the ownership in the hands of the spouse in the lower bracket. However, where there will initially be losses (especially those resulting from soft costs or interest on money borrowed to acquire the property) one has to consider a trade-off. On the one hand, it is advantageous to have the losses from soft costs, interest, and other operating expenses claimed by the taxpayer in the higher bracket. However, at the time of sale, the penalty is that this taxpayer is forced to report all the profit.

Generally, when advising my own clients, I try to determine whether the holding period is anticipated to be short or long. If the holding period is short, then the tax advantages of deductible expenditures may be more than offset by the opportunities to split profits on sale. On the other hand, if a long-term holding period is contemplated, it may be more advantageous to have property owned by the taxpayer who is in a higher bracket, even though there can be problems later on when the property is sold.

However, even at this time, with proper planning, one may *still* be able to avoid the problem of having capital gains *plus* interest income taxable under an instalment sale.

Transforming a Cash Transaction into an Instalment Sale

As mentioned previously, instalment sales involving principal and interest receivable by any *individual* should be avoided. Let us return to the example where a farmer sells land with a tax cost of $250,000 for $750,000. If the sale is made for *cash*, the farmer may take his proceeds and lend the *full amount* to his family or to a family corporation in order to effect future income splitting. The *family* would then earn interest income on these funds. The farmer could then borrow money and buy an income-averaging annuity to spread his capital gain. In this way, the farmer would not be taxed on any interest income and the family or family corporation could repay the funds needed by the farmer to pay his taxes over the period of the annuity. The point of such an arrangement is that the capital would be available to the family from the outset to achieve income splitting. The family would receive interest income, while the farmer pays tax on his capital gain.

Unfortunately, under most arrangements, a purchaser would not ordinarily be willing or able to pay the entire purchase price for property. It would still be possible, using creative tax planning, to segregate capital gains from interest income. An arrangement of this nature would involve the following steps:

1. The purchaser would borrow the full purchase price (assumed to be $750,000) from a lending institution for one day.
2. The purchaser would then pay cash to the farmer for the property.
3. The farmer would then lend the cash received to a family corporation on a non-interest-bearing basis.
4. The farmer would then borrow funds to acquire an income-averaging annuity to offset his capital gain.
5. The family corporation then lends the full purchase price back to the purchaser and takes back a mortgage on the property.
6. The purchaser would then repay his interim (one-day) financing.
7. Then, over a period of time, the purchaser would make payments on account of principal and interest to the family corporation, and the family corporation, in turn, could repay whatever principal is needed by the farmer to pay taxes as his annuity is received. The corporation may then be used (as described in the next chapter) as a vehicle to split the interest income among the family members.

I have used this arrangement on many occasions to keep capital gains separate from interest income. All it takes is a little effort and imagination.

Step 1

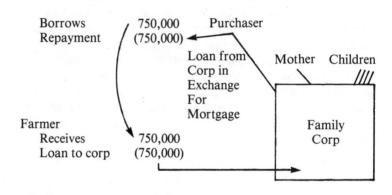

Borrows   750,000   Purchaser
Repayment   (750,000)

Loan from
Corp in   Mother   Children
Exchange   ////
For
Mortgage

Family
Corp

Farmer
Receives   750,000
Loan to corp   (750,000)

Step 2

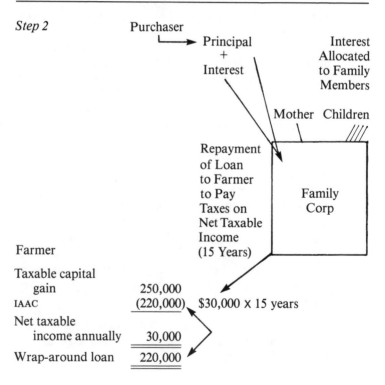

Purchaser

Principal   Interest
+   Allocated
Interest   to Family
                          Members

                      Mother   Children
                             ////

Repayment
of Loan
to Farmer
to Pay
Taxes on   Family
Net Taxable   Corp
Income
(15 Years)

Farmer

Taxable capital
  gain   250,000
IAAC   (220,000) $30,000 × 15 years
Net taxable
  income annually 30,000
Wrap-around loan   220,000

122

Summary

One of the major advantages of holding property in your own name is the potential use of an income-averaging annuity contract to shelter profits on an eventual sale. A second advantage is that when property is sold either to family members or outsiders, you can use income tax reserves to shelter profits. While the vendor may legitimately postpone the recognition of his income, the purchaser will achieve a tax cost equal to the current fair market value of the property at the time the transfer takes place. There is, therefore, no double tax when the property is subsequently resold.

In Chapter Eight, we will examine the use of real-estate holding companies. We will see that while there are some significant potential advantages, there are also some pitfalls which should be avoided.

Real-Estate Holding Companies—
When and How to Use Them

One of the common mistakes that Canadians often make is to incorporate companies too soon—while the penalties outweigh the advantages. For example, whenever a new real estate or other venture is getting under way, there is a good chance that it will incur some losses at the outset. This is especially true in cases where income tax write-offs for soft costs are available. In addition, it is quite common for real-estate projects to have negative cash-flows for a period until rents can be increased to cover the costs of operations. If you hold your real-estate investments personally, your tax losses will be fully deductible, so that you can shelter other personal sources of income from tax. However, if your investments are held by a corporation, only the corporation will be able to deduct its own losses. If the corporation has no other income, the best that you could hope for is to carry back the operating loss to the preceding taxation year (if there was income in that year) and forward up to five years against future income. Even if the losses will be usable over the five-year carry-forward period, you must always consider the time-value of money. In other words, the idea is to use your losses as quickly as possible.

As we will see in this chapter, one of the best tax-planning strategies is to hold property as an individual during the construction period and over the first few years until the property starts to generate profits. Later, one would then consider "rolling over" these real-estate holdings to a corporation in order to split future income from the property and gains arising from its sale among members of the entire family—especially if they are in lower tax brackets.

You should note that a corporation cannot buy an income-averaging annuity, although when property is sold on an instalment basis, a corporation (like an individual) can spread its tax on capital gains over the payment period. As we will see in Chapter Nine, you would not ordinarily use a corporation as a vehicle to own your personal residence. The general capital gains exemption in Canada on the disposition of a principal residence does not apply unless the home is owned by an individual. In this chapter, you will see that transferring property *into* a corporation is usually quite straightforward. However, incorporation is very much a "one-way street". While the rules for transferring in are quite generous, there is no way that an *individual* can extract property back out of a corporation without severe tax penalties if the property has appreciated in value. In general, the corporation would be deemed to have sold its property at market price, and the value of the assets themselves would create a taxable dividend for the individual, to the extent that he receives more than what he paid for the capital stock of the corporation in the first place.

How to Incorporate a Real-Estate Holding Company

As discussed, you would usually begin by owning property as an individual. If a group of individuals is involved, the ownership may be structured as a partnership through which losses would be allocated among the partners. When the property starts to generate a profit, Section 85 of the Income Tax Act may be used as the vehicle to transfer it to a Canadian corporation, without triggering either recaptured depreciation or capital gains. The corporation can also be structured to pass on *future growth and income* to other family members.

Section 85 and Its Applications

While the concept of transferring property on a tax-deferred basis to a corporation is simple, the actual operation of Section 85 is quite complex and a "rollover" should not be undertaken without professional advice from a tax accountant or lawyer. There are many rules which must be followed. Specifically, the corporation itself must be a Canadian corporation set up under either federal or provincial law. One cannot use Section 85 in order to transfer property which has appreciated in value to a foreign corporation without triggering income taxes. This point is extremely significant where a Canadian holds real estate outside Canada. As we will see in Chapter Thirteen, for example, if a Canadian wishes to acquire property in the United States through a U.S. company, he would be well-advised to purchase the property through that corporation in the first place. The individual could not otherwise transfer the property at a later date (once there has been substantial appreciation) without having the transfer being treated as a disposition at fair market value for Canadian tax purposes.

A second important rule is that there must be no retroactive gift conferred on family members at the time the rollover takes place. The Income Tax Act recognizes that a corporation is an acceptable vehicle for splitting *future*—not past—income and growth. In order to structure the rollover, a Section 85 transfer is usually accomplished by giving back to the transferor "non-share consideration"—that is, cash or a loan equal to the tax cost of his property—and shares with a fair market value equal to the difference between the property's tax cost and its fair market value. Very often, the shares taken back have no future growth attached to them and the family members then subscribe to other classes of shares which would provide them with subsequent growth and dividends. Notwithstanding the fact that the transferor takes back the equivalent of the fair market value of the transferred property, under Section 85 the transfer will have taken place for income tax purposes at the transferor's cost.

If the corporation subsequently disposes of the property, the corporation will then realize the income-tax gain that would have been taxable to the transferor, while if the shareholder ever disposes of his shares in the company, he will realize a similar profit for income-tax purposes. This arrangement is illustrated in the series of examples which follows:

Assumptions: Father wishes to transfer a real-estate investment to a family corporation to arrange future income-splitting.

	Cost	Fair Market Value
Land	$100,000	$ 180,000
Building—cost	600,000	1,100,000
Building—undepreciated capital cost	450,000	
Mortgage payable	375,000	

Phase 1

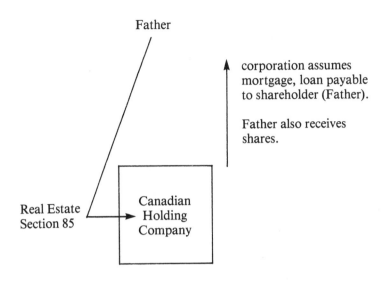

Father

corporation assumes mortgage, loan payable to shareholder (Father).

Father also receives shares.

Real Estate
Section 85

Canadian
Holding
Company

Balance Sheet

	Current Value	Tax Cost	
Land	$ 180,000	$100,000	
Building	1,100,000	$450,000	(U.C.C.)
	$1,280,000		
Mortgage payable	$ 375,000	$375,000	
Loan payable shareholder	175,000	$175,000	
Preferred shares (voting; non-growth)	730,000	Nil	
	$1,280,000		

If the corporation ever sells the property for $1,280,000, it will realize recaptured depreciation of $150,000 ($600,000 − $450,000) and a capital gain of $580,000 ($1,280,000 − $700,000).

If Father ever sells his shares, he will have a capital gain of $730,000 for income tax purposes.

Phase 2

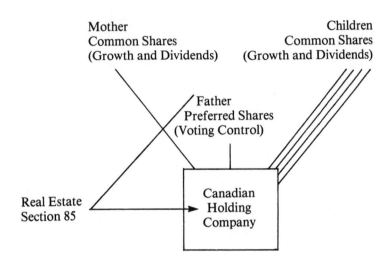

Mother
Common Shares
(Growth and Dividends)

Children
Common Shares
(Growth and Dividends)

Father
Preferred Shares
(Voting Control)

Real Estate
Section 85

Canadian
Holding
Company

The family members now invest $10,000 for common shares entitling them to *future* growth and dividends.

Balance Sheet

	Current Value	Tax Cost	
Cash	$ 10,000	$ 10,000	
Land	$ 180,000	$100,000	
Building	1,100,000	$450,000	(U.C.C.)
	$1,290,000		
Mortgage payable	$ 375,000	$375,000	
Loan payable shareholder	175,000	$175,000	
Preferred shares (voting; non-growth)	730,000	Nil	
Common Shares	10,000	10,000	
	$1,290,000		

Since Father took back total consideration equal to the full fair market value of the property (less mortgage owing) at the time of transfer, there is no retroactive gift. However, the family members will receive all future growth and dividends as a result of their *relatively* nominal share-capital investments.

This is only one illustration of how a Section 85 transaction, followed by the introduction of other family members into the arrangement, can be structured. In this case, the other family members would receive all future growth and dividends. It would be possible, however, to arrange the transaction so that Father could also benefit from at least a portion of future appreciation if he wanted to do so. Again, because of the complexity of Section 85, professional advice must be sought before undertaking any transfers of property to a corporation.

Section 85—a Caution to the Potential User

There is one special problem in connection with Section 85 transfers which even professional advisers often fail to consider. While the provisions of Section 85 are quite broad and many types of properties qualify for "rollover" treatment, there is one significant exception. Specifically, these provisions cannot be used to transfer *inventory* of real estate (held specifically for resale) on a tax deferred basis. In drafting the tax rules, the government was afraid that a trader in real estate might consider transferring his property to a corporation immediately before a contemplated sale and then follow this up by a transaction involving shares. In this way, the real-estate trader would hope to obtain capital-gains treatment on the disposition of his shares, instead of ordinary taxable income on the sale of the property itself.

While the restriction against inventory clearly discourages professional real-estate traders and speculators from rolling over property to a corporation immediately before sale, the implications may, however, be even broader. You will remember from Chapter Six that in Canada, one is not always certain whether a real-estate profit gives rise to capital gains or ordinary income. Therefore, what are the tax consequences if real estate is held for several years by an individual and is then "rolled over" to a corporation immediately before its sale? It appears to me that Revenue authorities might consider the proceeds from an immediate sale following the initial transfer to be ordinary income. In other words, Revenue officials could argue that the property was acquired by the corporation specifically for resale at a profit. Thus, the entire gain may be taxed as income to the corporation. Moreover, the authorities could go so far as to deem a "change of use" to have taken place immediately before the transfer took place. Thus it is possible that at the time of rollover, the real estate could also be deemed to be inventory to its transferor. Thus, the rollover itself could be negated with the profit becoming taxable at the time of transfer. This is because in the absence of Section 85, all transfers from an individual to a corporation are deemed to take place at fair market value. *There is, consequently, a significant exposure to double taxation!*

At this point, there have been no tax cases on the subject, but I for one am somewhat concerned. Therefore, as a general guideline, I do not recommend a Section 85 transfer of real estate to a Canadian corporation where such transfer would be followed shortly thereafter by a sale. My suggestion is that the property should be retained by the corporation at least one or two years after the rollover so that, using hindsight, it is clear that the corporation had acquired a capital asset instead of a trading property. Having met this holding period, capital gains treatment should result on a sale and the corporation can be used to allocate the capital gain to the family members holding the common or growth shares.

A taxable capital gain is considered to be "investment income" when earned by a private corporation. The next portion of the chapter will review the corporate tax structure for investment income as it passes through the corporation to the individual shareholders. It should be noted that a private company is very much an extension of its owners. Thus, the tax-free half of a capital gain may be extracted from a private corporation completely without taxation. No penalty therefore results from having earned a capital gain through a private company.

The Corporate Tax Structure for Investment Income

Investment income such as interest, rents and the taxable half of capital gains is initially taxed at approximately 50% (the actual rate varies slightly from province to province) when earned by a corporation. The Income Tax Act then permits the remaining 50% to be reinvested. Because at least 50% tax is paid from the outset, the government does not mind if the shareholder would otherwise have paid higher (personal) taxes. Since maximum personal tax brackets rarely exceed 65% (except in a few provinces) the government does not try to prevent the deferral of up to 15% of tax.

Thus, even before engaging in any sophisticated tax planning, it is evident that it is generally to the advantage of individuals in brackets higher than 50% to earn their income from their real-estate investments corporately. The opportunity to invest excess dollars not otherwise available personally can provide a significant tax advantage.

Although an investment company can only "keep" 50% of what it earns, at any time dividends are paid to shareholders an amount equal to 16⅔% of the investment income is then refunded back to the corporation. In other words, the net *permanent* corporate tax is only 33⅓% and 66⅔% of each dollar's earnings is eventually available for distribution. These rules can be summarized as follows:

Investment income	$100
Corporate tax	50
Net corporate retention (maximum)	50
Refundable tax (16⅔% of $100)	16.67
Available for dividends	$ 66.67

Canadian Dividends Received by an Individual

The tax treatment of dividends received by a Canadian individual from a Canadian company may seem quite strange to many people. When an individual receives a Canadian dividend, the dividend is included in the taxpayer's income. In addition, he is then required to include in income a *further* 50% of the amount actually received. This extra 50% is called the "50% gross-up".

The grossed-up dividend (150% of the actual) is then taxed in the individual's marginal bracket for that year. Initially, this appears to create a penalty situation where more than what is actually received is taxed. However, in arriving at the individual's taxes payable, there is a dividend tax credit which is *equal* to the 50% gross-up. (The federal dividend tax credit is 75% of the gross-up, while a provincial dividend tax credit covers the balance.) These rules are illustrated in the schedule below.

If you examine the schedule, it becomes apparent that the tax treatment of dividends does not result in a penalty to the shareholder who receives them. Although one initially pays tax on an amount greater than what is actually received, the dividend tax credit *more than compensates* for this inequity. If, for example, you are in a 40% tax bracket and you receive $100 of additional income from any other source *except* Canadian dividends, you would expect to pay $40 on this *incremental* income. However, on a Canadian dividend, the tax is only $10. Similarly, a taxpayer in the 50% bracket only pays $25 on a $100 dividend, while someone in a 60% bracket pays only $40.

The favourable tax treatment of dividends from Canadian companies takes into account the fact that a dividend is a distribution out of profits on which a corporation has previously paid tax. *The dividend tax credit is intended to compensate the individual shareholder for at least a portion of the corporate tax previously paid.*

Actually, the "gross-up and credit" system is designed to exactly compensate a shareholder for a permanent corporate tax of 33⅓%. Thus, when anyone receives a dividend of $66.67 out of $100 of investment income initially generated through a private corporation, this provides the *same after-*

SCHEDULE OF TAX PAYABLE ON $100 CANADIAN DIVIDEND

	$20,000	$45,000	$77,000
Taxable income level			
Individual's marginal tax bracket	40%	50%	60%
Cash dividend	$100	$100	$100
50% gross-up	50	50	50
Additional taxable income	$150	$150	$150
Tax in marginal bracket	$ 60	$ 75	$ 90
Dividend tax credit (combined federal and provincial)	50	50	50
Net tax payable	$ 10	$ 25	$ 40

tax retention as would have been the case if the owner of the corporation had received the $100 directly.

As mentioned previously, if the shareholder of a corporation is in a tax bracket higher than 50%, he can use the corporation to obtain some tax deferral advantages. At some future time, when he decides that he wishes to draw out dividends, he is *no worse off* than he would have been had he owned the investment *personally* in the first place. There is an illustration of the two alternative approaches on pages 133-34. (The reader should note that this example ignores the effects of the $1,000 investment-income deduction.)

COMPARATIVE AFTER-TAX RETENTION ON INVESTMENT INCOME

Alternative A—Investment income (e.g. interest, rents, royalties, taxable capital gains) is earned personally

Investment income	$100	$100	$100
Marginal tax bracket of investment holder	40%	50%	60%
After-tax retention on $100	$ 60	$ 50	$ 40

Alternative B—The investment income is earned by a private corporation

Investment income	$100			
Less: Approximate effective federal and provincial corporate tax*	50			
Retained earnings	$ 50			
Shareholder's tax bracket		40%	50%	60%
Tax deferral (prepayment) under Alternative B		$ (10)	$ Nil	$ 10

*The company has a potentially refundable dividend tax on hand of $16.67. This amount is refundable at the rate of $1 for every $4 of dividends paid.

Retained earnings in corporation	$ 50		
Add: Refundable tax	16.67		
	66.67		
Less: Dividend in cash	(66.67)		
Corporate net retention	Nil		

	40%	50%	60%
Shareholder's tax bracket			
Dividend in cash	$ 66.67	$ 66.67	$ 66.67
1/2 gross-up	33.33	33.33	33.33
Income for tax purposes	$100.00	$100.00	$100.00
Tax at marginal rates	$ 40.00	$ 50.00	$ 60.00
Less: Effective dividend tax credit (equal to gross-up)	33.33	33.33	33.33
Net tax	$ 6.67	$ 16.67	$ 26.67
Net retention (dividend in cash – net tax)	$ 60.00	$ 50.00	$ 40.00
Net retention without corporation (Alternative A)	$ 60.00	$ 50.00	$ 40.00

The Use of Investment Companies

The gross-up and credit systems, which provides that 50% of all amounts actually received as dividends from Canadian companies is first added to income and is then deducted directly off taxes otherwise payable, has a very interesting by-product. This by-product is a major factor in tax planning for Canadian corporations and their shareholders.

Specifically, up to $30,000 of Canadian dividends can be received each year by an individual *totally tax-free* as long as he or she has *no other income*. This is illustrated in the example on page 135, which uses average tax rates applicable across Canada. The example shows a dividend of $30,000 that is grossed up by an extra $15,000. However, after applying personal exemptions and other deductions, the tax otherwise payable is completely offset by the $15,000 dividend tax credit. The net effect is to reduce taxes to nil.

Remember that the concept of tax-free dividends only applies where a taxpayer has no other income. If the taxpayer in our example had an *extra* $1,000 from *any source whatsoever*, the taxable income would become $41,000 instead of $40,000. In this case, since the individual is already in a 46% combined federal and provincial tax bracket, the extra $1,000 of income would cost $460 of taxes. There would be no further dividend tax credits available to offset this additional burden.

Thus, if you receive dividends as well as other income, the other income "floats to the top" and gets taxed at your highest marginal bracket with no relief. If you have substantial other income, you should be aware that the tax advantages of Canadian dividends are greatly reduced. You should also note that there is no direct relationship between dividends and other income. Therefore, you could *not* receive, for example, $15,000 of salary and a further (tax-free) $15,000 of dividends. The interactions of various mixes of dividend and other income must be determined on a trial-and-error basis with the aid of your own accountant.

IF THE TAXPAYER HAS NO OTHER INCOME,
$30,000 OF CANADIAN DIVIDENDS ARE TAX-FREE

Dividend	$30,000
1/2 "gross-up"	15,000
Net income	45,000
Less: Estimated personal exemptions	5,000
Taxable income	$40,000
Estimated federal and provincial taxes	
On $25,000	$ 8,100
On $15,000 (tax bracket 46%)	6,900
On $40,000	15,000
Less: Dividend tax credit (combined federal and provincial)	(15,000)
Net tax payable	$ Nil

Opportunities for Income-Splitting Through a Corporation

The tax rules for investment income were designed to produce an equitable treatment where income is earned and is then passed on as dividends *to the person who injected the capital into a corporation in the first place.* The legislators probably failed to adequately consider the opportunities which exist to use a corporation as a vehicle to collect income and then *deflect it to family members in low tax brackets.* This is illustrated in the form of a diagram (below), and in the example on page 137, which outlines the incredible tax advantages obtainable by simply putting together the investment income rules explained previously.

In the example shown, Father incorporates a private company to hold the real estate investments which he would otherwise retain personally. He exchanges his investments for a combination of non-interest-bearing loans and shares. Outside of the Province of Quebec, there is no requirement that

INCOME SPLITTING THROUGH A CORPORATION

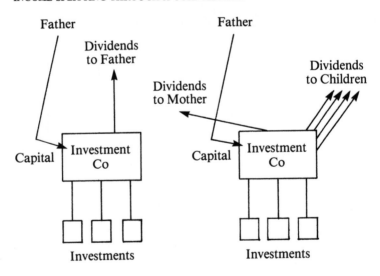

Intention of Rules   *Opportunities for Tax Planning*

Assumptions:
Father is in the 65% bracket and has $2,000,000 of real estate earning rental income (net of expenses) at 10%. He is married and has four dependent children. His wife and children have no income.

Alternative 1—Rental income is earned personally

Income on $2,000,000 at 10%	$200,000
Less: Income taxes thereon at 65%	130,000
Net retention (35% of total)	$ 70,000

Alternative 2
- A corporation is formed and the real estate is transferred by Father to the company under Section 85.
- Father subscribes to preferred shares with voting powers sufficient to control but with no "growth potential".
- Mother and the children subscribe to common shares.

Income on $2,000,000 at 10%	$200,000
Less: Corporate tax at 50%	100,000
Retained earnings	100,000
Add: Refundable tax to corporation when dividends are paid (16⅔% × $200,000)	33,000
Cash available for dividends	133,000
Less: Dividends to wife and four children	(133,000)
Remaining cash available for dividends	Nil
Dividend to each of wife and four children ($133,000 ÷ 5)	$ 26,600
Net tax payable by each	Nil
Net retention by family (5 × $26,600)	$133,000
$133,000 ÷ $200,000	66.5%

Father charge the corporation interest on loans which he has advanced. In addition, if Father does not charge interest, there are also no tax requirements that interest be imputed. (For Quebec tax purposes, one would have to transfer the assets into the corporation in exchange for some sort of non-dividend or low-dividend-bearing preferred share. These shares would have to be structured so as not to involve substantial future growth or income potential.)

At the time of incorporation, Mother and the four children simultaneously invest a relatively nominal amount of money and subscribe to the common shares. Growth and dividend benefits would attach to these shares. In order to avoid "income attribution" it would be important for the family members to invest their own funds or use money borrowed from outsiders. If necessary, Father could guarantee their loans without creating any adverse tax situation.

Since the investments are now held by the corporation, the company would begin to earn the rental income which would otherwise have been Father's. Initially, the corporate tax rate is approximately 50%. Even if no further steps are taken to split income, there is a $30,000 after-tax advantage, since the corporation would retain $100,000 (50% of $200,000) as compared to only $70,000 that would otherwise have been retained by Father personally. This illustrates the tax-deferral advantages for individuals in brackets over 50% who use corporations to limit their tax exposure on investment income.

In addition to the fact that the corporation can retain 50% of its investment earnings, the company also has the ability to pay out 66⅔% of its profits by way of dividends. This is because of refundable tax considerations. In this case, at the time dividends are paid, $33,000 out of the (previously paid) corporate tax of $100,000 is refundable to the company. This would enable the company to pay Mother and the four children dividend payments of approximately $26,600 each. If none of them has other income, the net tax payable after gross-up and credit will be nil. Thus, $133,000, or 66.5% of the total earnings, is available for reinvestment purposes.

To reiterate, a corporation is therefore a vehicle for collecting income from real-estate investments that would otherwise be taxed in one person's hands at high marginal rates. The income can then be recycled and reallocated to other family members who are in low brackets, and significant absolute tax savings can be achieved.

Capital Gains Sheltered

While the previous examples in this chapter assume a rental yield, income splitting through a corporation is viable for all sorts of investment activity. If, for example, the family corporation sells real estate or marketable securities, the tax burden of capital gains can also be reduced greatly. This is because the taxable half of a capital gain is taxed as investment income, while the tax-free half of the gain is not only tax-free to the corporation, but can also be extracted by the shareholders personally, with *no tax payable*, on a special dividend basis. The example on page 140 illustrates how a *taxable* capital gain of $50,000 may be sheltered where investment assets are held through a family corporation.

Of course, the potential to tax shelter all kinds of investment income will vary from case to case and depends primarily on the number of family members that one has available for this purpose. The opportunities are, however, astounding.

Control of the Investment Corporation

The preceding discussions have assumed that Father would control investment policies and dividend-payment decisions through his voting preferred shares in the family company. The family members would own the common shares, which would participate in growth and which would facilitate income splitting.

How can one ensure that family members will reinvest their dividends back into the company, short of using violence or other unsavory methods of coercion? Actually, Father has several alternatives. First, he can cause the corporation to be capitalized with a special class of shares—non-voting redeemable preferred shares. Then, instead of causing the company to pay cash dividends to trigger a refund of taxes, he could have the company pay stock dividends to his family members in the form of these non-voting redeemable preferreds. The corporation would still obtain its 16⅔% refund of tax, but all that the family members would receive is pieces of paper. Although a stock dividend from a private company is technically taxable, as long as the amount is less than $30,000 per person, the tax payable would be nil. Since Father would always have voting

Assumptions:
1. Father makes a capital gain of $100,000 on the sale of real estate of which $50,000 would be taxable. He is in the 65% tax bracket. Without the benefits of a corporation, his tax would therefore be $32,500.
2. Father is married and has four children—none of the other family members have any income.

If a family investment-holding company had made the gain instead:

Taxable gain	$50,000
Less: Corporate tax at 50%	25,000
Retained earnings	25,000
Add: Refundable tax to corporation when dividends are paid (16⅔% × $50,000)	8,333
Dividend to other family members	$33,333
Dividend to each ($33,333 ÷ 5)	$ 6,666
Net tax payable by each	Nil
Final corporate tax ($25,000 – $8,333)	$16,667
Father's tax—if no corporation	$32,500
Corporate tax	16,667
Tax saving	$15,833

---

control of the company, it is he who would decide if and when these special preferred shares would be redeemed.

As a second alternative, the shares owned by Mother and the children could be of different classes. In other words, Mother could receive Class A common shares, child "number one" could receive Class B, and so on. The share structure could be designed so that dividends may be declared on *any class* to the exclusion of any of the other classes. Thus, if one of the family fails to reinvest funds as Father dictates, Father could then cut off the dissident shareholder from future income by refusing to cast his vote in favour of dividends on that particular individual's shares.

As a third alternative, a trust could be created to hold the children's shares while Father continues to control the flow of income and all investment decisions. Although establishing a trust is the most complicated method and involves the greatest amount of legal and other documentation, it is the preferred route to take—especially if the children are minors.

The Formation of Discretionary Trusts

Usually, a family trust involves three trustees, including Father, Mother and a close family friend, relative, or adviser. Generally, if Father is the one who is providing his capital to the investment corporation, he would have the right to replace either of the other trustees although they would not be able to replace him.

The trust would borrow funds in order to subscribe to the common shares of the investment corporation. This is done to avoid income attribution—especially where one or more of the children are minors. Dividends would then be paid by the corporation to the trust as illustrated previously.

If rental income is earned or the properties are sold and the trust receives a dividend, the trustees have two choices. First, they could have the trust pay taxes on the entire dividend. Obviously, this would not be a good choice, since on dividends in excess of $30,000, there are significant taxes payable. As a second option, however, the trustees are permitted to enter into what the Tax Act calls a "preferred beneficiary election". The preferred beneficiary election is simply a decision to *allocate* the dividends to the children for tax purposes. The allocation makes the children taxable instead of the trust. Of course, as long as the allocation on a per child basis is under $30,000, there are no personal taxes payable. In fact, however, no amounts are actually paid out. The trustees are then in the position of holding tax-paid money and they can reinvest the funds back into the holding company to compound future growth.

If a trust is set up as being "discretionary", this provides even further scope for tax planning. The discretionary feature means that the trustees are permitted to eventually distribute capital (generally upon the dissolution of the trust) to whichever of the preferred beneficiaries (and in whatever proportions) the trustees, at their discretion, may at *some future time* see fit. Thus, Father may freeze his estate and pass on growth, even if he is unsure of exactly where he wishes such growth to go! Perhaps the children are relatively young and their capabilities and personalities are still not known.

The key point is that there is no requirement that the preferred beneficiary election (which allows for equal allocations of income between the children) be tied in to ultimate distribution ratios. In an extreme situation, even though income may have been allocated to four children for many years, Father may decide that only one child should eventually receive *all* the funds. In fact, the rules permit a decision on distributions to be deferred for up to twenty-one years.

In order to discourage long-term "inter vivos" trusts, (that is, trusts formed by living persons) there is a deemed disposition of trust property at fair market value if the trust is still in existence on its twenty-first anniversary. The deemed disposition would ordinarily trigger capital gains and this should be avoided. Avoidance can be accomplished by simply winding up the trust shortly before the twenty-first anniversary and distributing its assets (the common shares of the investment corporation) to some or all of the children. Of course, if Father is still alive, he could continue to control the company and its portfolio through his voting preferred shares. However, within twenty-one years, he should be in a position to know which of his children are "worthy" of an (eventual) inheritance.

Discretionary trusts giving the trustees the power to make annual preferred beneficiary elections are becoming more and more popular in tax and estate planning. Care must always be taken to comply with the particular laws of the jurisdiction in which the trust is being set up. Accordingly, it is advisable at all times when one is contemplating such a trust to have the arrangement documented by lawyers and accountants who have had experience in such matters.

Capitalization of the Investment Company

When setting up an investment corporation, how much money should each of the shareholders contribute in exchange for their shareholdings? For example, can a family member invest only one dollar in the common share capital of a company and thereby receive dividends of up to $30,000 a year?

There has been only one reported tax case on this subject. The case involves two Alberta optometrists who incorporated a management company in 1970 to administer their practice. The company was controlled by these two individuals through voting, non-participating shares, but their wives also held shares which were non-voting but fully participating. The company paid management fees to the doctors and declared substantial dividends to the wives, who had invested very little in the first place. In fact, the wives apparently invested pennies, and over a three-year period, received over $90,000 in dividends.

The Minister of National Revenue argued that an indirect benefit had been conferred by the doctors on their wives and that the whole set-up was a sham. The Tax Review Board upheld the Minister on the basis that although there was a business purpose for the incorporation of the company, the declaration of these dividends to the wives was not a sound business practice.

The judge showed no distaste for income splitting and estate planning as a *concept*, but in his judgement, he gave the opinion that acceptable limits had been exceeded. He concluded that the scheme was simply intended to avoid income tax and that the dividends were rightly assessed as being income of the doctors. This case was appealed and eventually settled out of court.

In spite of this one case, many accountants and lawyers are still not overly concerned and investment companies are often set up with only nominal share capital. However, I personally recommend extreme caution in this area. If, for example, one is forming an investment corporation with the expectation of paying $30,000 a year of dividends to family members (either directly or through a trust) I think that the capitalization per person should be at least $10,000.

Thus, in a family corporation involving a wife and four children, common shares should be issued for a total consideration of, say, $50,000. To avoid income attribution, Father should not gift these funds to the family members. Rather, they should take a bank loan which, if necessary, could be *guaranteed* by him. The interest on the borrowed money would be tax deductible since the borrowings would be incurred for the purpose of earning income in the form of dividends. In addition, the infusion of an extra $50,000 of capital into the corporation would result in additional income being earned by the company. There would be no economic loss. Finally, the bank loan could always be repaid by the family members out of dividends over a period of one or two years.

The advantage of taking all these steps is that the Minister of National Revenue would probably be hard-pressed to allege that a transaction is a sham where $10,000 is invested for the purpose of earning $30,000. Unfortunately, there are no guidelines within the Canadian tax structure and any final decision as to capitalization of an investment company is a matter that must be resolved by the taxpayer and his own advisers.

Other Advantages of Real-Estate Holding Companies

Beyond the advantages of deferring taxes otherwise payable for individuals in high brackets and the opportunity to split income with family members, there are other benefits that incorporation provides. These include non-tax considerations such as anonymity—the ability for you, the owner of property, to keep a "low profile". Where your assets are held through a corporation, it is possible to arrange your affairs so that the extent and nature of your holdings would not be made public. You are also protected from personal harassment from irate tenants or perhaps even suppliers with which your corporation has a dispute.

Financing arrangements are also easier to make if a venture is incorporated. Lenders often prefer to loan money to corporations because of the many types of securities that a corporation may issue. A lender may, for example, obtain equity participation in the form of shares. In addition, if the shareholder himself dies, there is no loss of continuity and a lender is not in a position where he must begin to deal directly with the beneficiaries of the deceased shareholder's estate.

The Small Business Tax Rate

The 50% corporate tax rate and the concept of refundable taxes as described previously in this chapter apply to the investment income of a private corporation. However, it may be possible that rental activities carried on by a corporation would qualify as being part of an active business. Where this is the case, the small business rules may apply as long as the corporation is a Canadian-controlled private company. This means that not more than 50% of the voting shares may be held by non-residents. A Canadian small business pays income taxes at only 25% (again the rates vary slightly from province to province) on the first $150,000 of annual taxable income. The small business tax rate is available until a corporation has achieved cumulative pre-tax earnings of $750,000.

Ordinarily, rental income would not qualify for the small business tax rate. There is, however, an exception to this rule if the company has at least six full-time employees throughout a given taxation year, none of whom are related to the majority shareholder(s) and none of whom own 10% or more of any class of the company's stock.

Having six full-time employees may not be as difficult as it first appears. For example, a superintendent or caretaker on "full-time" call may be considered to be a full-time employee. Thus, if a corporation owns six apartment buildings, each of which has a separate caretaker or janitor, this may constitute an active business. Even if a corporation has as little as three buildings, the small business tax rate could still apply. This is assuming that, instead of one janitor per building, the corporation employs teams of husband and wife. One may argue that the wife is on full-time call during the daytime while the husband is on full-time call during evenings and weekends. Of course, one would have to be somewhat careful to insure that none of the superintendent-janitor couples split up during a given year. You should note that the tax requirement for the small business tax rate is for six full-time employees *through-out* the year. Thus, as an added precaution, you might be well advised to have the corporation acquire one extra building!

Avoiding the Restrictions on Capital Cost Allowances

As has been noted in previous chapters, a taxpayer's capital cost allowance claim on rental property is generally restricted to his net rental income after deducting expenses other than tax depreciation. In other words, capital cost allowance cannot be used to either create or increase a rental loss (MURB excepted).

However, a corporation can often be used to get around these rules. First, a corporation is not restricted from claiming capital cost allowances to create rental losses if its principal business throughout the year is any combination of leasing, rental, development, or real-estate sales activity. Although an individual may not shelter his own personal income when real estate is held through a corporation, it is possible that a company could retain a certain amount of other investments and shelter the income generated by these holdings without violating the "principal business" criteria. For example, a corporation which has, say, $2,000,000 of real estate assets might conceivably also hold $20,000 of term deposits bearing interest at 15%. The annual interest income of $3,000 could be offset by rental losses created through capital cost allowances. The alternative would be to hold these term deposits personally and have fully taxable interest income. There are no hard and fast rules as to how much non-rental income can be sheltered on this basis. However, as long as the corporation's chief activity (as measured by the value of its assets, gross revenues, and the amount of time and attention required to manage these) relates to real estate, the attempt to shelter should be successful.

With creative financing, however, it may be possible to go even further. You might consider setting up your corporation in such a way that you pay financing charges and carrying costs personally, while real-estate holdings are retained by the corporation. It may be possible for you to obtain a deduction for these financing charges while your corporation (which would then own the property on a debt-free basis) would have the opportunity to claim additional capital cost allowances. This would effectively avoid the capital cost allowance deduction restrictions discussed above. This is illustrated in the example on pages 147–48.

The arrangement illustrated below can be accomplished if the individual borrows money and then places the funds into a company in exchange for shares. The company then uses the funds acquired from its shareholder to buy the real estate. Where the individual retains the debt, the interest cost becomes deductible against personal income. This is because one can claim interest expense incurred in connection with the acquisition of shares—even if those shares do not bear dividends. Since the company would be without any debt obligations, it then would have more net income against which depreciation can be taken.

There may be a problem in that without security for the loan, the individual may not receive a favourable rate of interest. This problem could perhaps be circumvented by pledging the shares of the company as security or by raising the funds through a mortgage on one's home.

AVOIDING CAPITAL COST ALLOWANCE RESTRICTIONS

Assumptions: Cost of property (land and building)	$300,000
Undepreciated capital cost (U.C.C.) of building—Capital cost allowance (C.C.A.) 5%	220,000
Debt owning @ 18% interest	200,000
Annual rental revenue	43,000
Annual operating expenses (before interest)	6,000
Tax bracket of individual	60%
Tax rate of corporation	50%

ALTERNATIVE 1: Corporation owns property and incurs interest expense

Corporation's position:

Rental income		43,000
Operating expenses	$ 6,000	
Interest on mortgage (18% × $200,000)	36,000	
C.C.A. (5% × $220,000)—maximum	1,000	43,000
Net rental income		Nil

Net cash flow—before debt principal repayments:

Rental income	$43,000
Operating expenses and interest	42,000
	$ 1,000

ALTERNATIVE 2: Corporation owns property—interest expense is incurred by individual shareholder.

Corporation's position:

Rental income		$ 43,000
Operating expenses	$ 6,000	
Capital cost allowance (5% × $220,000)	11,000	17,000
Rental income		26,000
Income taxes—50%		(13,000)
Net rental income		$13,000

Net cash flow:		
Rental income		$ 43,000
Operating expenses and income taxes		19,000
		$ 24,000

Individual's position:

Interest on mortgage (18% × $200,000)	$(36,000)
Less: Income tax saving @ 60%	21,600
Net cash flow of individual	$(14,400)

Net cash flow of corporation	$ 24,000
Net cash flow of individual	(14,400)
	9,600
Net cash flow if debt is owed by corporation	1,000
Additional cash flow if debt is owed by the individual	$ 8,600

Revenue Canada is somewhat upset about any arrangement where the capital cost allowance restrictions are circumvented by a corporation claiming depreciation in excess of the maximum that would have been allowed had the corporation borrowed the money from the shareholder at a reasonable rate of interest. So far, it appears that the Revenue authorities would only be able to upset such an arrangement where the individual borrows money and simply lends the funds in turn to the corporation without charging interest. This is why it is important for shares of the corporation to be taken back, even if these shares do not provide for annual dividend payments.

Before this type of structure is implemented, professional counsel is certainly required. If, for example, the shares of the real-estate holding company are owned by other members of the family, there can be a tax problem if dividends are paid to other persons and not to the shareholder who injected the capital in order to acquire the property. Perhaps it would be best to pay corporate taxes on profits first, and then in subsequent years, pay dividends out of profits to the other family members.

Double Taxation—A Major Pitfall

One of the greatest problems which results from holding real estate through a corporation is that there is a potential double taxation on capital gains. This problem is all too often overlooked even by professionals when assisting clients in tax and estate planning. The problem arises because of the Canadian income tax rules on death. At that time, the general rule is that one is deemed to have disposed of all capital properties immediately before one's death at their fair market values. One can postpone all taxes payable by leaving property outright to a spouse or to a spousal trust, but, otherwise, there is a "capital gains reckoning" at the time of death.

Assume, therefore, that you form a corporation to acquire real estate. You invest, say, $100,000 and take back $100,000 of the corporation's shares. Suppose the corporation then purchases a piece of land for $100,000. Over time, assume that the land appreciates in value and is now worth $500,000. At this point, assume that you die and, to keep the example simple, suppose that your spouse had already died. For tax purposes, there is a deemed disposition of your shares. The fair market value is, of course, based on the underlying fair market value of the assets. Since the real-estate holdings are worth $500,000, you may therefore expect Revenue Canada to value your shares at this same amount. Since the tax cost of the shares is only $100,000, there is a $400,000 capital gain on death.

Then, what happens when the corporation subsequently sells its real-estate holdings several years later for $500,000 (ignoring any additional capital growth)? The corporation would then realize the *same capital gain which you realized previously*. In other words, the same gain is taxed twice. This is illustrated in table form on page 150.

Step 1—A corporation is formed

Cash	$100,000	
Capital stock	$100,000	(Tax cost of shares is $100,000)

Step 2—Real estate is acquired by corporation

Real estate	$100,000	(Tax cost is $100,000)
Capital stock	$100,000	

Step 3—The real estate appreciates and is now worth $500,000. The shareholder then dies without leaving a spouse.

Fair market value of his shares (i.e., the underlying fair market value of the property)	$500,000
Tax cost of shares	100,000
Capital gain on death	$400,000*

Step 4—The corporation sells its real-estate holdings after one year has elapsed (assuming no further appreciation).

Selling price of real estate	$500,000
Cost for income tax purposes	100,000
Capital gain to corporation	$400,000*

*The same gain is taxed twice.

You should note that the problem of double taxation can be avoided if the corporation is wound up within one year following your death and the assets are distributed to your heirs. The calculations to prove this are somewhat complex, and I have not included them in this text. Suffice to say, however, in the final analysis, there would only be one level of taxation. However, it is not generally feasible to wind-up a corporation within one year of the major shareholder's death, especially where its holdings are varied and complex.

Does this mean that you should not incorporate a company to hold growth properties? In practice, I rarely worry about the problem of double taxation where the person forming the corporation is, say, under age fifty-five. A person who is younger than age fifty-five presumably has a life expectancy of an additional twenty years or more. In my opinion, you shouldn't worry about a problem that could be postponed that far into the future. If the taxpayer is married, and his will provides that his property would pass to his spouse, there is insurance against even a premature death. This is because, as mentioned previously, capital property will pass from one spouse to the other without attracting taxation. Thus, only one of the two spouses has to be expected to live for a further twenty years to reasonably discount the impact of double taxation.

Even if both spouses are over age fifty-five and even if they are both in poor health, I might also not be too concerned about the potential for double taxation—as long as one of two situations can reasonably be expected to apply. The first is where an immediate wind-up within one year of death is, in fact, anticipated. The second is perhaps the exact opposite situation. This would be where the corporation is not only kept alive beyond the death of husband and wife, but would also continue to retain its property over an extended period of time. If the corporation is not wound up and continues to hold its assets for, say, an additional twenty years, again, you might not be too concerned about a problem that is deferred for that length of time.

The major concern arises in situations where an elderly individual wishes to incorporate his holdings and it is clear in talking to the potential heirs that they would wish to cause the corporation to sell at least some of the property a few years after they inherit it. In most cases, the sale and wind-up cannot be accomplished within one year and the potential for double taxation is quite severe.

Because of the possibility of double taxation, I often recommend to elderly clients who are attempting to plan their estates and freeze their growth that they use the direct transfer of property as described in Chapter Seven. By using income-tax reserves, it is still possible for them to postpone the recognition of income until death while the problem of double taxation is eliminated. Where there is a direct sale, the recipient of property acquires a cost base equal to the full fair market value of the property—even if he is not required to make an immediate payment of the purchase price. Thus, only one level of taxation is encountered.

Corporations of course play an important role when it comes to effective planning. However, you should be aware of the potential problem of double taxation before setting up any investment company for estate freezing and income splitting.

Summary

Making the "right" investment is, certainly, the most important ingredient when it comes to real estate. However, the way you structure your property holdings can be almost as vital in the final analysis. If your real-estate investments are extensive and they generate large taxable income, you may be well advised to wade through the complexities of corporations in order to use them to split income and growth with your family members.

There are, naturally, special circumstances which will apply in each case and there are usually some pitfalls. Make liberal use of the services of your accountants and lawyers. Bad planning may be worse than no planning at all.

CHAPTER NINE

Your Principal Residence

Possibly the best investment that any of us can make is to buy our own home. Recently, I met a dentist in Vancouver who told me that he had purchased his home for $200,000 in the spring of 1979, and that in May 1981, he turned down an offer of $800,000 for the property. If nothing else, high inflation has created a tremendous increase in residential property values in many parts of the country.

Nevertheless, for most Canadians, home ownership can be an extremely expensive proposition. This is because, in Canada, mortgage interest is not deductible where funds are borrowed to acquire personal property. Under Canadian tax rules, interest expense can only be deducted when one borrows to make an investment or to earn income from a business. Thus, if your mortgage payable is at 15%, and you are in a 50% tax bracket, you must earn a 30% pre-tax return on your investment capital to make it worthwhile to carry the mortgage on your home. Thus, for Canadians, proper planning dictates that you try to discharge a home mortgage as quickly as possible. Most mortgages will allow the borrower to prepay up to 10% per annum on the anniversary date each year. Therefore, I encourage my clients to pay off their mortgages over eight years instead of, say, twenty-five years. If you make ordinary payments on a monthly basis coupled with eight instalments of 10% of the original balance, your mortgage will then be eliminated within a period of approximately eight years.

For some lucky people, it may be possible to discharge a mortgage debt even more quickly. Assume that you have a mortgage of $50,000 at an interest rate of 15%. Assume, as well, that you also have $50,000 of cash which you have just recently inherited. Your mortgage costs you $7,500 a year in interest and this amount is not deductible. If, however, you take your $50,000 inheritance and invest it at the same interest rate of 15%, you will receive $7,500 of interest income. On the surface, there is an offsetting income and outflow. However, (ignoring the annual $1,000 investment-income deduction) the interest received is fully taxable. If you are in a 50% tax bracket, you will only keep $3,750 after taxes. There is certainly very little merit in retaining $3,750 while paying out $7,500. In this case, you should immediately use your inherited capital to discharge your debt. (The only exception might be if you are one of the few people with a low-interest "locked in" mortgage which dates back to the pre-inflation era.)

Deductible Interest

Once your home is paid for, you may *then* borrow the capital that you need for investments against your paid up home. If you borrow specifically for the purpose of making investments, *your interest expense becomes deductible.* Even if you are forced to borrow at an interest rate of 20%, remember that if you are in a 50% bracket, this represents a net after-tax outlay of only 10%. If the investment that you purchase appreciates by, say, 13½% per annum, you will be ahead of the game, even after taxes on capital gains.

Investment growth—before tax on capital gains	13.50%
Less: Tax on capital gain (½ X 13.5 X 50% tax bracket)	(3.37)
Net capital growth	10.13%
Gross interest expense	20.00%
Less: Tax saving in 50% bracket	(10.00)
Net cost to obtain capital growth	10.00%

The key point, however, is to establish equity in your house *before* you borrow for investment purposes, although you don't necessarily have to pay your house off in full before you can create tax-deductible interest. Let us assume that the balance on your mortgage is now $40,000, but that your house is worth $120,000. You could easily refinance the house when your mortgage comes up for renewal for, say, $80,000. Of this amount, half will be required to replace the financing previously owing. To this extent your interest expense will not be deductible. If, however, the remainder of the borrowed funds are used for investments, the interest on this amount *will* be deductible. You may be required to prove how you have applied your funds, but this should not prove to be too difficult.

Note that there is no shortcut to be taken. If you inherit money and use those funds for investment purposes without having first paid off the mortgage on your home, you will *not* be permitted to argue that you *could have* paid off the mortgage in the first place and then borrowed for investment capital. In tax cases that have come before the courts, judges have insisted on a proper "tracking". If you take a shortcut, be prepared to suffer tax penalties.

If you don't wish to borrow against your equity in the home, I suppose that you can rest on your laurels (having paid for the house in the first place) and use the extra cash flow from your job, profession, or business, to improve your lifestyle. However, if you are interested (as most of us are) in building up capital, you will probably never have a better opportunity to latch on to a large sum of dollars with which to pyramid your investment holdings. Remember that if an interest cost is halved for taxpayers in marginal tax brackets of 50% (or higher), the drain on cash flow is not nearly as great as the payment of non-deductible interest. Certainly, where your after-tax interest expense is no more than the annual inflation factor, the chances of coming out ahead on your investments become quite good.

Even if you are saddled with heavy mortgage payments for an extended period of time, an investment in your own home is probably a good one. This is because if you *rent* an apartment, duplex or house, you are also paying with after-tax dollars. At least, with ownership, you are rewarded for the non-deductible interest by gaining the appreciation on the property itself. If you pay rent, you are only subsidizing your landlord's capital growth. The appreciation factor is made even more significant because, in most cases, it is completely free from tax!

The Capital Gains Exemption for a Principal Residence

For a long time, Canadians have complained because mortgage interest incurred for the purchase of one's own residence is not deductible, in contrast to the situation that exists in the United States. The Trudeau government has maintained, however, that the Canadian treasury can ill afford to allow deductibility of home mortgage interest without a significant restructuring of the tax system to make up for lost revenues. In all fairness to Mr. Trudeau's position, it is very difficult, and indeed misleading, to try to compare certain isolated aspects of the tax systems of different countries. For example, although the U.S. system with respect to mortgage interest appears to be much more liberal, keep in mind that our basic personal exemption in 1981 is $3,170 while the equivalent personal exemption in the United States is only $1,000. Do the Americans complain and lobby for Canadian exemptions? This simple example shows how wrong it is to take selected items out of general context.

Moreover, as we will see later in this chapter, not only is a capital gain on the disposition of a principal residence tax-free under Canadian law, but, as well, it is generally possible for a husband and wife to *each* have a *separate* principal residence and thus double up on the tax exemption. There is also no dollar limitation on the amount of capital gains which may be exempted. In the United States, by way of contrast, only one principal residence is permitted for tax purposes between husband and wife at any given time. In addition, although it is possible to sell a house and acquire another one without paying taxes, there is only a single once-in-a-lifetime capital gains exemption. The maximum dollar limitation on this in the United States is $100,000 (per married couple) and one can only take advantage of this exemption after age fifty-five. Thus, the Canadian principal-residence rules are in some respects much more *generous* than those in the U.S.

The Registered Home Ownership Savings Plan

In 1974, primarily as a concession to first-time home buyers, the Canadian government introduced the concept of the Registered Home Ownership Savings Plan (RHOSP). The RHOSP is available for any taxpayer eighteen years old and over who does not own residential property and is not married to a spouse who has an interest in residential real-estate. Where an individual is qualified, up to $1,000 a year can be contributed until $10,000 (plus interest) is accumulated. The maximum length of time that one can keep a RHOSP open is twenty years.

If funds are withdrawn from this plan and are used to purchase a home (that the owner will occupy), the withdrawal is tax-free. You should note that home furnishings no longer qualify and contributions are only deductible for a given year if made before December 31. One is permitted to contribute in the year of acquisition of a home although the contribution should be made before one takes title to that residence.

Whenever funds are withdrawn and are not used during that year or within sixty days thereafter to acquire a home, the withdrawal becomes taxable. Proceeds withdrawn and not used to purchase a home to be occupied by the owner may be rolled over into an income-averaging annuity. Although funds may be moved from one RHOSP to another, once a withdrawal is made, a taxpayer may never reinstate. In this respect, you are only allowed one RHOSP in a lifetime. Since the intention of the program is to provide tax-free income towards the acquisition of a home, Revenue Canada adopts the position that interest on money borrowed to contribute into an RHOSP is *not* deductible.

As I already indicated, one is not qualified to contribute to an RHOSP if the taxpayer or his spouse has "an interest in residential real estate". This restriction covers more than situations where the taxpayer already owns a home. For example, if you have an interest in a multiple unit residential building as a tax shelter, or even an interest in a Florida condominium, you become disqualified from participation in an RHOSP. It appears to be permissible, however, for an individual to own vacant land only or shares in a corporation where the corporation holds residential property.

A Look at RHOSPs

There are several reasons why RHOSPs are not very effective. First of all, one does not usually think about saving towards the purchase of a home too many years before the home is actually bought. Thus, it is unusual to find a taxpayer who has had the foresight to put more than two or three annual contributions into his plan. Even between husband and wife, it would be unlikely to find more than $5,000 or $6,000 in total.

In addition, even if a taxpayer waits ten years and contributes $1,000 per annum, he could only expect to have approximately $18,000 (with interest) available at the end of that time. However, over that same ten-year period, it is likely that house prices would have doubled or even tripled. Thus, the individual is no closer towards the acquisition of his residence than he would have been ten years earlier. It is my opinion, therefore, that the RHOSP will not make a home significantly more accessible to the average Canadian. Certainly, however, the RHOSP should be used for its short-range benefits. If a couple decides in November, 1982, that the following spring would be a good time to buy a first home, and if both husband and wife have income, it would certainly pay for each to contribute $1,000 in 1982 and again in 1983. That way, there would be $4,000 of (tax-free) money available towards the purchase. Certainly, this is better than having no subsidy at all.

The RHOSP as a Gifting Program

Many middle-income and upper-income taxpayers can obtain some unintended benefits with respect to their children from the home ownership savings program. With escalating housing prices, it is not uncommon to find parents providing the downpayment for their children's homes. Let us take an example in which the parents are willing to provide $10,000 to their twenty-eight-year-old son towards the acquisition of his home. Outside Quebec, a gift of cash between parents and children is not taxable. In this case, the parents do not get a tax deduction and their son does not have to take anything into income. The reason for these rules is that cash simply represents income on which taxes have already been paid. Presumably, the parents (if they are in 50% tax brackets) will have had to earn $20,000 by that time in order to have $10,000 of after-tax capital available to give their son.

With a little advance planning, however, the gift of the downpayment for the home *could have been tax deductible*. Let's assume the parents start a gifting program in the year that their son turns eighteen. If that year is 1981, the exemption that the father would get for his son would be $1,090. This is provided that the son's net income is not in excess of $2,180. What if the son is still going to school, but has earned a net income of $3,270 after tuition fees? At this point, his father will have lost a personal exemption of $1,090. If the father is in a 50% bracket, the additional tax cost to him would be over $500.

On the other hand, if before December 31 the father gifts $1,000 to his son, the son could take these funds and purchase an RHOSP. The RHOSP contribution would be tax deductible and would reduce the son's net income to only $2,270. This would reinstate a deduction to father of $1,000 and would consequently result in a $500 tax saving. Thus, the cost of having made a $1,000 gift in the first place becomes only $500. In this manner, the RHOSP can be used to provide a very efficient Christmas gift.

If the father is concerned that his son might withdraw the funds from the home ownership plan, he can explain that every taxpayer is only permitted one RHOSP in a lifetime. Thus, a withdrawal of funds without the father's permission effectively ends any further contributions. In most cases, the child will co-operate for his (or her) own good.

In cases where the child is not a student but is in his (or her) late teens or early twenties and is working, the gifting program still has merit. If, for example, the son is now twenty-two years old and is earning $14,000 a year, even at this relatively modest income level, he is still in approximately a 35% tax bracket. In addition, the son is not likely to be thinking seriously about the possibility of buying a home in several years. However, the father can still make the annual gift of $1,000. Even in the son's tax bracket, if the gift is reinvested into an RHOSP, there will be a tax saving to him of $350. These dollars could then be *gifted back* to his father and the net cost of the gifting program for that year becomes only $650.

An RHOSP can be used very effectively to reduce the cost of providing a downpayment for a home to one's children. This may have not been intended by the legislators, but it nevertheless works.

The Taxation of Principal Residences

While the general rule is that capital gains realized after 1971 are taxable, a special exemption applies to a gain on the sale of a principal residence. A principal residence is an accommodation owned by a taxpayer (either alone or jointly) which is "ordinarily inhabited" by him, his spouse, a former spouse or a dependent child at any time during the year—as long as the taxpayer designates the property as his principal residence.

The accommodation can take any form such as a house, apartment, farm, condominium, or even a share in a co-operative housing corporation. A principal residence will also include not only the building, but also the land on which it is situated, up to a limit of one acre. For any additional land to be treated as part of the principal residence, the owner must establish that it is "necessary to the use and enjoyment of the housing unit as a residence".

So far, there has been little case law on the subject of excess land. However, it would appear relatively certain that if one lives in a community where the minimum lot size is, say, five acres, the extra land would fall under the exemption as well. In other cases, it remains to be seen whether or not Revenue officials will take a harsh or lenient stand. Present policy of Revenue Canada is that excess land must be "needed" in order for the building to function properly as a principal residence and not simply be "desirable". In an Interpretation Bulletin on the subject of principal residences, Revenue gives some examples where land in excess of one acre would be necessary. These include situations where municipal or provincial laws require residential lots to be in excess of one acre and where severance restrictions apply, and also where the size or character of a housing unit together with its location on the lot makes such excess land essential to its use and enjoyment as a residence. In addition, excess land is acceptable as forming part of a principal residence where the location of a housing unit requires such land in order to provide the taxpayer with access to and from public roads.

Certainly, if one disposes of a property which is a principal residence and which includes more than one acre of land, it would be advisable to have as much evidence as possible to substantiate a position that excess land was, in fact, required for personal use and enjoyment. For example, if the land is suitable for snowmobiling or cross-country skiing, and the taxpayer and his family have pictures to show that their property was used extensively for these purposes, they would have a much better case than a purely verbal argument two or three years after the sale when their claim for a complete capital gains exemption is reviewed. The old saying "a picture is worth a thousand words" could well apply in this case.

If a taxpayer owns two residences, only one of them may be designated as his principal residence for any given year. Where a husband and wife own their home jointly, each of them will have to designate the property as his or her principal residence for the entire gain on eventual sale to be exempt from tax.

In contrast, however, if one spouse owns and designates the city home as the principal residence, while the other spouse owns another property, the second property may also be designated as a principal residence provided it meets the test of being "ordinarily inhabited". A seasonal residence, such as a summer cottage or ski chalet, will apparently meet this test unless the principal reason for owning it is to produce income. It should be noted that there is no requirement under the Income Tax Act that a principal residence be situated in Canada. Thus, a condominium in Florida or Hawaii could also qualify for Canadian principal-residence exemption. (Whether or not a gain on a disposition of such property is exempt from U.S. tax is another story. This will be covered in Chapter Twelve.)

To tax plan properly, it is mandatory for husband and wife to separate their ownerships where there are two properties and a capital-gains-tax exemption is desired for both. The couple may start off jointly owning a city house and later decide to acquire a second residence. Before the latter acquisition, I suggest that one of the two spouses sell his or her interest in the city house to the other. The seller would then be the person who acquires the second property. The gain on the sale by husband to wife (or vice versa) of the interest in the city house would be exempt as a principal residence sale. In addition, there are generally no capital gains implications, in any event, on transactions between a husband and wife. Subsequently, when the city house is sold, the owner can then argue that the property was *always* his (or her) principal residence and that the gain on sale should be tax-free. Also, when the country house is sold, it would have qualified as well as a principal residence (to *its* owner) throughout the period of ownership.

Failure to structure ownership advantageously at the time of acquisition of the second property will, however, result in the gain on one of the two properties being at least partially taxable.

Technically, one's capital gain must be calculated in the same way as gains on other assets. However, there is a formula exempting a portion of the gain, based on the number of years during which the property was designated as a principal residence as a proportion of the total number of years of ownership. For purposes of these calculations, only years after 1971 are taken into account.

Since one's entire gain is normally exempt, Revenue officials do not require any designation of property as a principal residence to be filed from year to year. It is only when property is disposed of and where a *taxable* gain results, that a designation must be filed with one's tax return for that year.

There are also rules which allow a taxpayer to have up to two sales of principal residences in the same taxation year. Thus, if an individual moves from Montreal to Toronto, and then on to Vancouver, all in the same year, it is possible for the disposition of both the Montreal house and the Toronto house to be tax-free. (Actually, there is no requirement that these houses be situated in different cities.)

Purchase of Vacant Land—Construction of a Principal Residence

A tax problem may arise where an individual acquires land in one year and constructs a residence on it in another year. Unfortunately, the taxpayer may not designate the property as his principal residence until the year in which he commences to ordinarily inhabit the residence. However, the prior years when he owned only the vacant lot (or the lot with a residence under construction) would still be taken into account when working through the formula in order to calculate the portion of the gain which is taxable and the portion which is exempt. For example, where a taxpayer acquires a vacant lot and holds it for three years, and then builds a residence which is kept for seven years, the principal residence exemption on the sale of the property would be limited to only 70% of the gain on eventual sale. (Actually, the exempt portion of the gain would be 80%, since the formula for calculating exempt gains contains a "bonus" provision. Through the "bonus" provision, one automatically gets an *extra* year added on to the period of ownership as a principal residence.)

A Principal Residence on Land Used in a Farming Business

Where an individual owns a principal residence situated on land used in a farming business, he may use one of two methods to calculate his capital gain on the disposition of his property.

First, the individual may regard his land as being divided into two portions: one containing the home and adjoining land that may reasonably be regarded as contributing to the taxpayer's use and enjoyment of the residence; and the other containing the remainder of the land, part or all of which is used in his farming business. Under this method, the capital gain is calculated by subtracting from both the selling price and the tax cost of the property a reasonable factor for the principal residence portion.

The second method involves a calculation of capital gains based on the entire difference between the selling price of the property and its cost for tax purposes. The gain for income tax purposes is, however, decreased by $1,000 for each year after 1971 during which the taxpayer lived on the farm. There is also a bonus reduction of an extra $1,000 from the net gain as calculated. The reason one would only take into account the years after 1971 is because the cost base of a farm which was owned prior to 1972 would be the value of that farm at the end of 1971 and not its original cost. Thus, the accrued gain before 1972 is tax exempt in any event.

Losses on Disposition

Where a residence has been held primarily for the personal use or enjoyment of the owner and his family, the property is considered to be "personal-use property". As such, the Income Tax Act does not allow deductions for any loss on disposition.

Renovation of Homes—An Interesting "Hobby"

From time to time, there are newspaper and magazine articles about people who have a rather interesting hobby. They buy older homes, move into them, fix them up, and resell them at a profit. If a taxpayer undertakes such a venture only sporadically, he can still expect to qualify for the principal residence exemption for his gain on sale. However, if a taxpayer develops the habit of buying, fixing and selling a different house each year, Revenue officials will consider these transactions to be a business. As such, one's *entire* gain could become taxable. A number of tax assessments have resulted from investigations initiated from information which appeared in newspaper articles. Thus, anyone who is a habitual renovator should either maintain a low profile or be prepared for the possible adverse tax consequences that sometimes result from human interest stories.

Revenue Canada's Loss

In my opinion, probably the biggest mistake that is made by the Department of National Revenue is the rather lax position which is taken administratively with respect to reporting requirements on principal residences. As I mentioned previously, no designation of a property as a principal residence is required and no disclosure is necessary unless a taxable gain results from the disposition.

I guess that everyone knows that in any society where taxes are levied, there is an inclination for some people to cheat. If undisclosed income is received, however, one of the problems that the cheater faces is finding a way to use his funds without his investment income becoming visible. A sudden increase in interest or dividend income from one year to the next will often result in a form letter from Revenue Canada requesting information as to the source of sudden investment capital. Thus, one of the favourite methods of burying undisclosed income is to acquire an expensive home or to place "black" money into extensive renovations.

Revenue Canada would probably gain a substantial amount of tax revenues by simply adopting a mandatory reporting requirement for residence dispositions. Consider, for example, the case where a taxpayer reports a sale of a principal residence for, say, $300,000 where the cost of property three years previously was only $200,000. On audit, let us assume Revenue officials determine that the individual had only reported average annual gross income of $15,000 a year in the five years preceding the year of sale. The question would then logically arise, how could he afford to have purchased the home in the first place? Second, if Revenue Canada made use of statistical averages on a city-by-city basis, they might find that, for the particular municipality, one would only have expected a 30% increase in housing values during the period that the taxpayer owned the property. Thus, one would have ordinarily assumed that a house purchased three years previously for $200,000 would only be worth $260,000. It is then quite possible that the remaining increase in value represents the recovery of renovations and improvements which were made during the ownership period. Of course, if the taxpayer had only reported gross income of $18,000 a year for the three years, how could he have put in $40,000 of renovations? In any event, if the administrative policies are changed in the next couple of years, perhaps I will be able to derive the satisfaction of knowing that "the other side" reads my material!

Changing the Use of a Principal Residence

To accommodate people who are subject to temporary transfers, the Income Tax Act permits a taxpayer to move out of a home and still designate the property as his principal residence for up to four years. In order to make this election, the taxpayer must remain resident in Canada and must not designate some other property as his principal residence. If the designated property is rented out over that time, capital cost allowances may not be claimed to reduce rental income, although all other expenses, including mortgage interest, are permissible. It appears, however, that there can be a substantial benefit if the designated property is owned by either husband or wife and not jointly. There appears to be no prohibition against the second spouse acquiring a principal residence quite apart from the designated property. It may, therefore, be possible to eventually obtain two capital gains on a tax-free basis.

If an election to continue to designate a property as a principal residence is not made, there will automatically be a deemed disposition of the principal residence at fair market value as of the date habitation ceases. The resulting gain will ordinarily be tax exempt, although any future growth in value will become taxable when the property is either sold or reinhabited. The election to continue to deem the property as a principal residence gives the taxpayer a reprieve. If he reinhabits the property within the four years, the "chain" of ownership as a principal residence remains unbroken. If, on the other hand, the property is rented out beyond four years, there will only be a deemed disposition at the end of the fourth year. Then, only proceeds greater than the fair market value at the end of the fourth year would eventually become subject to ordinary capital gains treatment. The growth during the four years would, however, be tax-free.

The opportunity to take advantage of these rules can best be illustrated with an example. Assume the case of a university professor in Vancouver who accepts a two-year visiting fellowship at a university in Toronto. Instead of selling his Vancouver house, he rents it out for the two-year period. Upon reaching Toronto, his wife acquires a residence in that city and the couple inhabits this latter property during the term of his limited engagement. When a subsequent sale of the Toronto property takes place, the professor's wife treats the gain as exempt on the basis that the property was her principal residence. When the Vancouver home is then reinhabited, it continues to qualify as the professor's principal residence and, upon subsequent sale, the entire gain on that property is exempt as well.

One can obtain an extension to the rule which would permit a principal residence designation to continue *indefinitely* beyond four years in cases where an individual (or his spouse) is transferred by an employer and later reoccupies the home. This is provided that the residence is reoccupied no later than one year following the year in which employment with that employer terminates.

These rules are designed to provide tax relief where property was first a principal residence and later becomes a rental property. Unfortunately, no similar alleviating provisions exist for the reverse situation.

Income-Producing Property Converted to Principal Residence

If a property starts off as a rental property and *then* becomes a principal residence, the owner has a problem. The rules of the Income Tax Act provide that, at the time of change of use, there is a deemed disposition of the rental property at current fair-market value. This will trigger recaptured depreciation and capital gains even though there is no change in ownership. The taxes will have to be paid without any corresponding in-flow of cash. The only consolation, of course, is that future growth in the value of the property will then be exempt from tax under the principal-residence rules.

There is no way out of this dilemma, and you should at least be aware of the problem. You might still wish to acquire a rental property now rather than waiting until you are ready to buy a house for personal occupancy. A delay could result in the penalty of having to pay a much higher price for the property in the future. You might consider buying a duplex, living in half and renting out the other suite. When you eventually sell, part of your gain will then qualify for the principal-residence tax exemption. One step that should be considered to reduce tax exposure would be to refrain from claiming depreciation during the years that property is rented out. You would have to weigh the alternatives for yourself— the potential tax benefits of having initially claimed depreciation against the detrimental effect of a subsequent recapture.

In some cases, you may be able to solve your problem by first moving in when you acquire a property, before you begin to rent it out. Then, technically, at the time you vacate the house and begin to earn rental income you can make the election to deem the property to continue to be your principal residence for up to four subsequent years. In this manner, if you reinhabit your home within that time, you can elect to have the entire ownership period be considered as one of principal residence.

Of course, whether or not the house initially qualifies as being "ordinarily inhabited" is a question of fact. I don't think that it would be sufficient for you to buy a property and spend one or two evenings curled up in a sleeping bag in your living room in order to substantiate occupancy. To be safe from reassessment, I expect that a three-month occupancy (at a bare minimum) would be more realistic. In order to qualify as a principal residence, it would also be a good idea if you arrange for a telephone listing at that address in your name and change over billings for credit cards and other monthly accounts to that residence. Then, after several months, if you find that you no longer wish to live in that house because it is too large, too small or too expensive, there is nothing wrong with taking advantage of the rules by renting it out from that time on while electing to maintain a principal-residence status for up to four subsequent years.

Partial Use as a Principal Residence

As would be expected, whenever a taxpayer occupies part of his property and rents out the other part, the "housing unit" will consist of the portion occupied by him and the rental portion is subject to capital gains treatment when a disposition takes place. If a housing unit is used for non-residential purposes, such as where a doctor carries on his practice using a part of his home, only that portion occupied by the owner as a housing unit will be eligible to be treated as a principal residence. Any gain on disposal of the non-residential portion will be subject to normal taxes.

Ownership of a Principal Residence by a Corporation

Perhaps one of the most important points with respect to the whole concept of principal residences is the fact that to qualify for capital gains exemption, a property must be owned by an individual and not a corporation. If a corporation owns residential property which is rented out to a shareholder as the shareholder's principal residence, the corporation will still be subject to capital gains taxes at the time the property is sold. Thus, it appears that there is a significant disadvantage to corporate ownership. In some cases, however, corporate ownership should be considered. While a decision can only be taken on the facts of each particular case, I have, over the years, developed certain personal guidelines that might be useful.

If you are considering buying a "conventional" home in either a low or middle price range in comparison to other housing in your municipality, my general inclination is to favour personal ownership even if you have a corporation which could make the acquisition on your behalf. This is because if the corporation acquires the property you will still have to pay a fair rent or face an assessment from Revenue Canada as having received a taxable benefit. The rent, of course, is non-deductible in the same way as the mortgage payments would not be deductible if the property were owned personally. Thus, either way, ownership is somewhat expensive, but at the time of sale, there is the benefit of receiving a capital gain tax-free if the property is in your personal name.

However, if you control a private corporation which qualifies as an active business for income tax purposes, there might be a better alternative. The general tax rate on business profits across Canada is only approximately 25%. (The low rate of tax only applies to the first $150,000 of business profits and until $750,000, before tax, has been earned cumulatively.) A complete analysis of the Canadian small business tax rates is not relevant to this particular book. Nevertheless, you should note that the purpose of the low corporate tax rate is to encourage business expansion. The idea is to allow after-tax profits of seventy-five cents on the dollar to be used to finance receivables and inventories and for acquisitions of business machinery and equipment. However, there is no actual requirement that the after-tax profits be reinvested in business-related assets. It is perfectly permissible to use these profits to generate investment capital instead. Thus, where a business earns large profits which are not required for expansion and where the owner would like to buy a high-priced home, he might consider corporate ownership. The corporation could pay for the house using 75% of its profits towards that objective instead of paying salaries or dividends and having the individual acquire the property with only fifty cents or forty cents on the dollar after high personal taxes.

This concept can be illustrated with a simple example. Assume that a very successful insurance brokerage business is owned by an individual and that the business is incorporated. The business earns $250,000 each year after paying all operating expenses but before any remuneration to the owner-manager. Since the owner-manager lives very well, he takes a salary of $100,000 a year before taxes. At this point, he is already (in most provinces) in a 60% personal tax bracket. The corporation, on the other hand, with pre-tax profits of $150,000, pays only 25% tax.

On each $150,000, after a corporate tax of 25%, the annual build-up of retained earnings is $112,500. After only four years, the corporation has retained profits of $450,000. Assume that the individual now wants to buy a home which would cost $300,000. Since an insurance brokerage business is not a heavily capital-intensive operation, it is possible that the corporation itself could spare the full $300,000 out of its retained profits of $450,000. The corporation then buys the home and rents it to the shareholder.

By way of contrast, if the shareholder wanted $300,000 to pay for his house personally, being in a 60% bracket, he would have otherwise had to draw a total of $500,000 of dividends from his company in order to net $300,000 after taxes. (The tax cost of a dividend to an individual in a 60% bracket is 40% after applying the dividend tax credit.) Thus, the "earning power" required to finance the acquisition of the home becomes substantially more expensive.

Given a $200,000 saving in cash flow from the very beginning, the shareholder may not be concerned that he will have to pay non-deductible rent to the company over the entire period of ownership and that the capital gain at the time of eventual sale would become taxable. After all, even if half the gain were taxed at the top corporate rate of 50%, the effective tax (on half the gain) would only be 25%.

Granted, the foregoing example is somewhat specialized. Even if an individual "owns" a successful small business corporation, the opportunity to use after-tax corporate profits to acquire a residence is not necessarily available unless the company has no need for its profits for business expansion. In the above example, if the business were an expanding manufacturing concern, it might not be desirable to reduce working capital by $300,000.

Loans by Corporations to Employees and Shareholders for Home Purchases

As an alternative to corporate ownership of a principal residence, which automatically results in the loss of a capital-gains exemption, you might consider a corporate *loan* to yourself as an employee or shareholder in a business for the purpose of buying a house.

If a business makes a loan to an employee, there is nothing in the Income Tax Act requiring that the loan be repaid within any specific time frame—as long as the employee is not a shareholder of the corporation. Thus, a loan from an employer corporation to an employee can be made for an indefinite period and can remain outstanding as long as both parties agree. If the loan is ever forgiven, the forgiveness of debt would at that time create income from employment. This rule is to prevent tax-exempt and other non-profit organizations from making advances to their employees (instead of paying salaries) and forgiving these loans later on. A non-profit organization would not need a tax deduction and, in the absence of the above rule, an employee could escape taxation.

Where an employee is also a shareholder there are, however, some very strict repayment rules that ordinarily apply when a loan is made. The reason for these rules is that the government does not want shareholders borrowing money initially taxed at comparatively low corporate rates without the imposition of personal taxes. In the absence of any special rules, a corporation with profits of $10,000 would have as much as $7,500 of funds available for shareholders' loans after paying Revenue Canada as little as 25% of its profits.

The general rule on shareholder loans is that if a loan is

outstanding on two successive year-end balance sheets of the company, it is retroactively included in the shareholder's income. Thus, the maximum length of time that a loan can remain unpaid is two years less one day. (The "two years less one day" would only apply if the loan were taken out on the first day of a company's fiscal year).

One cannot subvert the system by simply repaying the loan just before the deadline and then borrowing back the funds. Other provisions within the Tax Act provide that "a series of loans and repayments" is equivalent to not having repaid the loan at all. In addition, one cannot use family members for purposes of taking these loans for extended periods of time. A loan to a member of a shareholder's family is basically the equivalent of a loan to the shareholder.

There are, however, several specific exceptions to the above rules which provide the individual with an opportunity to borrow money for a longer period of time. The most significant of these is that a corporation is permitted to make a loan to a shareholder *who is also an employee* to acquire or construct a house for himself and his family to live in. The Income Tax Act does, however, require a reasonable repayment schedule to be decided upon at the time the loan is made and to be subsequently adhered to.

Thus, in the case of a privately owned company, one of the best tax deals available in Canada is the opportunity that exists with respect to housing loans. The first advantage of such a loan arises because corporate tax rates, as was mentioned previously, tend to be significantly less than personal rates. Where the employer is a privately owned company and pays only 25% tax, 75% out of each dollar of profits can then be used as an advance to the owner for purposes of buying a home. This is much cheaper than using only fifty cents (or less) out of each dollar of after-tax personal earnings.

The second advantage is that the employee-shareholder obtains the use of corporate dollars *today* which he must only repay over a period of time, presumably with "cheaper" dollars because of inflation. A reasonable repayment program for the principal itself might be ten or fifteen years.

If you own a controlling interest in an incorporated business, you would be well advised to speak to your advisers

Personal after-tax funds:

Salary to shareholder-employee	$100,000
Less: Personal taxes of 50% (minimum)	50,000
After-tax funds available to purchase a home	$ 50,000

Corporate after-tax funds:

Earnings taxed in corporation	$100,000
Corporate taxes (25%)	25,000
After-tax funds available to shareholder as a loan for his home	$ 75,000

---

with regard to such a loan *before* you purchase or build any residence. The residence need not be a city home. A country house (or second home) will also qualify as long as it will be owned primarily for personal use and could not be construed as a rental property.

Note that the very generous provision in the Income Tax Act permitting such a loan applies only in situations where a house is being built or bought. It does not apply to the refinancing of an existing home. However, if your intention is to make a major extension to an existing residence, it may be possible to get an advance ruling from Revenue Canada allowing a company loan for that purpose under the same favourable tax conditions.

Interest Implications of Loans

While the housing loan itself is an excellent benefit, a discussion of this topic is not complete unless interest implications are taken into account. There is no requirement that interest be charged in Canada on any loan from a corporation to an individual. However, where interest is not charged by the employer, it must be "imputed" as a taxable benefit at the average bank prime rate of the preceding year and added on to the individual's earnings for that year. For 1981, the rate of calculated interest is 12%. (There are, however, several exceptions such as where the loan is very small or where the loan is in conjunction with a stock-option or stock-purchase agreement.)

Interest need not be charged, nor is it imputed on a "relocation loan". The rules allow a corporation to make an interest-free relocation loan of up to $50,000 (per family unit of husband and wife) if an employee has been moved from one place in Canada to another in connection with change of job location. The proceeds of the loan must be used to acquire a residence that is at least 40 kilometres closer to the new work location than the employee's old residence would have been. The purpose of such a provision is to encourage employee mobility. The housing relocation loan is available as a benefit not only to employees who are being transferred from one place to another, but also to individuals who are being "head hunted" by companies operating in other cities. This loan can be used to induce an individual to accept a new job that also involves a move.

The best advantage, however, is obtained where a privately owned business decides to expand its base of operations. For example, take the case of a business operated out of Toronto by two partners. A decision is made to open a branch in Hamilton approximately 100 kilometres away. One of the owners agrees to move from Toronto to Hamilton to run the new division. Although housing prices in the two cities might be comparable, the corporation could still make a loan of up to $50,000 to the individual moving from Toronto to Hamilton. Since this person is a shareholder, a reasonable repayment period (i.e., ten to fifteen years) is required for the principal. However, because it is a relocation loan, no interest need be charged or imputed.

Even where a loan is made to an employee under conditions where interest must be calculated, it is important to note that there is still an opportunity for the individual to derive a significant benefit. This is because the only cost to the employee is the tax on the amount added to his income. Take the example of an individual in a 50% bracket who has been promoted but has not been asked to relocate. As a fringe benefit, the company offers him a loan of, say, $50,000 towards the acquisition of a new home. Here are the tax consequences of that loan.

Loan made	$50,000
Imputed interest factor (1981)	12%
Taxable benefit	6,000
Less: Automatic basic exemption	500
Net taxable benefit	$ 5,500
Out-of-pocket cost to employee in 50% bracket	$ 2,750
Earnings required to pay taxes of $2,750	$ 5,500

If that same employee were to get a raise in salary, and would then borrow $50,000 for his new home from a lending institution, the following would result:

Loan obtained from lending institution	$50,000
Interest rate (minimum)	17%
Interest cost (non-deductible)	$ 8,500
Earnings required to pay interest of $8,500	$17,000

In this case, the earning power needed by the employee to finance his house is over three times as high as under the alternative of a loan from the employer. Clearly, the employee should be willing to forgo some increase in salary in order to benefit from the use of company funds.

If a loan is made, the employer would be incurring an "opportunity cost" of otherwise having $50,000 in investments. The company would, however, save a corresponding outlay in the form of additional salary. Often, using the services of the company's accountant, who knows both the relevant corporate tax rate and the employee's personal tax bracket, an arrangement can be worked out which will be advantageous to both parties.

In some cases, the employer's policy is to charge a low rate of interest on loans to employees. There does not, however, appear to be much logic in this practice where the loan, in turn, is to be used for personal purposes. Under such an arrangement, the employer must recognize interest income which is fully taxable, while the employee's tax relief is limited to a $500 annual exemption. It would be better to reduce the employee's salary by the amount of the interest otherwise charged to offset any loss to the employer. Coping with a taxable benefit is much cheaper than an actual outlay of cash.

Summary

At some point, most Canadians must decide whether to buy a home or to rent. Certainly, there are many factors that must be taken into account, not the least of which are the various income tax consequences of different alternatives. The major point in defence of home ownership is, of course, the fact that a personal residence is the only major asset on which profits can be realized without a part being caught up in the taxman's net.

CHAPTER TEN

Recreational Property—
Is "Timesharing" a Better
Alternative?

One of the major benefits when Canadians acquire recreational real estate is the opportunity to structure ownership so that the capital gain on eventual disposition becomes tax-free. This is because, as was discussed in the previous chapter, a husband and wife can each own a principal residence. It should be noted, however, that a second home is a rather expensive proposition. This is because the interest expense in financing such a property is *not* deductible. Remember, that to pay one dollar of non-deductible interest means that you must earn (at least) two dollars of pre-tax income to subsidize your expenditure. In the long run, it may be of small consolation that your capital gain is tax-free.

This can be illustrated by way of a simple example. Assume that you buy a vacation cottage at a cost of $60,000 and that you finance the entire acquisition at an interest rate of 17%. Assume, as well, that you are in a 50% tax bracket and that you keep the cottage for ten years. At the end of that time, you sell it for $180,000, or triple your purchase price. If you examine the table on page 178, you will see that at the end of ten years your capital appreciation (including principal repayments on the mortgage) will amount to $124,260. However, during that same period you will have made payments of $100,200, leaving you with a net profit of only $24,060.

By way of contrast, assume instead that you purchased a recreational property primarily for rental purposes and that you only used it personally once in a while. Assume that the property is purchased primarily for capital appreciation, but that it is potentially possible to generate $3,000 each year of rental income. (If this property were truly a rental property

EXAMPLE 1: PROFIT FROM SALE OF RECREATIONAL PROPERTY (NO RENTALS)

Purchase price of recreational property	$ 60,000
Monthly payment (17% mortgage, 25-year amortization)	835
Payments over 10 years ($835 × 12 × 10)	100,200
Principal outstanding at end of 10 years	55,740
Selling price (gain is tax-free as a principal residence)	$180,000
Less: Mortgage owing	55,740
	124,260
Less: Payments made over 10 years	100,200
Net profit from ownership over 10 years	$ 24,060

---

without any personal use, the rental income would probably be substantially higher.)

From the second example, it is evident that the cash flow from rental income and the tax saving from the rental loss will together heavily subsidize the carrying cost of the property over the period of ownership. On a sale at the end of ten years, even though there would be an estimated $30,000 of taxes on capital gains, the net profit from ownership is more than double the net profit reflected in the first instance where the property was acquired for recreational purposes only.

You should note that this is only a hypothetical example. There is, for example, the possibility that the rental loss would be disallowed by Revenue Canada on the basis that (because of low rents) there is no reasonable expectation of profit. A good deal would depend on the amount of time that the property is used for personal purposes relative to the period during which it is rented out. On the other hand, consider the additional benefits which would result under the second alternative from deducting real-estate taxes, utilities and repairs and mainte-nance over the ten-year period. (These expenses would be the same whether the primary function of the property was for personal use or for rentals.)

The point that I wish to make is that it *may not* necessarily be advantageous to sacrifice interest and other deductible expenses on an ongoing basis in exchange for a long-range capital gain which is tax-free.

City House vs. Country House

The major difference between the "primary" principal residence and a "secondary" principal residence is the question of need. When it comes to a primary home, we all need a shelter to come in out of the rain and snow. As I said in the last chapter, when it comes down to a choice between non-deductible mortgage interest and non-deductible rent, I for one would rather pay the interest cost in exchange for (tax-free) capital appreciation.

EXAMPLE 2: TAX SAVINGS FROM RECREATIONAL PROPERTY
(WITH RENTALS)

Purchase price of recreational property purchased primarily for rental purposes		$ 60,000
Monthly payment (17% mortgage, 25-year amortization)		835
Payments over 10 years ($835 × 12 × 10)		100,200
Principal outstanding at end of 10 years		55,740
Rental income—per annum		3,000
Rental income over 10 years	$ 30,000	
Less: Mortgage interest ($100,200 – $4,260 principal repayments)	(95,940)	
Net rental loss	(65,940)	
Less: Tax savings thereon (50%)	32,970	
Out-of-pocket rental loss	$(32,970)	

On Sale:		
Selling price		$180,000
Less: Mortgage owing	$ 55,740	
Tax on capital gain 50% × ½ ($180,000 – $60,000)	30,000	(85,740)
		94,260
Add: Rental income over 10 years		30,000
		124,260
Less: Mortgage payments		(100,200)
		24,060
Add: Tax savings from rental loss		32,970
Net profit from ownership after 10 years		$ 57,030

A recreational property, on the other hand, is an entirely different situation. One usually does not "need" a second residence. If your lifestyle is such that you would actually make use of a cottage for a substantial portion of the year for personal purposes then, by all means, if you can afford it, go ahead and buy. Under those circumstances, you wouldn't want the property to be rented out and if you are willing to use after-tax dollars to subsidize your ownership, this is a personal choice that only you can make. On the other hand, if you are interested in recreational property for only a few weeks each year, you might be better off channelling your dollars into a property which is purchased primarily for rental purposes and is only used personally on occasion. The trade-off is that you would have to be willing to pay tax on an eventual capital gain in exchange for the immediate and on-going benefits of deducting your rental loss.

Timesharing—Another Alternative

If your lifestyle is such that there is ample activity in your hometown to keep you busy during most weekends and you only take vacations at specific times in the year, you may want to consider timesharing as an alternative to the ownership of a recreational property. Under a timesharing arrangement, you acquire an interest in recreational property for that part of the year that you want to vacation. You do not tie up funds (or borrowing power) in an expensive facility which will sit vacant during most of the year.

The concept of timesharing began in Europe more than a decade ago when Europeans found themselves prepaying for hotel and resort accommodations in order to secure future occupancy. The idea spread to Florida in 1972 and was introduced to the U.S. market by developers who were trying to sell condominium units within a then generally depressed Florida real-estate market. The idea proved to have several benefits unique to North America and it soon spread as both consumers and developers recognized the potential advantages. The idea behind a timeshare is that the consumer does not necessarily have to own an entire condominium or other resort lodging to be able to have a facility available for use at the time it is wanted. The original intention was to help make vacation costs somewhat inflation-proof in future years. However, as an additional benefit, consumers began to realize that each timeshare week purchased represents an investment—because a unit can conceivably be sold at a potential profit. Recent statistics indicate that annual sales of timeshare units in the United States were estimated at some $25,000,000 in 1975, soaring to nearly $800,000,000 in 1979 and over $1,000,000,000 in 1980. Resort timesharing is still quite new in Canada although the concept is starting to take hold.

Types of Timesharing

Timesharing falls into two broad categories:

(1) *Fee simple ownership*—where the consumer owns his own week in the same way as he may own a house or any other real estate. The owner can keep it, sell it, rent it, gift it, or bequeath it to his children.

(2) *Right to use*—this represents ownership for a specific period of time, usually anywhere from fifteen to fifty years. This is very much like owning a lease. The right to use the weeks may also be sold, gifted or bequeathed subject only to restrictions on the length of time under contract. At the end of the period, possession reverts back to the owner.

From a Canadian perspective, timesharing makes sense to me because if I buy a week's use of property for personal purposes, I then tie up only a minimum amount of my investment capital or borrowing power in a project where my interest cost is non-deductible. This allows me to use my resources (including borrowing power) to acquire other property where the cost of ownership is subsidized largely by income tax write-offs. In other words, instead of tying up $60,000 in a vacation property which would only be used two weeks a year, I would instead invest only $15,000 in timeshare units, leaving $45,000 of my borrowing power available for a revenue property.

If inflation continues, both types of timesharing should appreciate in value. Thus, the investor should be able to recover his investment and perhaps even make a capital profit. For example, under the "fee simple" arrangement, as land prices and construction costs increase, new units will become more expensive. This means that the value of a unit which is already built should be worth more in subsequent years. Even under the "right to use" concept, there is potential for appreciation. If, for example, I pay $8,000 for the right to use a condominium unit one week a year for the next forty years, I would expect to be able to sell that right for at least the same $8,000 twenty years from now. This is because, with inflation, a right-to-use for a further twenty years (from that time on) should be worth at least the same $8,000 that forty years' use is worth today.

Regardless of the type of timesharing week that is available (fee simple or right to use) all timeshare ownerships have a number of common financial obligations:

1. Timeshare weeks are all priced differently. You pay more for a week in high season than you do for a week in low season.
2. Every timeshare owner is obligated to pay an annual maintenance fee. The concept of paying maintenance fees is similar to the obligations which arise under normal condominium ownership. All of the expenses associated with running the resort—insurance, grounds-keeping, utilities, building maintenance, cleaning costs, real-estate taxes, etc., are divided between all of the unit holders, generally on an equal basis. Usually, an extra charge is levied as a reserve for furniture replacement. In some cases, such as where utility costs vary dramatically depending on the season, the users during the high cost periods will pay an extra charge.
3. Generally, the purchaser of a timeshare week will pay cash for the week bought, although financing is often available. A downpayment would usually run about 25% of the purchase price and financing would be over a five-year term. At the present time, during a low-season period, one might pay as little as $5,000 for a

timeshare week. High-season rates may, however, be more than double this amount.

There are several ways of allocating the weeks of the year to the timesharer for his vacation. The most frequent ways are:

1. *Fixed time.* The fixed-time concept means that one buys a specific time period which recurs every year. Of course, under a fixed-time arrangement, the timesharer would pay a premium to secure a time period in the peak holiday season. On the other hand, someone who prefers to vacation in the low season would generally pay less. Under a fixed-time arrangement, one is guaranteed the same time each year without the need to make any reservations.

2. *Floating time.* A floating-time project will allow the use of a given number of weeks each year. The actual dates would be determined under some type of reservation system. With floating time, all timesharers may purchase at a similar cost but would have to make application each year to reserve their vacation time. There is, of course, the danger that you may not be able to secure the period which you desire. In some cases, there might be an arrangement which would facilitate swapping with other members to a more suitable time period.

In 1974, the first of two international exchange organizations was created to provide timeshare owners with an opportunity to exchange their intervals between resorts and between owners. Thus, if one owns a week of timeshare in British Columbia, it may be possible in a given year to exchange that week for a week's holiday in Mexico, Hawaii or anywhere else. The opportunity to exchange is contingent on space being available at the other location. Thus, it is generally suggested that you list several acceptable alternative locations and even time slots as part of your application for an exchange. If you own a unit at peak vacation time, you are more likely to have your request for an exchange honoured than if you have a unit in low season.

A Major Pitfall

The big problem with any timesharing arrangement is the question of ongoing management. Remember that an owner of a timeshare week would share his unit with perhaps forty to fifty other owners. There is no guarantee that furniture or facilities won't be abused or that the timeshare promoters will actively manage over a period of forty or fifty years. In my opinion, the best timeshare arrangement would be where the units are connected to a resort with varied facilities and where the owners of the timeshare project are also the owners of the resort. In this way, there is a vested interest in maintaining the timeshare units properly. The users would presumably patronize the resort facilities and would provide additional revenues to the owners.

Timeshares as an Investment

It is perhaps somewhat difficult to evaluate the investment potential of a timeshare. You could take the position, for example, that if a timeshare unit cost $8,000, you might be better off investing these funds at 15% interest and using the investment income to spend on a holiday. The only problem, of course, is that interest income is taxable, and if you are in a 50% bracket, what starts out as $1,200 annual interest income becomes only $600 after taxes. Also, with inflation, the value of your cash decreases by approximately 12% per annum (at current rates). Thus, the buying power of your capital suffers through erosion by inflation.

On the other hand, if you invest the same $8,000 in a forty-year vacation lease, the value of your investment should, for at least the first ten or twenty years, keep pace with inflation. Thus, the actual cost of the holiday becomes only the weekly maintenance charge. You avoid both taxable interest income and also the necessity of paying for a vacation with dollars that are not tax deductible.

The major advantage of timesharing is, however, the one to which I referred previously. Specifically, it enables the investor to tie up a relatively small percentage of his borrowing power in an investment which is of a personal nature. This provides greater flexibility to acquire investment property.

Timeshare Ownership for Businesses

Timeshare ownership may also evolve into an important employee benefit program for corporations. A business might provide its employees with accommodations, as an employee incentive. The unit could also be used for entertaining clients, for housing executives attending board meetings, and to generate rental income. If the timeshare unit were owned by a corporation and were used for business purposes, the corporation could capitalize the cost and depreciate it over the ownership period. In addition, interest charges incurred to finance the acquisition become tax deductible as well as maintenance fees and other related costs. Where a timeshare unit is provided to an executive and/or employee for his personal vacation use, there would be, naturally, a taxable benefit to the individual. The taxable benefit under the Income Tax Act is supposed to be calculated as the value of the benefit to the employee—which may be substantially greater than just the annual maintenance cost which is paid by the company. On the other hand, if the facilities are used in conjunction with conferences and seminars, the adverse tax consequences may be reduced greatly or may even be eliminated.

Timesharing as a Tax Shelter Project

Possibly the best opportunity with respect to timesharing revolves around the potential of such a project as a tax shelter to any builder who develops one.

First of all, during the construction period, the owners of the project can claim all of the soft-cost write-offs described in Chapter Four. Second, if the project is structured on a right-to-use basis, the units are marketed in the form of long-term leases. In other words, the property itself is not sold by the developer, but is instead retained and leased out. The monies received from the "consumers" thus becomes *prepaid rental income* and, under the Canadian tax rules, can be reported as income over the entire period of the lease. Then, for example, if the units are marketed on a forty-year basis, the owner of the project recovers his costs "up front", but only has to pay tax on his receipts over the ensuing forty years. This provides the most beautiful Canadian tax shelter imaginable—a write-off of soft costs to minimize the initial investment, as well as a quick recovery of all project costs, together with a profit which is not taxable except over a long-term period. At the end of the timesharing interval, even if the buildings are then worthless, one may presume that the appreciation in land values would more than offset the original cost of the structures. From the developer's standpoint, there is an overall anticipated capital appreciation.

On paper, it generally appears that a timesharing project has no down-side risk to its developers. If the average week sells at, say, $8,000 and there are fifty weeks available during the year (allowing two weeks annually for maintenance) simple arithmetic shows that a unit which might otherwise be worth $100,000 or $150,000 can actually be "sold" for up to $400,000. However, there are two additional factors that must be considered. First, the marketing costs of timesharing projects tend to be quite high. I am told that these costs including advertising, commissions to sales persons and other related expenditures often amount to about 40% of a unit's selling price. Second, there is no certainty, in Canada at least, that all fifty weeks can be marketed. Unfortunately, because of the climate which generally prevails in this country, there appears to be little demand for vacation time during the months of, say, October, November, April, May and June. It may therefore be difficult to have all or substantially all of the weeks sold. Although I have not investigated this matter in any great detail, I would suggest that a timesharing unit would only be viable if, as I mentioned previously, the project is connected to a resort—especially where such a resort also caters to convention and seminar business. Under these circumstances, the units could be rented out from day-to-day during the low vacation months, which happen to coincide with peak seminar and convention periods.

The opportunity to create a very attractive tax shelter through timesharing is something that is probably uniquely Canadian. First of all, as we will see in Chapter Twelve, the U.S. (by way of contrast) does not provide nearly the same soft-cost write-off opportunities as we have here in Canada. Second, I understand that the owners of a U.S. timeshare project must report their proceeds as income either immediately or over a short period of time, even if "right to use" units are sold. In the U.S., one cannot simply adopt the position of treating proceeds as long-term rents to be taken into income over forty or fifty years. In Canada, on the other hand, there is no restriction against creating long-term leases so that income recognition is deferred. (One would expect, however, that if income is postponed, related expenses such as marketing costs and commissions would also have to be deferred over the period for which the rents are collected.)

You should note that even in Canada, only "right to use" timeshares would qualify as a shelter. If the arrangement were a fee simple project, then the developer would merely be in a position of selling units upon completion. Thus, his gain or loss would become ordinary profit from the business of building units for resale. The entire shelter would be negated because the soft-costs would only be recaptured.

Summary

It is possibly a little early to try to assess the long-term consequences of the timesharing phenomenon. Certainly, the concept does have appeal for Canadians—especially because of the fact that interest expense incurred for personal purposes is non-deductible and the cost of most vacation property is therefore quite expensive. It remains to be seen, however, whether timesharing units will actually appreciate by an amount at least equal to the inflation factor. If this is the case, the concept will probably become quite popular. Of course, as I mentioned earlier, timesharing is not advantageous to someone who has a holiday home and truly uses it all year round. I have been quoted statistics, however, which indicate that Canadians use their second homes an average of only seventeen days (or two and one-half weeks) per year! Thus, for most Canadians (even wealthy ones) a vacation home becomes an expensive luxury.

CHAPTER ELEVEN

For Real Estate Developers and Their Advisers...

A book on Canadian real estate couldn't be complete without a discussion of some of the various ways in which developers and large investors can structure their transactions to minimize taxes and maximize returns. This chapter will deal with many of the important "tricks of the trade". While these topics may be somewhat unrelated to one another, they are nevertheless of interest to the sophisticated taxpayer and his advisers.

Maximizing Tax Advantages from Capital Cost Allowance Write-Offs on Real-Estate Holdings

In Chapter Four, we reviewed the Canadian tax restrictions against any real-estate loss being created or increased by capital cost allowances (unless the project qualifies as a MURB). However, I pointed out that these prohibitions do not apply to a corporation whose principal business is real-estate ownership, development, leasing or any other related activity. The term "principal business" is not defined. Presumably, in the event of a dispute between taxpayers and the Minister, a court would probably look at the gross real-estate assets in comparison to other assets as well as gross rental income compared to other sources.

For at least some investors, there may be a very interesting benefit in transferring personally-held real estate into a corporation along with a simultaneous transfer of other investment assets. Let us examine a typical situation. Assume an individual has a rental property (which is not a MURB) with a cost of $500,000 and a fair market value of $750,000. The individual is in a 55% combined federal and provincial marginal tax bracket. The property has been owned for some time, and for the first few years operated at a negative cash-flow. The taxpayer quite rightly has retained this property in his own name in order to deduct the cash-flow losses against rental income. In a sense, he has obtained a substantial shelter because the after-tax loss has been relatively small in comparison to the capital appreciation. As one would hope and expect, over the past few years rental income has now increased to the break-even point. Thus, there are no longer any shelter benefits available because a loss cannot be created from capital cost allowances. Assume, as well, that the same taxpayer has $173,333 invested in term deposits at 15% and his annual interest income is $26,000. Of course, the first $1,000 of annual interest income will automatically qualify for the "investment income deduction" when he files his return. However, even with the deduction, the taxes payable on $25,000 of interest income in a 55% bracket are $13,750.

I suggest that *both* the real estate and $166,666 of term deposits should be transferred to a corporation simultaneously. Using Section 85 of the Income Tax Act (already described in Chapter Eight) the taxpayer can elect to "roll over" the real estate into the corporation at his cost for tax purposes. In other words, the $250,000 capital gain does not have to be realized. In addition, a transfer of term deposits at face value does not involve any adverse tax implications. (In passing, it should be noted that an individual would always wish to hold back sufficient investment assets to trigger $1,000 of Canadian investment income each year. In this case, $6,667 of term deposits are retained personally.)

In my opinion, the corporation will qualify as one whose principal business involves real-estate activities. Thus, in the first twelve months, it will be able to claim 5% of $500,000 as capital cost allowances, or $25,000 in total. If the property simply carries itself and rental income just covers operating expenses, the capital cost allowance claim will therefore create a rental loss of $25,000. This amount can completely offset the interest income generated by the term deposits. Under this arrangement, the taxpayer will be able to defer $13,750 of taxes otherwise payable personally.

I refer to the above amount as a tax *deferral* instead of as a pure saving. Of course, if the real estate is eventually sold, it can be assumed that the capital cost allowance previously claimed will be recaptured. At that point, the income taxes payable will probably approximate that which would have been paid had the property been held personally. If the property is retained for an extended period, the impact of the future tax will be relatively small—especially if high inflation continues. The following table illustrates this example.

Taxpayer's marginal tax bracket (assumed)	55%
Cost of property (Class 3)	$500,000
Fair market value of property	750,000
Rental income net of expenses before capital cost allowance (C.C.A.)	Nil
Term deposits at 15%	173,333
Annual interest income	26,000

With no corporation:

Rental income*	Nil
Term deposit interest	$ 26,000
Less: Annual investment income deduction	1,000
Taxable interest income	$ 25,000
Taxes payable @ 55%	$ 13,750

If real estate *and* $166,666 of term deposits are transferred to a corporation:
Interest income of individual
$$(\$173,333 - \$166,666) \times 15\% =$$
$$\$6,667 \times 15\% = \qquad \$ \ 1,000$$

This is offset by the annual $1000 investment-income deduction

Corporation's tax position:

Rental income net of expenses before C.C.A.	Nil
C.C.A. Permitted (5% × $500,000)	$ 25,000
Rental loss	$ (25,000)
Interest income ($166,666 × 15%)	$ 25,000
Taxable income	Nil
Corporate income taxes payable	Nil
Income taxes deferred** through C.C.A.	$ 13,750

*C.C.A. cannot create a rental loss
**If the real estate is subsequently sold, there will be a recapture of depreciation. Therefore, the example refers to a tax deferral instead of a tax saving.

It should be noted that this example represents only one of many opportunities which can conceivably arise to shelter miscellaneous income that an *individual* cannot otherwise offset against losses on personally-owned real estate. In similar manner, it would be possible to shelter Canadian dividends, royalties from oil and gas properties, or even, in some cases, earned income from professional fees or commissions.

Principal Business Corporations for Developers

The concept of using the excess capital cost allowance potential of a corporation whose principal business is real estate is an important factor in tax planning for real-estate developers— especially where the business consists of developing property *both* for resale and retention.

When a builder sells property, it is often customary for him to "take back paper". In other words, the developer enters into an agreement for sale or a second mortgage which bears interest. Unfortunately, high interest rates on second mortgages create an impediment against sales. However, what if a development company has excess capital cost allowances available on property purchased or built for retention? Under those circumstances, the corporation can shelter interest income on second mortgages against capital cost allowances on its own properties.

To put this concept into simple numerical terms, if a large development company (that is not eligible for small business tax rates) wishes to earn a 13% *net* rate of return on invested capital, the gross rate of interest must, of course, be 26%. However, if a 13% gross rate of interest is sheltered by capital cost allowances, the gross and net rates become the same. Thus, a corporation whose business consists of building both for resale and (partially) for retention has a "competitive edge". The corporation can afford to dispose of certain properties under very favourable conditions by sheltering interest income against capital cost allowances. By being able to offer low rates of interest, it becomes much easier to undercut the market and compete effectively.

Extending the Lifespan of Class 6 and Class 32 Properties

As discussed in Chapter Four, the Canadian government decided in 1977 to phase out the availability of 10% capital cost allowances on rental buildings. No new construction of Class 32 MURBS was permitted after 1977. Similarly, no one is permitted to purchase or acquire a Class 6 building after 1978. If a property originally qualified for 10% depreciation, the right to claim such write-offs continues to apply as long as the owner retains possession. The owner is also permitted to pass on the property as a Class 6 or Class 32 asset to members of his family. In addition, if a taxpayer "rolls over" such property to a corporation under Section 85 of the Income Tax Act, the properties retain their depreciation status. However, as soon as there is an arm's-length change of ownership, a Class 6 or Class 32 property would fall into a buyer's Class 3 or 31.

There are some minor exceptions to the rules prohibiting 10% tax depreciation. Class 6 will still contain certain properties whose acquisition is connected with income from farming or fishing, or structures which have no footings or other base support below ground level. One is also permitted to make additions or alterations to a Class 6 building to the extent that the total cost of such additions and alterations does not exceed $100,000.

There may, however, be a very simple method to extend the lifespan of Classes 6 and 32 even in circumstances where there is an arm's-length sale. This could be accomplished by structuring a two-step arrangement. First, the owner of the property would use Section 85 of the Income Tax Act to transfer his holdings to a new corporation. Ordinarily, under a Section 85 rollover, the transferor and transferee would elect to transfer at the undepreciated capital cost of the particular property. This is because, on such a transfer, one would not normally want to record income for tax purposes. However, there is no restriction against transferring property to a Canadian corporation under Section 85 at an agreed upon amount equal to the fair market value of the property! It should be noted that if the vendor really wanted to sell his property to a third party in any event, he would have to be prepared to recognize recaptured depreciation and capital gains. Thus, if a Section 85 election is made at fair market value, this would result in the *same* recapture and capital gain which would otherwise arise in an arm's-length sale. The advantage of such arrangement, however, is that, if Section 85 is used, the Canadian corporation would assume an undepreciated capital cost for the building at its *current fair market value and* the property would continue to be treated as Class 6 or Class 32. Then, the shareholder could sell his shares in the corporation to the arm's-length buyer and, indirectly, the latter would acquire a Class 6 or 32 property.

You should be aware that such an arrangement is not necessarily right for everyone. If the prospective buyer is an individual who is looking for *personal* tax shelter, it may not

---

A TWO-STEP ACQUISITION OF A CLASS 6 OR 32 BUILDING

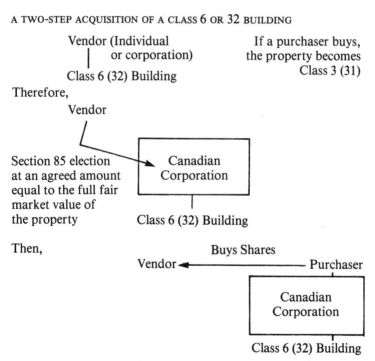

The purchaser then "injects" income into the Canadian corporation to be sheltered by a 10% capital cost allowance, or amalgamates this corporation with another corporation.

benefit him to have a Class 6 or 32 property in a Canadian corporation. On the other hand, it may be possible for the buyer to funnel some of his other income into that corporation and shelter *it* with the capital cost allowance. Alternatively, if the buyer is a corporation, one could follow up the purchase with a statutory amalgamation of two companies. Under those circumstances, the new company (formed solely for the purpose of the Section 85 rollover) would immediately disappear and the Class 6 or 32 property would retain its status on the books of the buyer company.

There is always some danger that the Minister of National Revenue may deem such a series of transactions to be only a ploy to avoid the intent of the Income Tax Act (which it is). Whether or not such an arrangement could be successfully attacked is, however, a matter of conjecture. The steps certainly fit within the letter of the law—if not the spirit. In any event, it may be something worth exploring if your particular circumstances warrant—whether you are a prospective buyer or seller.

How to Evaluate Capital Cost Allowance Potentials

Quite frequently, real-estate holdings in Canada are structured in corporate form. Usually, over a period of time, rental properties will start to carry themselves and, once positive rental incomes are generated, capital cost allowance is generally claimed in order to shelter rental income. At some time, the owner of the property may decide to sell. There are two ways in which this can be accomplished. First, the corporation itself can sell its land and building to the (arm's-length) purchaser. As an alternative, the purchaser can acquire the shares of the corporation which owns the property in the first place.

Of course, if the purchaser buys the shares of the corporation which owns the property, he then (indirectly) acquires the building at its undepreciated capital cost. In other words, although the purchase price for the shares may be based on the fair market value of the underlying assets, the excess price paid for the shares is *not* subject to any tax write-off. On the other hand, if the purchaser acquires the building directly, he is

TWO METHODS OF ACQUIRING CORPORATE PROPERTY

Before:

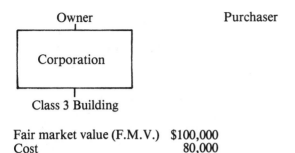

Owner   Purchaser

Corporation

Class 3 Building

Fair market value (F.M.V.) $100,000
Cost   80,000
Undepreciated capital cost
   (U.C.C.)   60,000

After:

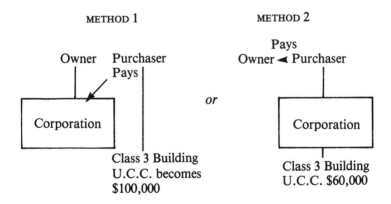

METHOD 1   METHOD 2

Pays
Owner   Purchaser   Owner ◄ Purchaser
        Pays

                    or

Corporation   Corporation

        Class 3 Building
        U.C.C. becomes   Class 3 Building
        $100,000   U.C.C. $60,000

---

entitled to start claiming capital cost allowances based on the full purchase price of the property itself. Common sense would dictate, therefore, that a buyer would pay more for the property than for the shares of the corporation which owns that property. The question then arises, how much more?

The example above, which explains the two alternatives in diagram form, assumes that a building has a fair market value of $100,000, a cost to the vendor of $80,000, and an undepreciated capital cost of $60,000. If the purchaser buys the building itself at fair market value, he will therefore obtain an additional $40,000 of potential income tax write-offs. The extra amount that the purchaser should be willing to pay for the building (and not the shares) is represented by the present value of his potential tax saving from being able to write off *an additional* $40,000 for income tax purposes over a period of time. You should note that the building itself is not worth $40,000 more than the shares of the company which owns it. Being able to write off only 5% per annum means that the tax value of the extra $40,000 is considerably less than this gross amount.

Fortunately, there is a very simple formula which will enable the purchaser to calculate the present value of his potential tax savings from writing off a greater amount of capital cost allowance. The formula applies where the particular asset being acquired is subject to depreciation for tax purposes in accordance with the declining balance rules, and it only works where the purchaser has sufficient taxable income in each year to absorb the full write-off. (Certain property such as leasehold improvements and the cost of patents, rights and licenses are written off on a straight-line basis for income tax purposes. The formula described in this section would not apply.) The formula can be expressed mathematically as follows:

$$\text{Present value of tax savings} = \frac{C \times T \times R}{R + I}$$

Where,
C = cost of additional depreciation base
T = purchaser's tax rate
R = rate percentage of capital cost allowance
I = after-tax cost of capital to the buyer

I am not particularly inclined towards higher mathematics and I have no idea why the formula works—nor do I care as long as it does. The application, however, simply involves a few numerical computations with the aid of a pocket calculator. In the example referred to previously, the cost of the additional depreciation base would be $40,000. Let us assume that the purchaser's tax rate is his marginal tax bracket of 50%. The capital-cost-allowance rate percentage for a Class 3

196

building is, of course, 5%. The only difficult step in applying the formula is to determine the after-tax cost of capital to the buyer. In my own practice, I would ask the purchaser what his borrowing rate is if he wished to obtain financing. Assume that his banker is charging him 20%. Naturally, if funds are borrowed for investment purposes, the interest is deductible, so that (in a 50% tax bracket) the after-tax cost of capital would be only 10%. Thus, the value of the extra $40,000 of depreciation base if the property itself were purchased (instead of shares) can be calculated as follows:

$$\text{Present value of tax savings} = \frac{\$40,000 \times .50 \times .05}{.05 + .10}$$
$$= \$6,666$$

In this case, the buyer should therefore be willing to pay up to $93,334 for the *shares* of the company that owns the building, discounting the underlying fair market value of the property ($100,000) by the loss of $6,666 of tax savings. If a $40,000 difference can be reduced to only $6,666, it becomes evident that negotiating differences between a prospective purchaser and vendor can be kept to a minimum. Needless to say, the smaller this difference the more likelihood there is that a deal can be structured.

Transactions Involving Land and Buildings— Saving Taxes Through Demolition

When land and building are sold together, a vendor would generally ask to have the contract drawn so that most of his proceeds are allocated to land. This is because a profit on the sale of land usually gives rise to capital gains, only one-half of which is taxable. If the contract allocated most of the purchase price to the building, this would create (fully taxable) recaptured depreciation and a capital gain would only result to the extent that the proceeds exceeded original cost.

A purchaser, on the other hand, would usually ask to have the contract drawn so that only a small amount is allocated to land, since he would obtain no tax write-offs whatsoever on land costs. If he can ascribe a high purchase price to the building, this could provide a significant advantage from future capital cost allowances. In normal circumstances, if a buyer argues in accordance with his own advantages while a vendor tries to defend his position, one expects to end up with a transaction allocating costs between land and building at relative fair market values.

However, in many instances, a purchaser only buys a property in order to acquire land for future development. In other words, it is the purchaser's intention to demolish any buildings on the site, perhaps shortly after the acquisition is completed. Where a purchaser acquires a building just prior to demolition, he will not obtain a depreciation base for that building. In numerous cases, the courts have denied a tax write-off where a building is demolished shortly after its purchase. This is because capital cost allowance write-offs are predicated on requirements that the particular asset must be used by its owner in carrying on a business or must have been acquired for the purpose of earning income from the property itself. In demolition cases, the courts have held that the cost of a building is simply added to the buyer's land cost and no tax relief is available.

There is, however, an opportunity for some constructive tax planning. Where a demolition is intended, have the vendor knock down the building *before* a sale takes place. This would provide the vendor with a higher capital gain on land, which will then be at least partially offset by a *fully deductible* "terminal loss" on the building. In other words, in the year a building is demolished, the undepreciated capital cost of the property can be written off *completely*. The tax advantages are compounded because only half the gain on the land is taxable while the terminal loss is fully deductible.

If there are several potential purchasers bidding on a property, a vendor might even be willing to accept a lower offer from one of the purchasers who will buy the property free and clear of buildings. This is as long as the tax advantage more than offsets the lesser price. In the past, Revenue authorities have been somewhat upset with vendors who have demolished buildings simply to accommodate purchasers. In some cases, attempts have been made to disallow a deduction for the terminal loss. However, as a result of a 1979 Supreme Court decision (Her Majesty the Queen vs. Malloney's Studio

Limited), this matter appears to have been resolved once and for all. Specifically, the court held that if a building is truly demolished before a property sale takes place, the transaction can only be viewed realistically as a sale of bare land. Therefore, the vendor should be entitled to a terminal loss deduction which could then be used to shelter part of his gain on the disposition of land.

This discussion reinforces one of my major points—that an arrangement between a buyer and seller can best be structured for mutual advantage when the lines of communication are held open.

The Art of Valuing Leasehold Interests

One of the most underrated opportunities to tax plan effectively in conjunction with the purchase and sale of a business revolves around the subject of leasehold interests. Normally, when any business is sold, a vendor would like to have as much of the proceeds as possible allocated to those assets where only half his gain will be taxed. Such assets would include land and business goodwill.

On the other hand, paying a high price for land and goodwill is not attractive for the purchaser. Land costs do not involve any tax write-offs whatsoever while the tax rules permit only one-half of the cost of goodwill to be amortized at 10% per annum. A buyer would much prefer to see a contract for the purchase and sale of a business drafted in such a way that the bulk of the purchase price is allocated to assets such as inventories and depreciable property where there are high write-offs. As mentioned previously, where both vendor and purchaser negotiate for their own advantages, the result is likely to be a transaction at true fair market values. Generally, I believe that many accountants and lawyers make a grave mistake in helping their clients structure business arrangements. Usually, where assets are bought and sold, the allocation specified in the contract is first made to tangible assets (up to their fair market values) with the remainder of the purchase price simply being charged to goodwill.

A major area of flexibility, however, arises with respect to the valuation of leasehold interests. Often, one of the assets that the purchaser buys is the vendor's lease. Perhaps, for example, a purchaser, in taking over a vendor's business, assumes a lease which was negotiated two years previously with three years still to run. The base rent is $10,000 per annum. Perhaps, if the purchaser were forced to negotiate a new lease for this three-year period he would have to pay $13,000 each year for the identical space. Thus, one of the assets which the purchaser is buying is the right to pay $3,000 less rent each year for three years. The total saving of $9,000 has a present value. Maybe, as illustrated below, the present value is $6,800. (The actual present value is dependent on the prevailing rate of interest.)

Year of Lease	3	4	5
Rent payable	$10,000	$10,000	$10,000
Fair market value rent if lease were renegotiated	13,000	13,000	13,000
Savings	$ 3,000	$ 3,000	$ 3,000
Present value of savings	$ 6,800 = $ 2,700 +	$ 2,300 +	$ 1,800

Therefore, instead of allocating the entire purchase price over and above the fair market value of tangible assets to goodwill, a special allocation of $6,800 should be made to the value of the lease. This would reduce the goodwill allocation by that same amount.

Let us first consider the vendor's position. Where goodwill is sold, one-half of the gain is taxable. Similarly, if a leasehold interest is sold, this too would result in capital gains treatment. It should be noted that although a leasehold interest falls into Class 13, one only worries about recapturing depreciation where depreciation had been claimed in the first place. In this instance, the sale for $6,800 represents a capital gain on the sale of property with a "nil" cost. (After all, the vendor did not actually pay for the lease—he simply negotiated it.) Thus, the vendor realizes the identical taxable income whether he is selling a leasehold interest or goodwill!

Now consider the buyer's position. If the leasehold interest were ignored and an extra $6,800 were allocated to goodwill, only half the cost could be written off at 10% per annum. On the other hand, where the allocation is to the value of the leasehold interest, the *entire* amount can be amortized over the remaining term of the lease.

Of course, the transaction would have to be structured in such a way that the fair market value of the lease is not *overstated*. Even in an arm's-length transaction, the Minister has the right to disregard the terms of a contract where he feels that the parties have colluded to misstate relative allocations under a contract in order to provide undue tax advantages.

The Use of Real-Estate Partnerships, Joint Ventures and Syndicates

Very often, real-estate construction ventures are carried out in partnership form. A partnership is a conduit through which incomes or losses are allocated at the end of each fiscal period to the partners. There is often a loss in the early stages of real-estate development. The loss is created by soft-cost write-offs during construction as well as negative cash flows that arise subsequently, especially if the project is heavily financed. If a project is held by a corporation with no other sources of revenues, the losses are not deductible until some future year. Therefore, in order to obtain an immediate tax write-off, a partnership or joint-venture arrangement is usually employed. Participants thus get an immediate tax deduction which is shared according to the rates of percentage ownership.

At some future time, once a project is operating profitably, Section 85 of the Income Tax Act can then be used to roll over the assets into a corporation. If the syndicate is very large, it may even be possible to structure the corporation as a public company. Under these circumstances, partnership units are converted into marketable securities. This adds the advantage of liquidity to the other advantages of tax deductibility, capital growth, etc.

One of the problems that accompanies the use of a basic partnership structure is that each and every partner can technically be held liable for all the debts and obligations of the partnership. The "unlimited liability" exposure can be rather dangerous and a "limited partnership" is, therefore, generally used as a vehicle for structuring real-estate projects.

A limited partnership is a cross between a partnership and a corporation. Under such an arrangement, there is a general partner (often a dummy company with no other assets) which assumes overall liability for the entire debts of the partnership. Each limited partner is then only liable for his own proportionate share of the debts of the enterprise as well as his own capital investment. In other words, exposure to losses is limited, while the tax benefits of the partnership arrangement flow through.

The tax consequences just discussed are essentially the same whether an arrangement is called a partnership or joint venture. The term "partnership" is not defined in the Income Tax Act. Generally, a partnership is merely a relationship that exists between persons carrying on business in common with a view to profit. A mere co-ownership of properties not associated with a business (i.e. a joint tenancy) does not, of itself, create a partnership in spite of the fact that the co-tenants may agree to share profits or losses. Basically, the undertaking can take any form that the participants desire. The major impact of calling the arrangement a partnership, is that *capital cost allowances* would then be claimed at the *partnership* level and the resulting net income or loss would be allocated to the member partners. By way of contrast, under a joint venture arrangement, each participant is free to claim *capital cost allowances personally* based on an allocated share of the undepreciated capital cost of the assets. (In addition, income would be recorded by each participant as of his *own* year-end, instead of having income allocated at the end of the *partnership's* fiscal year.)

There are a number of situations where the requirement to claim capital cost allowance at the partnership level could result in an unfavourable tax treatment. Examples where this would happen include the following:

1. One partner may have losses or other deductible items from sources outside the partnership that are not available to all the partners. If the arrangement were not a partnership, he could utilize these losses and deductions to offset his share of the partnership income without "using up" his share of the capital cost allowance.

2. It may be that the partnership itself does not have sufficient income to absorb all of the available capital cost allowances. Assuming the income of a partnership is derived from rental properties, capital cost allowance is generally limited to the net rental income after all other operating expenses. In other words, losses created from excessive capital cost allowances could not be allocated to the member partners in such a situation. A member partner, however, may have income from personally-owned rental property which could otherwise absorb the available tax depreciation if it could be claimed directly by himself. The requirement to claim capital cost allowance at the partnership level and the restrictions in respect of rental income will prevent this taxpayer from reducing his tax liability under such circumstances.

Certain favourable tax consequences can also result from the formation of a partnership. For example, if a partnership arrangement is generating profits for tax purposes, the partnership can have a fiscal year which is different from that of the partners themselves. This can result in a deferral of tax. For example, if a partnership which begins operations on February 1, 1982 picks a January 31, 1983 year-end, the income for the period February 1, 1982 to December 31, 1982 is only recognized in 1983. A partner who happens to be an individual will not have to report this income until he files his 1983 personal income tax return in March or April 1984. Similar advantages also apply where the partners are corporations.

With the exception of differences arising out of capital cost allowance claims and the question of when incomes or losses are deemed to be distributed, it really doesn't make much difference whether an arrangement is called a partnership, joint venture or syndicate. In an Interpretation Bulletin Revenue Canada advises:

> For guidance on whether a particular arrangement at a particular time constitutes a partnership, reference should be made to the relevant provincial law on the subject, and such law will be viewed as persuasive by the Department of National Revenue. Formal registration of a partnership or

limited partnership is not in itself decisive because a declaration of this type does not prevail in partnership law over the actual facts of a situation.

Each case must, therefore, be examined on its own particular merits and a conclusion can only be reached as to whether a partnership exists on the basis of the factual setting. This places an emphasis on the element of intention as well as the necessity for careful legal draughtsmanship.

Summary

The old adage "there is more than one way to skin a cat" applies equally to real-estate transactions. With proper planning, buyers and sellers can together use the tax rules to obtain mutual benefits. Any time you are planning to enter into a deal, ask yourself whether there are other alternatives which might produce the same economic result but with greater tax advantages. Often, the best place to start is by keeping the lines of communication open between yourself, your business associates and your advisers.

CHAPTER TWELVE

A Guide to U.S. Real-Estate Investment and Development Activities by Canadians

Investment in U.S. real estate seems to be increasing in popularity all the time. There are several reasons for this phenomenon. First, the climate in many parts of the U.S. is certainly milder than here in Canada and U.S. property is being acquired for personal reasons such as vacation and retirement purposes. Also, during most of this last decade, U.S. interest rates have been lower than Canadian rates and cheaper financing costs make such property more attractive. As well, the U.S. dollar has been quite a bit stronger in the last few years than has its Canadian counterpart. Finally, in the past, non-resident aliens have been exempt from U.S. capital-gains tax on the sale of their property as long as that property was not connected with a U.S. trade or business during the year of the sale.

Types of Investments

Broadly speaking, U.S. real-estate investments can be broken down into the following four categories:

1. The condominium, which is owned either for personal use or for a combination of personal and rental purposes. Often, such an investment will be situated in a "sun and sand" location.
2. Property development activities. This category refers to construction projects undertaken by Canadians either for resale or for retention—including office buildings, apartment blocks, warehouses, or shopping centres.
3. Purchases of already-constructed projects for medium- or long-term holdings. This includes properties pur-

chased primarily for the purpose of earning rental income as well as those acquired primarily for the capital gain on eventual sale.

4. Raw land purchased for resale. This component will be dealt with separately to distinguish it from raw land held for *development*, which is included as part of the second category above.

Methods of Holding Properties

There are four basic methods that can be used to set up U.S. real-estate activities. These include:

1. Direct investment by an individual
2. Ownership through a Canadian incorporated company
3. Ownership through a U.S. incorporated company
4. Ownership through a U.S. subsidiary of a Canadian incorporated company.

Special other techniques may also be used, some involving corporations organized under the laws of third countries where there is a favourable interplay of tax agreements between Canada, the United States and these other jurisdictions.

Choosing the Proper Method

It appears that many Canadians are seeking guidance as to the "best" method of structuring their investments in the United States. In this chapter and the next, we will examine some of the more important considerations. Here we will analyze the ingredients which must be considered *before* an owner, or prospective owner, can make a decision on how to structure his holdings. In the next chapter, we will examine the pros and cons of direct investment versus corporate ownership. Each alternative has its benefits and its pitfalls. In the final analysis, you will probably choose to structure U.S. real-estate holdings using the alternative which presents the least of all difficulties in your situation. Certainly, one of the key points in deciding on a suitable method is a knowledge of both the Canadian and U.S. income tax implications and how they interact.

This subject is even more complex today than it was two or three years ago, because the Canada—U.S. Tax Convention, which was previously put into place in the 1940s, has recently been renegotiated. A new Treaty was signed on September 26, 1980. However, at the time this is being written, the new agreement is still waiting ratification by Parliament in Canada and the U.S. Senate. It is anticipated that the new Tax Treaty will take effect sometime in 1982 or 1983.

Decision-making also requires an awareness of recent income tax amendments in the United States under the Foreign Investment in Real Property Tax Act of 1980 (FIRPTA). These provisions were passed into law on December 3, 1980, and are retroactive to June 18, 1980, unless the provisions of this legislation are overridden by an income tax treaty. You will see that FIRPTA will have a tremendous impact on the tax consequences of real-estate property dispositions in the United States.

I have often suggested that you should discuss this book with your own advisers. In this case, because of the complexity of the material, you might want to buy them a copy! Seriously, when it comes to U.S. real-estate investments, you should note that, while this book will provide basic guidelines, *no final decisions should ever be made without consulting with U.S. tax counsel.* If your activities are confined primarily to "border" locations, you might expect your advisers in both countries to have adequate familiarity with the interaction between Canadian and U.S. tax law. However, if you are involved (or planning involvement) in areas such as Hawaii, Texas, Colorado or Florida, it is quite possible that counsel in those states has had very little exposure to some of the relevant factors. As you will see, the key to getting the right answers is to ask the right questions.

U.S. Development Activities—A Canadian Tax Shelter

In my opinion, possibly one of the most exciting aspects of making certain kinds of U.S. real-estate investments is the opportunity to use these to shelter Canadian income. In Chapter Four, we examined the topic of soft-cost write-offs for both real-estate developers and investors. We saw that, for

Canadian tax purposes, up to 20% of project costs can be written-off during a construction period.

I pointed out that the references in the Canadian Income Tax Act to the soft-cost write-off components do *not* require that these expenses be incurred in Canada in order to be tax deductible. A Canadian resident (individual or corporation) is taxed on world income, and the term "income" includes negative income, or a loss, as well. Thus, a foreign property or business loss is deductible in arriving at income for Canadian tax purposes, and if a real-estate construction project is situated in the United States, there is no reason why the soft-cost components could not create a Canadian tax shelter.* What is required, is simply that in accounting for construction period costs, the allocations be consistent with Canadian classifications. The soft costs would be written off and the hard costs would be capitalized.

Ownership of Development Projects

Even without going any further, we can immediately draw conclusions as to how a U.S. development project should be owned. Obviously, the owner (at least initially) *has* to be *the Canadian individual or corporation which requires the shelter*. In other words, if a U.S. development project is carried on by a brand new company without any income— whether Canadian or American—the Canadian taxpayers who need shelter would not be able to use the soft costs for themselves.

As we will see later on, however, if the taxpayer who needs the shelter is a Canadian individual, it may be advantageous at some future time to transfer the project—preferably after it has begun to generate a positive cash flow—to a corporation. This is because of potential exposure to U.S. estate taxes which would arise if the individual were to die with U.S. real estate in his or her own name. This will be discussed in much more detail in the next chapter.

*Actually, there are no provisions which limit the shelter to either the United States or Canada. A project could be located anywhere in the *world* and still provide a tax shelter for Canadians. However, for many of us, the investment world is limited to North America and you must always make your investments where you are most comfortable.

Notwithstanding the availability of Canadian write-offs, these same soft costs would be capitalized in the U.S. For foreign tax purposes, a Canadian does not generally "require" a loss. As long as his net rental income from U.S. sources is nil, no foreign taxes should become payable. Capitalizing the soft costs would, therefore, provide a higher future depreciation base to shelter U.S. rental income once rents are generated.

In the final analysis, the taxpayer will end up with two sets of books. While the phrase "two sets of books" has sleazy overtones, in this case it is quite legitimate. On the Canadian books, the soft costs will have been written off over a short period of time; while, for U.S. purposes, the soft costs are capitalized over a more extensive period. The following table summarizes the U.S. tax consequences of incurring soft cost expenditures where the owner of a project is an investor who is not carrying on a development business.

U.S. TAX CONSEQUENCES OF SOFT-COST EXPENDITURES

Description of Cost Component:	U.S. Tax Consequences:
First mortgage insurance fee	Amortize over life of loan
Second mortgage guarantee fee	Amortize over guarantee period
Legal fees re: Mortgages, construction and management agreements and tenants' leases	Capitalize. (The cost of obtaining tax advice is deductible)
Initial services fee	Capitalize
Initial leasing and marketing fees	Amortize over life of leases
Costs of obtaining financing	Amortize over life of commitment (if incurred in a trade or business)
Insurance	Capitalize
Cash-flow guarantee fee	Amortize over life of guarantee
Landscaping	Capitalize—write-off over 20 years
Real-estate taxes during construction	May either be capitalized, or amortized over ten years
Interest on interim financing	May either be capitalized, or amortized over ten years

209

The most significant of the soft costs in almost any project will be the initial services fee as well as interest on interim financing. In both cases, the U.S. tax provisions call for a long-term write-off. There is, however, an interesting option with respect to real-estate taxes and interim financing costs during the construction period. The Internal Revenue Code permits these expenditures to be amortized over a ten-year period instead of having them capitalized and written off over the entire lifespan of a project. Thus, it would be important for an investor to make medium- to long-term projections of his rental income and expenses. If it is anticipated that a project will begin to generate taxable revenues within only a few years, an election should be made to amortize construction-period taxes and interest over ten years. On the other hand, if annual expenses (including depreciation) will be sufficient to shelter rental income over the medium- to long-term, it may be better to capitalize the taxes and interest and write these off over fifteen years, which is now the general write-off period for buildings.

Developer's Soft-Cost Write-Offs

There are, as also discussed in Chapter Four, some specific soft-cost write-offs that only Canadian real-estate *developers* are allowed to offset against their business income. These are expenses of representation, site investigation costs and utilities service connections. The U.S. does not have any similar legislation permitting such expenditures to be written off. Instead, they are capitalized unless a project is abandoned, at which time the rules do permit a tax write-off.

An Overview of U.S. Depreciation Policies

If you build or buy real estate in the United States, you must consider accounting for depreciation. As is the case in Canada, you must first segregate land from building. Where an already-developed property is purchased, this can be done in several ways, including:

1. Arm's-length negotiation between buyer and seller
2. Real-estate tax assessors' breakdown
3. Independent appraisal

As in Canada, only building components (as well as such things as furnishings) are depreciable.

The Reagan administration has recently introduced legislation which greatly alters and simplifies the U.S. tax depreciation system. In the past, the actual useful life of each property determined the period over which tax deductions for depreciation were taken. Now, assets will be grouped into broad categories with fixed write-off periods: in general, three years for automobiles, light trucks and special tools; five years for other equipment and machinery; and *fifteen years* for most buildings.

Under the previous system, buildings were written off over about thirty-two years to forty-three years and equipment over five to fifteen years.

Depreciation Methods

A key difference between the Canadian and U.S. systems is that, for U.S. purposes, tax depreciation is *not* elective. One *must* take full depreciation each year.

Because depreciation is *mandatory*, there are *no restrictions* against using it to create or increase a rental loss. However, where a taxpayer (especially a non-resident) acquires property and the operating expenses are already sufficient to shelter all rental income, the requirement to take depreciation may be a curse instead of a blessing. This is because of the potential for recaptured depreciation in the year of sale. Certainly, you would not want to suffer a recapture if you never obtained a tax benefit from the write-off in the first place! If a property owner is a U.S. resident, it is unlikely that the requirement to claim depreciation would create adverse consequences. This is because, in all probability, the owner would have sufficient other income to absorb a rental loss. However, if we consider the position of a Canadian investor, the story is quite different. It is quite conceivable that a Canadian's only connection with the United States is his investment in real estate. Therefore, a loss created by depreciation would provide no tax benefits in the absence of other U.S.-source income.

In the United States, disposals will generally result in an immediate recognition of profit or loss. The amount of recaptured depreciation will depend upon the nature of the property that was sold. For equipment and fixtures, any gain is taxed as ordinary income to the extent that the depreciation was not warranted. However, for buildings, straight-line depreciation simply reduces the tax cost of the property and "creates" a larger capital gain. Thus, for a Canadian investing in U.S. real estate, the worst exposure will be to recapture depreciation at capital gains rates.

First-Year Depreciation

The U.S. and Canadian rules are also quite different with respect to first-year depreciation. For Canadian purposes, the general rule is that a full year's capital cost allowance may be claimed on any assets owned at the end of a year—as long as the *taxpayer's* year is twelve months long. (The foregoing is, of course, subject to the general restrictions which exist against creating rental losses.)

For U.S. purposes, however, depreciation in the year of acquisition must be assessed proportionately, that is, *prorated*. Usually, if someone requires a depreciation shield for U.S. purposes, the normal tax planning would be to acquire property *early* in a given year. This is in direct contrast to the Canadian concept of acquiring property late in the year that shelter is required.

The Investment Tax Credit

A tax credit is a direct reduction against income taxes otherwise payable. In the U.S., there is a 10% investment tax credit which applies to new and used "personal property" regardless of business activity.

The term "personal property" in the U.S. has an entirely different meaning from this term as used in Canada. For Canadian purposes, personal property is something that is owned for personal use and enjoyment and no depreciation write-offs are permitted. However, the term in the United States simply denotes property which is moveable (as opposed to real estate, which is immoveable). Thus, personal property would include refrigerators, stoves, carpets, drapes, removeable partitions, and other equipment acquired in conjunction with real-estate investments. Buildings are *not* covered. Only up to $125,000 of the cost of used personal property presently qualifies annually. Recent amendments will raise this ceiling to $150,000 in 1985.

Generally, two-thirds of the cost of eligible property is considered in computing the credit. The calculation of the credit therefore can be illustrated as follows:

Cost of new refrigerators, stoves, etc. purchased as part of an apartment building construction project	$300,000
Estimated useful life	12 Years
Calculation of investment tax credit ($300,000 × ⅔ × 10%) =	$ 20,000

The credit does not affect the asset's cost for depreciation (again in contrast to the investment tax credit rules here in Canada) but is limited to the first $25,000 of U.S. federal tax otherwise payable plus 80% of any excess in 1981 (90% in 1982).

Where an industrial or commercial building is more than thirty years old and is not expanded, all rehabilitation expenditures having a lifespan of more than five years will now qualify for a 15% credit. The credit rises to 20% for buildings at least forty years old and is 25% for older residential or historic structures. As a result of recent legislative amendments, buildings less than thirty years old no longer qualify. An investment tax credit that is not utilized may be carried back three years and *forward for up to seven years*. Thus, the credit can be used by a Canadian to shelter U.S. taxes which might otherwise arise on property dispositions. It is extremely important, therefore, to make the necessary calculations in the year that "personal property" is acquired and to keep track of the specific carry-forwards.

The Energy Tax Credit

The United States also has a 10% tax credit for investment in various types of energy conservation devices. Structural components such as solar heating panels will qualify, and there is no limit on the amount of tax which may be offset. Where an asset has at least a three-year life expectancy, 100% of the costs qualify for the credit.

Capital Expenditures vs. Repairs and Maintenance

As in Canada, the U.S. tax system permits current repairs to be deducted in arriving at income, provided that the expenses are incurred to earn income, do not materially add to an asset's value, and do not prolong its useful life. Capital expenditures are charged to capital costs and are depreciated. The U.S. does, however, have certain statutory guidelines which have no counterpart here in Canada. For example, in the U.S., a current expense is not permitted where the expenditure either changes an asset's use or increases productive capacity by more than 25%. There are also restrictions against "loading up" with heavy repairs in any given year in order to shelter non-recurring income. Excess repairs may not be written-off, and are subject to amortization as capital. If you are thinking of acquiring property in the United States which requires substantial repairs or renovation, you would be prudent to seek U.S. advice with respect to the anticipated tax consequences *before* making your expenditures.

Deemed Dispositions

One of the most striking differences between the Canadian and U.S. tax systems is with respect to the topic of non-arm's-length transactions. For Canadian tax purposes, when gifts are made between any two individuals (other than husband and wife) there is normally a deemed disposition at fair market value. Similarly, gains can arise when property is converted from personal to business use or vice versa. By contrast, the U.S. will ordinarily deem a conversion to occur at the lesser of an asset's fair market value or its tax cost and no gains are therefore recognized. When assets are acquired in the U.S. by gift or bequest, the recipient will generally assume the donor's undepreciated cost as his (her) new basis, although a spouse will achieve fair market value in a divorce or separation settlement. The Internal Revenue Code tries to avoid fair market value determinations in non-market transactions.

214

Capital Gains

For investors, the tax burden of a long-term capital gain is now quite a bit less in the U.S. than in Canada. For example, if an individual is in a high tax bracket in Canada, half his gain could conceivably be taxed at around 60 to 65%. This produces an effective tax cost of between 30% and 32½%. In the U.S., 40% of a long-term gain is taxable but the top marginal tax rate is now only 50%. Thus, the effective maximum tax rate becomes 20% (40% x 50%).

The U.S. tax system has an especially interesting rule which has no Canadian counterpart. Arbitrarily, unless one is a trader in property, the cut-off between ordinary (fully taxable) income and capital gains occurs after a minimum one-year holding period. Thus, the tax consequences of a disposition are much more readily ascertainable in the U.S. than they would be in Canada. You will recall from Chapter Six that the Canadian authorities will often deem a real-estate profit to be income from an "adventure in the nature of trade" even after a holding period of several years.

An Overview of the U.S. Tax Rules
for Non-Resident Aliens and Foreign Corporations

Where a non-resident alien individual (that is, a non-resident of the U.S. who is also not a U.S. citizen) or foreign corporation derives income from U.S. sources, the U.S. imposes taxes. If the income derived from the U.S. is business income (referred to in the Internal Revenue Code as income which is "effectively connected with the conduct of a trade or business within the U.S."), tax is imposed at normal graduated rates on taxable income. The tables on page 216 summarize the U.S. tax rate structure for both corporations and individuals.

Several points should be noted. First, the tax rate schedule for individuals is based on 1980 rates for unmarried persons. Actually, the personal tax rate structure in the U.S. depends on the taxpayer's filing status. In contrast to the Canadian rules, the U.S. permits married persons to file "joint returns", and a separate tax rate structure then applies where the income of husband and wife are pooled. There is also a special table for married persons filing separately, as well as for unmarried "heads of household".

For Corporations		*1981*	*1982*	*1983*
First	$ 25,000 of taxable income	17%	16%	15%
Next	$ 25,000 of taxable income	20%	19%	18%
Next	$ 25,000 of taxable income	30%	30%	30%
Next	$ 25,000 of taxable income	40%	40%	40%
Excess over	$100,000 of taxable income	46%	46%	46%

For Single Individuals (Selected Tax Brackets)

Taxable income		
	$ 2,300–$ 3,400	14%
	$ 10,800–$ 12,900	24%
	$ 18,200–$ 23,500	34%
	$ 34,100–$ 41,500	49%
	$ 55,300–$ 81,800	63%
	$ 81,800–$108,300	68%
	$108,300–Up	70%

There is also another very important difference between Canadian and U.S. tax laws when it comes to rate structures. In Canada, provincial taxes are a significant factor when one considers the total tax burden for both individuals and corporations. Thus, whenever rates are quoted, they represent *combined* federal and provincial taxes.

On the other hand, U.S. state income-taxes tend to be relatively small in relation to federal taxes. Moreover, a state income-tax is deductible on the federal return, thus reducing its impact even further. Therefore, whenever rates are quoted in the U.S., these rates are usually federal tax rates only. You are cautioned to investigate the actual tax rates levied by any state or states where you are interested in doing business or acquiring property.

To summarize, then, business income is subject to graduated tax rates. A non-resident alien individual or foreign corporation would be required to file an annual tax return and pay taxes on business profits at these rates.

Passive Investment Income

If a non-resident's U.S.-source income is from passive investments, tax is imposed at a flat rate of 30% on the *gross* income received, without any allowances for deductions. However, the 30% rate is modified if the U.S. has a tax agreement with the country in which the non-resident alien or foreign corporation lives. Between Canada and the U.S., the Treaty rate of withholding is generally only 15%.

All income from U.S. real property, whether from sale, rental, or otherwise, is considered to be U.S.-source. In order to avoid a flat rate withholding tax of 15% on gross rents, provisions of the Canada-U.S. Tax Agreement and the Internal Revenue Code permit a non-resident alien to pay regular graduated tax on *net* rental income after deducting all expenses attributable to earning that income. Thus, if net rental income after depreciation is nil, there is no U.S. tax liability.

It is somewhat academic whether or not the opportunity to pay graduated taxes on net rental income (instead of suffering a withholding tax on gross rents) is optional or mandatory. Since expenses incurred to earn rental income are usually significant in relation to the gross, it generally pays to file on a net basis. (There is, perhaps, an exception in the year property is sold. See page 220.)

U.S. Capital Gains

Until 1980, non-business-related capital gains of a non-resident alien were generally exempt from U.S. tax—even if the capital gain pertained to the disposition of U.S. real estate. As long as the property itself was not connected with a U.S. trade or business in the year of sale, a non-resident alien or foreign corporation thus recognized no U.S. tax liability. (Of course, if the taxpayer was a Canadian resident individual or corporation, the gain would still be subject to *Canadian* taxes.)

The Foreign Investment in Real Property Tax Act of 1980 (FIRPTA)

On December 3, 1980, both Houses of Congress passed provisions which included the Foreign Investment and Real Property Tax Act of 1980 (FIRPTA). President Jimmy Carter signed the Bill before he was succeeded by President Ronald Reagan. Under the FIRPTA legislation, any gain from the disposition of a U.S. real-property interest by a foreign investor will now be treated as a gain that is effectively connected with a U.S. trade or business. Consequently, a foreign investor will be taxed on capital gains from U.S. real property interests in essentially the same manner as a resident of the United States or a U.S. corporation.

U.S. real property interests that are now subject to tax under U.S. law when disposed of by a foreign investor include almost any direct interest in real property or mineral deposits located in the U.S., and any interest in a U.S. corporation where real-estate holdings amount to 50% or more of its non-liquid assets. A U.S. real property interest held by a partnership, trust or estate will be treated as being owned proportionately by the partners or beneficiaries.

The FIRPTA legislation will not, however, tax profits from the disposition of shares of a *foreign* corporation which owns U.S. real estate. Thus, if a Canadian company owns real estate in the U.S. directly and disposes of the property, the gain is subject to tax. However, if the owners of the corporation dispose of the *shares* of the Canadian company, they will only be subject to Canadian taxes.

The Act also imposes a number of new reporting requirements. A U.S. corporation that has a foreign shareholder is required to report unless it establishes that it is not a U.S. real-property holding corporation. Other entities must report if they have a foreign investor whose proportionate share of the entities' real property interests exceeds $50,000. Thus, even Canadian companies must report where there are significant U.S. real property holdings. In addition, a reporting is required from foreign investors who hold direct interests in U.S. real property. Failure to comply with these requirements can result in fines of up to $25,000.

The new capital gains provisions generally apply to dispositions after June 18, 1980. The effective date is, however, delayed through to January 1, 1985 in the case of a conflict between the Act and an applicable income tax treaty. If the treaty is renegotiated to avoid conflict with the Act, the January 1, 1985 delayed effective date can be extended up to an additional two years. The reporting requirements first apply to calendar 1980.

FIRPTA and the Canada–U.S. Tax Convention

On September 26, 1980, a new Tax Treaty was signed between

Canada and the United States, although almost a year later, as mentioned previously, this document has not as yet been ratified. Under the provisions of the new Treaty, rental income from real property will be taxed in the country where the property is situated. If the owner is subject to taxes in the other jurisdiction, that other jurisdiction will allow a foreign tax credit. The new Treaty also contains capital gains provisions which are compatible with the FIRPTA legislation. Specifically, first claim for taxes will go to the country where the property is located.

Reprieve from U.S. Capital Gains

However, until such time as the new Tax Treaty becomes effective, which may not be until sometime in 1982 or 1983, the provisions of the former Treaty will apply. Under the existing Canada–U.S. Treaty, the U.S. cannot tax a capital gain on the disposition of real estate owned by a Canadian individual or corporation unless the owner has a "permanent establishment" in the United States. If a permanent establishment does exist, the Treaty will *not* provide protection and the new FIRPTA rules are applicable immediately. It should be noted that an exemption for U.S. taxes on capital gains will not apply even if the property sold is not connected with that particular permanent establishment.

A permanent establishment includes a branch, warehouse, office, or other fixed place of business, but does *not* include the existence of a subsidiary corporation. The use of substantial equipment and machinery within the United States at any time in the year by a Canadian enterprise also constitutes a permanent establishment for that year. Where a Canadian carries on business in the United States through a U.S.-based employee or agent who has *general power to contract* for his employer, the Canadian is deemed to have a permanent establishment. *Thus, even if one owns a managed condominium, the fact that the manager may make all decisions with respect to the property could conceivably create capital gains exposure if the property is sold.* Under the terms of the new Treaty, where a resident of Canada becomes a subject to U.S. capital gains on real estate owned on September 26, 1980, (the date the treaty was signed), computations of gains will only be based on increases in value after 1980. Gains will be assessed on a monthly basis calculated with reference to length of time of ownership unless the U.S. Secretary of Treasury can be convinced that a greater portion of the gain should be exempted.

Until recently, Canadians holding real-estate assets in the United States were generally able to escape U.S. capital gains for two reasons. First, the Canada–U.S. Tax Treaty provided an exemption as long as the taxpayer did not have a permanent establishment in the U.S. Second, even if a permanent establishment did exist, unless the particular property itself was effectively connected with a U.S. trade or business, the gain was not taxable under U.S. domestic law. Since U.S. real estate is now automatically deemed under FIRPTA to be connected with a trade or business, the only defence against U.S. capital gains which is still available is under the "old" Tax Treaty. At this time it remains to be seen whether or not the U.S. authorities will wait for the new Treaty to be signed or whether they will attempt, in some cases, to collect capital gains taxes from Canadians immediately. For example, under the terms of the existing Treaty, where a Canadian investor hires a U.S. real-estate agent to manage his property and gives that agent general power to contract, he is considered to have a permanent establishment in the U.S. Thus, even if a Canadian owns a condominium in Florida or Hawaii which is used for personal purposes three weeks a year and is rented out the balance of the year as part of a rental pool, the owner could likely be deemed to have a permanent establishment. If a disposition takes place, the gain may now be subject to U.S. tax.

The Interaction Between Rental Income and Capital Gains

As mentioned on page 217, both the Internal Revenue Code and the "old" Canada-U.S. Tax Agreement contain options which allow the owner of real estate to pay graduated taxes on net rental income. The relevant provisions under the Code prescribe a lifetime election (which can only be revoked with the consent of the U.S. Secretary of Treasury) while the option under the Treaty is on an *annual* basis. As you will see below, the Treaty option is much more flexible and should always be the one chosen.

If an election is made to pay tax on net rents, the owner is deemed to be carrying on business in the U.S. through a permanent establishment. This means that a sale of property in that year would *automatically* result in exposure to U.S. capital gains.

Therefore, in the past, tax planning has dictated that the annual Treaty election to pay tax on net rental income be made each year *except* in the year of sale. If, in the year of sale, no permanent establishment *actually* exists (and no election is made) the gain has historically been exempt from U.S. tax. In general, a taxpayer would try to sell early in a given year to reduce the burden of a 15% tax on gross rents for that year.

Under the new Treaty, this opportunity to avoid U.S. taxes will disappear since real-estate rental income and capital gains will *both* be subject to tax in the country in which the property is situated. There is no election to be taxed on a net basis on rental income in the new Treaty. Accordingly, it will be extremely important to exercise the election available under the Internal Revenue Code after the effective date of the new Treaty.

Avoiding U.S. Capital Gains—Much Ado About Nothing?

At this point, it may be interesting to think about whether or not it is worthwhile to go to all kinds of trouble to avoid U.S. capital gains on dispositions of real estate. If U.S. property is owned by a Canadian individual or corporation, a gain on sale will be subject to Canadian taxes in any event. This is because a Canadian is subject to tax on world income. If the same gain is taxed in the U.S., Canada will generally allow a foreign tax credit for the U.S. taxes paid. As long as the U.S. tax is less than the Canadian tax, there will be no double taxation. In fact, if the Canadian's tax bracket is higher in Canada, it could be that part of the tax would be paid to the U.S. and the balance payable to Canada.

The only advantage in trying to avoid U.S. taxes on real-estate capital gains is in circumstances where the Canadian individual or corporation can also shelter this income from taxes here in Canada. There is no point in concocting schemes to avoid U.S. tax if the same dollars are going to be paid out in any event. The only difference between paying in the U.S. or paying in Canada is perhaps a function of patriotism. Whether or not this is significant depends on you.

Holding U.S. Real Estate Through a U.S. Corporation

If there is no advantage in trying to avoid U.S. capital gains for you (because of exposure to Canadian taxes in any event), you may consider using a U.S. corporation as the vehicle for holding the property. A long-term capital gain of a U.S. corporation is now taxed at a top rate of not more than 20%. This is substantially less than the tax liability which would arise in Canada.

One of the advantages of using a U.S. company is the fact that rental profits generated would qualify for the U.S. low rates on the first $100,000 annually. (See table on page 216.) If annual expenses offset rental revenue, there would be no tax exposure except in the year of sale. If profits are minimal, you might consider extracting management salaries from the U.S. company into Canada. There is a special provision under the present Canada–U.S. Tax Treaty which will allow an individual to claim exemption from U.S. tax on compensation for personal and professional services performed in the U.S., if he is present in the United States 183 days or less *and* the compensation does not exceed $5,000. Under the new Treaty provisions, the $5,000 limit is to be doubled to $10,000 (U.S. funds). Of course, such compensation will be taxed in Canada, although the individual may be able to arrange his affairs to reduce his Canadian-source employment income by an equivalent amount. This type of arrangement would work very well where the individual controls both Canadian and U.S. businesses and the Canadian business already has losses for tax purposes and doesn't need a salary expense as a deduction.

Foreign Accrual Property Income

There is, however, one very important set of Canadian tax rules that must be considered before choosing a foreign corporation as a vehicle to earn passive investment income. These are the Foreign Accrual Property Income (FAPI) rules. Under the FAPI provisions, passive foreign income of certain "foreign affiliates" is imputed back to the Canadian shareholders to prevent tax avoidance. *The FAPI of a "controlled foreign affiliate" is included in a Canadian taxpayer's income whether these profits are distributed or not.* A foreign affiliate is a corporation not resident in Canada in which a Canadian resident owns directly or indirectly a 10% interest in any class of shares. A controlled foreign affiliate is a foreign corporation which is controlled by a Canadian taxpayer directly or indirectly either alone or together with not more than four other Canadian resident persons. For purposes of the definition of control, a related group of persons is considered as the equivalent of a single person.

The purpose of the FAPI rules is to prevent Canadians from incorporating offshore companies in tax-haven jurisdictions in order to earn investment income free from tax. Actually, the FAPI rules will not have a significant effect where investment income (such as rentals or capital gains) are earned through a U.S. corporation. This is because, under the calculation of imputed income, a special deduction is permitted against Canadian taxes which takes into account the underlying foreign income taxes already paid. For individuals, the deduction is equal to *twice* the foreign taxes paid by the foreign affiliate in the first place.

EFFECT OF FAPI

Assumed FAPI income	$100
Less: Corporate taxes paid	50
Retained earnings of foreign affiliate	$ 50
Calculation of imputed income:	
FAPI income	$100
Less: 2 X $50	(100)
Balance imputed	Nil

The effect of the special deduction is to remove any Canadian tax liability where the foreign tax rates approximate the Canadian rates. Where the owner of the foreign affiliate is a Canadian corporation (and not an individual), a similar formula applies.

In order to avoid bookkeeping for insignificant amounts, the Canadian tax rules also provide that there is *no attribution* where annual FAPI otherwise allocated to a Canadian is under

$5,000. Furthermore, attribution only applies to passive income of a foreign affiliate and not active business income. Income from services (fees or commissions) earned by a foreign affiliate is excluded from FAPI where there are a significant number of business transactions.

The Canadian tax rules are structured so that dividends *received* by Canadian residents out of previously taxed FAPI will not be taxed a second time. In addition, there are provisions so that FAPI excludes dividends from one foreign affiliate to another or investment income which is incidental to an active business carried on by the foreign affiliate (for example, interest on overdue accounts receivable).

Impact of FAPI

If you re-examine the U.S. corporate tax table on page 216, the impact of FAPI earned by a U.S. corporation can be determined. On taxable income over $100,000 the U.S. tax rate is almost 50%. Thus, the amount that would be imputed to Canada after the formula (which permits a deduction for approximately twice the U.S. corporate tax paid) is essentially nil. In addition, as already mentioned, where the net profits of the U.S. company are less than $5,000, the FAPI provisions do not apply in the first place. The impact of FAPI is therefore only felt to the extent of U.S. profits *between $5,000 and $100,000*. The effect of earning FAPI in that range is that the Canadian "owner" loses the benefits of U.S. low-rate taxation. It is true that taxes on the first $100,000 will be low in the U.S. However, the difference between the U.S. tax paid and a 50% tax otherwise payable on investment income will become due here in Canada. You should also note that if a U.S. corporation is extremely profitable and has holdings in the many millions of dollars, the impact of FAPI is negligible. Moreover, if the operations of the U.S. company can be categorized as an active business, the provisions of FAPI would not apply at all. The distinction between active business and passive investment is not necessarily clear-cut. As a guideline, however, it is my understanding that FAPI will not apply where a U.S. corporation has at least six full-time employees all dealing at arm's length with the controlling shareholder—all of whom are involved in the rental activities.

While the FAPI rules may appear to be somewhat complex, you should realize that the only real difficulty, in most cases, is compliance. The tax impact is not necessarily significant.

Summary

This chapter is basically a preamble to selecting a vehicle for holding U.S. real-estate investments. You have seen that U.S. construction projects can create a tax shelter for Canadians if structured properly. Decision-making will involve an understanding of the U.S. tax rules governing property dispositions under the FIRPTA legislation. Also, where a Canadian individual or corporation holds property, the provisions of both the existing Canada–U.S. Tax Treaty and its replacement are relevant. Where a U.S. corporation is contemplated, some familiarity with U.S. corporate tax rates is important, as well as an understanding of how these interact with the Canadian FAPI provisions. Given this background, the next chapter will concentrate on providing specific guidelines.

CHAPTER THIRTEEN

Setting Up U.S. Real Estate Activities

Having dealt with most of the ingredients which must be considered before making a decision on how to set up U.S. real-estate activities, we are now in a position to analyse the different alternatives. These are, as already indicated, direct investment by a Canadian individual (or individuals); ownership through a Canadian company; acquisition by a U.S. company; and using a U.S. subsidiary corporation owned by a Canadian parent company. The alternatives are depicted schematically in the diagram on the next page.

There are, as well, other possibilities including corporations set up in third-country jurisdictions and investment through partnerships and co-tenancies. These will also be discussed in this chapter.

In establishing guidelines to determine the "best' alternative for holding U.S. real-estate investments, I must again stress the fact that each particular case has its own special circumstances and final decisions should never be made without consulting professional advisers on both sides of the border. As noted in the previous chapter, international investment involves many, often complex factors. However, what I propose to do here is to provide you with a *method of analysis*. Essentially, this involves examining each alternative in terms of "pros and cons". Often, a final decision will be based on the method which creates the fewest number of problems.

State Laws

In every case, U.S. state laws and restrictions must be considered first. Some states have restrictions prohibiting foreign ownership of property for investment or speculative

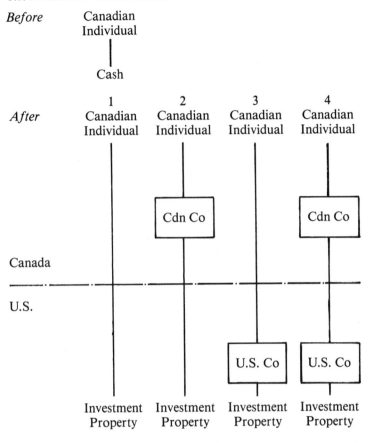

purposes. Other states restrict the type or amount of real estate which can be acquired by a non-resident alien. There may also be certain states where if a non-resident alien or foreign corporation wishes to acquire property, this must be done in a specific way. If, for example, the laws of a particular state require a non-resident alien to buy property personally, then most of this chapter becomes somewhat academic. The decision simply reduces itself to the question of whether or not to buy the property in the first place.

Types of Investment

For purposes of this chapter, the different types of real-estate holdings will be divided into four basic groups:

1. A single-family condominium—which may be owned for personal use only or for a combination of personal use and rental,
2. Real-estate development activities—which will generally involve Canadian tax-shelter implications,
3. Acquisitions of already-built property—such as shopping centres, office buildings or apartment houses, and
4. Raw land held for resale.

Direct Investment By an Individual—Advantages

Direct ownership by a Canadian individual has several advantages. These include the following:

Cash flow: This may be the most important consideration of all, if the intention of the owner is to bring his revenues back to Canada. In some instances, tax depreciation in the United States (and capital cost allowance in Canada) will offset profits from the property for income tax purposes. If there is a cash flow over and above that required for mortgage principal repayments, this may be returned directly to the investor without any immediate taxes.

If property is held by a Canadian company, the cash flow could be repatriated from the U.S. into Canada, but any distributions to an individual shareholder would still be taxable as a dividend. If a project is held by a U.S. company, there ordinarily would be no U.S. withholding taxes as long as the U.S. company has no retained earnings, but for Canadian tax purposes, distributions back to an individual would again be treated as a dividend.

Of course, in many cases, cash flow is only a theoretical advantage. A single-family condominium, even if rented out for a substantial portion of the year, does not usually generate a significant cash flow. Property development activities don't produce cash flow either—in fact, the opposite usually applies. Cash flow is also not an issue in considering holdings of raw land. It is only with respect to acquisitions of already-built property that cash-flow considerations may, in fact, be important. Even for these properties, one must consider the objectives of the owner. If his intentions are to reinvest surplus profits in the United States, as opposed to bringing them back to Canada, the opportunity to repatriate funds becomes somewhat irrelevant.

Start-Up Losses: When it comes to property development activities, you must always begin with a consideration of the potential tax shelter aspects. For Canadian purposes, very generous soft-cost write-offs will be available where the project is held by the taxpayer who requires the shelter. Once a project is completed, it is unlikely that there will be a significant positive cash-flow, at least in the early years. Any profits would presumably be offset by both capital cost allowance in Canada and tax depreciation in the U.S.

Even at this early stage of our analysis, you may safely conclude that U.S. development projects should be undertaken by the taxpayer who requires a shelter. The taxpayer may be an individual in a high tax bracket or a profitable Canadian corporation. This conclusion is drawn simply by the process of elimination—any other ownership structure would only "waste" the available tax write-offs. (Later on in this chapter, you will see that there can be some terrible disadvantages where development property is held on a long-term basis after completion by a Canadian individual. This is because of exposure to both U.S. estate taxes as well as Canadian taxes which arise on death. Thus, while *initially* development activities should be structured in the name of the taxpayer requiring shelter, it would probably be advisable to remove the property from an individual's hands at some future point. This will be discussed further on.)

The deductibility of start-up losses may also be relevant (at least to some extent) where a single-family condominium is owned for rental purposes. While the project would not qualify as a MURB for Canadian tax purposes, a rental loss can still be deducted against Canadian income. Even where the property consists of already developed real estate, there may initially be rental losses. This is especially true where the

229

project is heavily financed. For raw land holdings, on the other hand, interest and taxes will only be deductible for Canadian tax purposes if the owner is a property developer. If the land is held as a passive instrument for potential appreciation, the Canadian rules require that both interest and real-estate taxes be capitalized. Thus, the concept of start-up losses does not apply.

Low Set-Up Costs: Certainly, it is easier to structure the direct ownership of property than it is to structure Canadian and/or U.S. corporations. The simplicity of direct ownership is possibly the greatest advantage to be considered when deciding on an ownership method for a single-family condominium. In fact, as long as the disadvantages described below are not too severe, I often recommend that a single-family condominium be owned in your own name. This is especially advantageous where the property is used primarily as a vacation home and might, thus, qualify under the Canadian tax rules as a principal residence.

Exchange Controls: I am somewhat hesitant to include exchange controls as an advantage of direct investment. This is simply because, at the present time, there are no exchange restrictions and no rules which would prevent Canadian dollars being converted into U.S. dollars or being exported from Canada. However, I have, from time to time, come into contact with clients who are concerned with the possibility that the Canadian government might impose restrictions on the export of currency. I am not an economist and really have no strong feelings on this subject one way or the other. However, from a "comfort" standpoint, there may be a psychological advantage to direct ownership. If, for example, the Canadian dollar becomes completely worthless, then an individual could conceivably dispose of his property in the U.S. to realize U.S. currency. Of course, if U.S. currency becomes worthless as well. . . .

Disadvantages of Direct Investment By an Individual

Liability: Exposure to loss is always something that must be considered in determining a structure for both business and investment activities. For example, developing land before tenants have committed themselves could be somewhat dangerous. There is also exposure to risks arising during the construction period. In most cases, however, liability during a construction period will be covered by the general contractor's insurance policy, and in many large ventures, a limited partnership is often used. Under such an arrangement, as described in Chapter Eleven, an individual's risk is limited to his own capital investment plus, perhaps, a proportional share of the partnership's debt. Certainly, liability is not a serious disadvantage when considering the acquisition of a single-family condominium. As long as the owner feels capable of making his monthly mortgage payments and can afford the upkeep, exposure is negligible.

U.S. Personal Tax Returns: Whenever rental income is received from U.S. sources, it will be to the owner's advantage to file a U.S. tax return electing to pay taxes on net rental income instead of suffering a withholding tax based on gross. Of course, this is nothing more than a nuisance requirement in many cases—especially where the tax form ends up being a "nil" return because expenses offset income. Actually, this disadvantage may be somewhat insignificant, because even if a particular property were owned by a U.S. corporation, or a Canadian company, there would still be the same need to report to the U.S. authorities.

In cases where there is a U.S. tax liability, one would expect a Canadian individual to be able to offset this against his Canadian taxes otherwise payable. This is because, in general, a Canadian individual's domestic tax liability (on world income) will be significantly higher than his U.S. tax on only a portion of his earnings. You should note, however, that the application of foreign tax credits is somewhat complex. This is especially so if profits for Canadian and U.S. purposes are substantially different because of varying depreciation claims and timing differences for deductions. For example, in the United States, interest on money borrowed for undeveloped land is tax deductible until the construction period begins while, in Canada, unless one is a developer, interest on vacant land *must be capitalized*—until the construction period starts.

Exposure to Special Taxes on Death: The largest pitfall to discourage direct ownership by an individual is exposure to heavy taxation at the time of death. The U.S. imposes both state and federal estate taxes on assets situated in the U.S. which are owned by non-resident aliens. *These taxes are a non-recoverable expense for which there is no offsetting Canadian tax credit.* (One really cannot expect the Canadian government to give a taxpayer any relief where no similar Canadian taxes are levied in the first place.)

In addition to U.S. estate taxes, direct investment also exposes an individual to Canadian taxes on deemed dispositions of property. For Canadian tax purposes, this will result in capital gains and recaptured depreciation.

The table on page 233 summarizes the U.S. estate-tax structure for non-resident aliens. The tax is, as already mentioned, based on the net value of assets minus liabilities situated in the United States.

If the net value of U.S. assets is under $60,000 at the time of death, the automatic tax credit of $3,600 will eliminate any exposure for tax purposes. However, at the other extreme, if the net estate value is, say, $2,000,000, a tax of approximately $380,000 represents a 19% burden. On values over $2,000,000, a 30% tax is *equivalent* to paying full capital-gains taxes in Canada. In fact, between Canadian taxes on deemed dispositions and U.S. estate taxes, it is conceivable that more than one-half of one's U.S. assets can be completely eroded!*

Because of U.S. estate taxes, it is usually inappropriate to hold developed property that you have purchased, such as shopping centres or apartment buildings, in one's personal name. Even if, initially, these investments are heavily financed and the net value is small, there is tremendous exposure to a severe gradual erosion of one's capital appreciation. The same problem exists with respect to holdings of undeveloped land.

---

*If any solace is gained by contemplating the greater misery of others, consider and pity the plight of the poor U.S. citizen who is a landed immigrant in Canada. For him (her) the double-whammy of U.S. estate tax on worldwide assets and Canadian income tax on death can virtually obliterate the entire estate.

If the $ value of the
estate is: *The tax (in $) is:*

Not over – 100,000	6% of the taxable estate	
100,000 – 500,000	6,000 + 12% of excess over	100,000
500,000 – 1,000,000	54,000 + 18% of excess over	500,000
1,000,000 – 2,000,000	144,000 + 24% of excess over	1,000,000
Over – 2,000,000	384,000 + 30% of excess over	2,000,000

This rate schedule is adjusted by:
1. An automatic tax credit of $3,600
2. A credit for state death taxes

There are very few advantages resulting from direct ownership, and exposure to U.S. estate tax is a tremendous disadvantage.

However, what about property-development activities? We have already concluded that construction projects should be owned by the taxpayer who requires a shelter. Certainly, if that taxpayer is an individual, exposure to U.S. estate taxes then results. To solve the dilemma:

Initiate construction in the name of the individual who requires shelter and then, once the project starts to carry itself, roll it over to a Canadian corporation.

If an individual dies subsequent to the rollover of his property to a Canadian corporation, at the time of death there will be no change in ownership to trigger U.S. estate taxes.

Why would one roll over to a Canadian corporation and not to a U.S. company? A transfer to a Canadian company not only eliminates exposure to U.S. estate taxes, but it is actually the *only* choice which is available under the *Canadian* rules. You will recall that Section 85 of the Canadian Income Tax Act permits property which has appreciated in value to be transferred without tax to a corporation. The rules of Section 85 provide, however, that the recipient corporation must be a *Canadian* corporation. Therefore, property which has already appreciated cannot be transferred into a U.S. company without immediately generating taxable income in Canada.

You might question the U.S. tax consequences of such a rollover. Will capital gains taxes be imposed when ownership changes? At the present time, it is my understanding that if a Canadian reorganization qualifies as a tax-deferred rollover, the U.S. authorities will provide a similar ruling.

In fact, this rollover concept is contemplated in Article Thirteen of the new Canada–U.S. Income Tax Treaty. Article Thirteen refers to a procedure whereby an application for rollover treatment can be made to the U.S. Secretary of Treasury. It appears that a favourable ruling will normally be granted.

U.S. Estate Taxes and the Single-Family Condominium

Whether or not exposure to U.S. estate taxes is a significant factor in making a decision on the single-family condominium depends on the circumstances. If the net value of a property at the time its owner dies is, say, $100,000 after deducting outstanding mortgage liabilities, there is no real damage from a practical standpoint. Six per cent of $100,000 is $6,000 but after subtracting an automatic credit of $3,600, the net exposure is only $2,400. Presumably, you would not need to set up a fancy corporate structure solely to avoid such an insignificant amount of tax. On the other hand, if the net value of property is, say, $300,000 the exposure to U.S. estate tax becomes much more than a "nuisance".

In order to limit liability for U.S. taxes, you might consider an arrangement whereby a condominium property is owned jointly by husband and wife. Each party would then prepare his or her will in such a way so that if either one dies, the deceased's share in the property will pass directly to the children. In this way, one would not encounter the problem of having a half-interest pass from one spouse to the other thereby creating double the value on the second death. Presumably, the wills would incorporate provisions so that a surviving spouse would have the right to continue to inhabit the property for as long as he or she so desires.

Of course, joint ownership may be a disadvantage where there is another home in Canada, and where under separate ownerships, there could conceivably be two principal residences for Canadian tax purposes. Also, before structuring such an arrangement it would be advisable to communicate with U.S. counsel to determine whether this would work under state and local legislation.

JOINT OWNERSHIP CAN REDUCE U.S. TAX EXPOSURE

Assumptions:
Value of U.S. condominium—$120,000
Property is owned jointly by husband and wife

Alternative 1: Husband dies and leaves his share to his wife. Wife dies shortly thereafter.

Value of husband's interest on death		$ 60,000
U.S. estate tax (6%)		$ 3,600
Less: Automatic tax credit		(3,600)
Net liability		Nil
Value of wife's interest when she dies		$120,000
U.S. estate tax		
6% x $100,000	$6,000	
12% x $ 20,000	2,400	$ 8,400
Less: Automatic tax credit		(3,600)
Net liability		$ 4,800

Alternative 2: Husband dies and leaves his share to the children (life interest only to wife). Wife dies shortly thereafter.

Value of husband's interest on death	$ 60,000
U.S. estate tax (6%)	$ 3,600
Less: Automatic tax credit	(3,600)
Net liability	Nil
Value of wife's interest on subsequent death	$ 60,000
U.S. estate tax (6%)	$ 3,600
Less: Automatic tax credit	(3,600)
Net Liability	Nil

235

Canadian Deemed Dispositions on Death

Beneficiary	Type of Property	Deemed Proceeds
Spouse or Spousal Trust	Non-Capital ⟵ Capital ⟵ Depreciable	—No Tax Implications —Cost (Adjusted Cost Base) —Undepreciated Capital Cost (U.C.C.)
Anyone Else	Non-Capital ⟵ Capital ⟵ Depreciable	—No Tax Implications —Fair Market Value (F.M.V.) —$\dfrac{\text{U.C.C.} + \text{F.M.V.}}{2}$

Non-Capital	—Cash, Government of Canada Savings Bonds, term deposits, life insurance proceeds
Capital	—Most corporate bonds, land, personal effects (jewellery, art, etc.), shares in public and private corporations
Depreciable	—Buildings, machinery, equipment

The Canadian deemed-disposition rules on death are summarized in the schedule above. From this schedule, it is evident that the tax consequences of death in Canada depend on two factors: to whom is the property bequeathed and what kind of property did the deceased have. For non-capital property such as cash, Canada Savings Bonds and life-insurance benefits, there are no income tax implications whatsoever—no matter who one's beneficiary happens to be. This is because cash, Canada Savings Bonds and other non-growth assets represent income on which taxes have already been paid. In the case of life insurance, the proceeds are not taxable since policy premiums are not deductible. (The only exception to these rules is in the Province of Quebec where there is still a provincial succession duty based on one's entire net worth immediately before death.)

With respect to all other property, husband and wife are considered as being the equivalent of one person. No tax need be paid until the last of the two dies. Thus, whenever capital property is bequeathed to a spouse, there is a (tax deferred) transfer at cost. No gain is recognized until the recipient spouse either sells the property or, in turn, dies and passes it on to someone else. Similarly, depreciable property passes at undepreciated capital cost (cost minus accumulated depreciation for tax purposes).

If capital property is passed to heirs other than a spouse, there is a deemed disposition immediately before death at fair market value. This will trigger all accrued capital gains on the deceased's last tax return. Whenever *depreciable property* passes to other heirs (upon the death of either or both husband and wife) there is a deemed disposition halfway between undepreciated capital cost and fair market value. The "halfway" rule will cause the recognition of less income than would otherwise be the case on a disposition deemed to take place at fair market value. This is illustrated in the example below.

The reason for having special rules for depreciable property seems to be that this kind of property is less liquid than other growth assets and, as well, is less susceptible to being sold in part. For example, if one dies leaving 10,000 shares of a public company, 1,500 shares can always be sold if necessary in order to pay taxes. It is not quite as easy to dispose of a 15% interest on a building.

Although the deceased escapes full taxation, the rules go

DEEMED DISPOSITION OF DEPRECIABLE PROPERTY
TO HEIRS (OTHER THAN WIFE)

Fair market value (A)	$120,000	$140,000	$200,000
Cost	100,000	100,000	100,000
Undepreciated capital cost (B)	60,000	60,000	60,000
Deemed disposition = $\frac{A + B}{2}$	$ 90,000	$100,000	$130,000
Recaptured depreciation	$ 30,000	$ 40,000	$ 40,000
Taxable capital gain	Nil	Nil	15,000
Total "deemed" income	$ 30,000	$ 40,000	$ 55,000
If sold before death:			
Recaptured depreciation	$ 40,000	$ 40,000	$ 40,000
Taxable capital gain	$ 10,000	$ 20,000	$ 50,000
Total income if sold	$ 50,000	$ 60,000	$ 90,000

on to provide that the heirs will become liable to recognize the remaining income at the time they actually dispose of the property. Thus, there is no forgiveness of tax, only a deferral.

Summary

Direct investment in U.S. property by an individual should be avoided for substantial holdings of raw land and property on which there is already construction.

On the other hand, as long as exposure to U.S. estate taxes is small, personal ownership of a single family condominium is certainly the most simple approach, and may be taken as a matter of expediency. Where the net value of the property is large, however, personal ownership is not feasible.

With respect to development properties, initial ownership should be in the name of the individual if he requires a Canadian tax shelter. However, there is a tremendous risk in holding the property too long. In order to avoid exposure to U.S. estate taxes, a rollover to a Canadian corporation under Section 85 should be effected as soon as the property starts to carry itself.

Use of a Canadian Incorporated Company—Advantages

Unimpeded movement of cash flow across the border: Where a Canadian incorporated company is used to hold property in the U.S., the cash flow (if any) which may be sheltered by both tax depreciation in the U.S. and capital cost allowance in Canada can pass tax-free across the border. The dollars cannot, however, be passed on to individual shareholders since such distributions would be treated as a taxable dividend. Whether or not cash flow is significant depends on the circumstances (see page 228). One would also have to ask whether the intention of the owner is to repatriate funds into Canada or to reinvest in the U.S.

Exemption from U.S. withholding tax on interest and dividends paid to Canadian shareholders: In some cases, the U.S. tries to impose taxes where a foreign corporation pays dividends to foreign shareholders. Ordinarily, this will not apply where a Canadian company holds real estate in the U.S.

and dividends are paid, unless the ownership and management of that property constitutes an active business.

If, by way of contrast, property were held by a *U.S.* corporation, dividends and interest paid to Canadian shareholders would then be subject to withholding tax. Ordinarily, the rate of withholding between Canada and the U.S. is 15%, although under the new Tax Treaty, dividends paid by a closely-held U.S. corporation to Canadian shareholders will only be subject to a 10% rate.

Elimination of exposure to U.S. estate taxes if an individual shareholder dies: Where property is owned by a Canadian incorporated company, there is no U.S. estate tax payable upon the death of the individual shareholder since there is then no change in the legal ownership of the property itself. In fact, I highly recommend that ownership by a Canadian company should be considered in structuring arrangements for the single-family condominium. The elimination of exposure to U.S. estate tax is a significant benefit, and it is unlikely that any severe problems would be encountered during the ownership period. In most cases, there will be no net income on which taxes would become payable, while on the other hand, deductible losses would probably be small.

Where the owner of the condominium is engaged in an active business here in Canada, the condominium may also be a good investment for the business operating in Canada. This is especially significant if the Canadian corporation qualifies for low taxes on its business profits. The Canadian company could then purchase the condominium as an investment, using a portion of its retained earnings for that purpose.

Using A Canadian Incorporated Company— Disadvantages

A Canadian corporation would be subject to taxes in both the U.S. and Canada: If there are profits from U.S. real-estate operations, there would be no "small business" tax rates in Canada even if these profits are deemed to arise from an active business. This is because only *Canadian-source* income from an active business qualifies for the low rates.

Timing differences may arise between the recognition of income for tax purposes in both countries: Where a Canadian company has large U.S. real-estate holdings, both U.S. and Canadian tax rules must be considered for every transaction. Differences in the depreciation systems may result in a loss of potential tax credits. If profits do arise, the net effect will generally be to pay tax at the higher of Canadian or U.S. rates.

All assets of the Canadian company would be subject to liability for the debts of the U.S. branch operation: This particular point is virtually self-explanatory. If all the eggs are in one basket, one rotten egg might ruin the whole bunch. Whether or not this is a serious problem in practice will, however, depend on the facts of each case.

Inability to utilize start-up costs (including soft-cost write-offs) unless other income is earned by the same corporation: This particular point has already been covered several times and needs no further clarification here.

Summary

A Canadian corporation may be a suitable vehicle for holding a single-family condominium investment in the U.S. This structure will serve to eliminate exposure to U.S. estate taxes and there can be added benefits if the Canadian corporation already generates profits which can be used to pay for the condominium in the first place.

It is only suitable to hold development projects in a Canadian company if that company has substantial other income which can then be sheltered. Otherwise, as mentioned previously, the initial investment should be made by the taxpayer who requires shelter and a rollover to a Canadian corporation can be effected later on. In spite of the fact that the Canadian incorporated company would then run into some of the disadvantages described on pages 239–40, there really is no other choice if you wish to avoid U.S. estate taxes.

Direct ownership by a Canadian incorporated company is not, however, in my opinion, the best method to structure purchases of undeveloped land or holdings of already developed property (unless an overriding consideration is to repatriate funds into Canada). Every single transaction would be exposed to taxation in both countries and any profits would automatically be taxed at Canadian high rates. (See the first disadvantage.)

Use of a U.S. Incorporated Company Owned Directly by Canadian Individuals—Advantages

Having already dealt with what are probably the "best" alternatives for the single-family condominium and U.S. real-estate development activities, we can now concentrate more on deciding how to structure raw land holdings and purchases of previously developed property. Using a corporation set up in the U.S. has the following advantages:

Only U.S. tax returns must be filed for reporting real-estate activities.

Consolidated tax returns may be filed in the U.S. if different real estate ventures are carried on by different companies: The concept of consolidated income-tax returns does not exist here in Canada and one of the problems that often confronts corporate groups is the difficulty of offsetting tax losses in one business against profits generated by another. The U.S. rules are much more generous in this regard. In the U.S., it is permissible to use separate corporations for liability purposes while still retaining the option to offset losses in certain enterprises against gains earned by others. If one has extensive U.S. operations, a U.S. holding company should be formed along with various U.S. real-estate subsidiaries. For the consolidated tax return provisions to apply, there must be a common U.S. parent.

Greater flexibility for reorganizations and liquidations: The U.S. income-tax rules are much more flexible than the Canadian rules with respect to reorganizations and liquidations. For example, the U.S. will permit similar properties to be exchanged one for the other without recognizing gains. Thus, a shopping centre in Seattle could be exchanged for a similar property in Boston. For Canadian purposes, such transactions would be treated separately as a sale and purchase, with the sale giving rise to recaptured depreciation and capital gains. Another example of flexibility pertains to corporate wind-ups. In the U.S., a taxpayer is allowed to acquire shares in a real-estate company, and if the corporation is then liquidated, there is a "step-up" in the cost base of the property which the purchaser receives on liquidation. Thus, the Canadian concept of paying less for shares than for assets (as described on pages 193–96) would not apply.

(This means that any extra amount paid for shares representing the fair market value of the property over and above its undepreciated cost is added to the tax cost of the investment itself. This serves to minimize income taxes on any future sale.)

Elimination of timing problems between the recognition of income for Canadian and U.S. tax purposes: If a company is incorporated in the U.S., profits will then be determined in accordance with U.S. rules. This eliminates the problem of having the same income taxed twice in different years in both jurisdictions.

Favourable U.S. corporate tax rates on profits: If you refer back to the schedule of U.S. corporate tax rates on page 216, you will note that the first $100,000 of annual profits is subject to low tax rates in the U.S. If these profits were, however, earned by a Canadian corporation, these low rates would not apply. You should note, however, that the U.S. tax provisions are drafted to ensure that retained earnings are reinvested in business operations and are not simply used to build up passive investment capital. There is a special "accumulated earnings tax" under U.S. tax law. If retained earnings exceed $250,000 and excess profits are not reinvested in business assets, there is a special penalty tax on excess retentions. Exposure to accumulated earnings tax is not, however, a serious consideration where the intention is to reinvest profits in further real-estate properties.

Disadvantages of a U.S. Incorporated Company

Inability to use start-up costs (including soft costs) against Canadian-source income: This point has already been dealt with on pages 229–30.

The requirement that taxes be withheld on interest and dividends paid to the Canadian shareholders: This disadvantage is only relevant if the shareholders' intention is to repatriate funds into Canada. Even then, if the withholding tax can be claimed as a foreign tax credit for Canadian tax purposes, this disadvantage is not too serious.

Foreign affiliate considerations—FAPI: If the U.S. corporation is a "controlled foreign affiliate" (which is often the case), Foreign Accrual Property Income, or FAPI, is attributed to the Canadian shareholders even if dividends are not distributed. FAPI will include net rental income as well as capital profits on sale. As mentioned on pages 222–24, FAPI is only a problem to the extent that the passive income of a U.S. company is between $5,000 and $100,000. Thus, if the corporation holds vacant land, FAPI considerations are not relevant. Moreover, in the opposite extreme, if U.S. profits can be treated as arising from an active business operation (six or more full-time employees) then FAPI would not apply. Then, even if there are profits, one would have the advantage of paying U.S. low rates on the first $100,000 and the tax rate on excess profits would be no higher than Canadian taxes otherwise payable. (At 46%, they would, in fact, probably be a few percentage points lower.)

You should note that if FAPI does apply, and income is attributed back into a Canadian shareholder's hands in the year it is earned, dividends should probably be paid at that same time. Otherwise, a severe timing problem can arise. When dividends are paid, they are subject to U.S. withholding taxes. However, since these dividends will not be taxed (a second time) in the hands of the Canadian shareholders, there will be no credit available in respect of these withholding taxes. (This is because foreign credits against withholding taxes will

243

not be available in a year that there is no foreign taxable income for Canadian tax purposes.)

Difficulty in repatriating capital: Any time a U.S. incorporated company is used as a vehicle to hold property there is another basic difference between the Canadian and U.S. tax laws which must be considered. In Canada, the rules are structured so that a shareholder's capital investment can always be returned tax-free. In the U.S., however, surplus must always be distributed to shareholders before a return of capital is permitted. Thus, if a Canadian shareholder has his shares redeemed or his loans repaid to him, there may be exposure to U.S. withholding taxes on a *deemed dividend*. This can create a serious problem and must always be considered in cases where it is desired to repatriate funds back into Canada.

"Thin capitalization":   The tax laws of both Canada and the United States contain restrictive rules to deter non-resident investors from setting up companies with heavy (interest-bearing) debt structures and small investments of capital stock. Ordinarily, interest expense is tax deductible and a corporation paying interest can usually expect to save approximately fifty cents on the dollar. On the other hand, interest passing across the border is only subject to a 15% withholding tax. Therefore, both the Canadian and U.S. governments have a right to be concerned. It is certainly not a good trade-off from their standpoints to sacrifice the opportunity to levy a 50% corporate tax in exchange for only a 15% withholding tax.

Thus, if a corporation owned by non-residents is "thinly capitalized", excess interest expense is disallowed as a deduction at arriving at profits. Under Canadian law, the statute permits a debt-equity ratio of 3:1. Where interest-bearing debt owing to a non-resident shareholder (or related party) exceeds $3.00 for each $1.00 of shareholders' equity, the excess interest is disallowed as an expense.

For U.S. purposes, no statutory ratio exists, although it appears that the guideline of 3:1 is also employed. You must therefore be extremely careful in structuring the set-up of a U.S. company. If a Canadian lends interest-bearing funds to a

U.S. company to help finance a property acquisition, the indebtedness may be treated as an equity investment. This means that the interest expense would be disallowed to the U.S. company. It would also be treated as a dividend to the shareholder, subject to withholding taxes. *Moreover, if the U.S. company has retained earnings, the repayment of the debt itself may be treated as a dividend, which is subject to withholding taxes.*

I strongly recommend that specific tax advice be obtained from U.S. counsel any time one is preparing to set up a U.S. company. While the debt-equity ratio is significant, there are other factors which must be considered. These include the following:

1. Is there an unconditional promise to pay on or by a specific date at a fixed rate of interest?
2. Is the debt subordinated to other loans?
3. Is the debt convertible into shares?
4. Is the ratio of shareholdings the same as the debt-lending ratio?

If there is doubt, I suggest that your advisers obtain a tax ruling from the Internal Revenue Service.

There is also a further problem that must be considered for U.S. purposes. Specifically, if a Canadian shareholder guarantees a loan made by a lending institution to a U.S. subsidiary, the U.S. may deem that a loan has, in fact, been made by the lending institution to the Canadian shareholder, who in turn, may be deemed to have made a capital contribution to the U.S. company. Under these circumstances, the repayment of interest by the U.S. company to the lending institution may become a dividend to the shareholder. The interest expense would not be deductible and a 15% withholding tax would apply. This is illustrated in the diagrams on page 246.

In order to avoid the problem of thin capitalization, especially in cases where the U.S. company has enough deductible expenses so as not to require additional interest as a deduction, the Canadian shareholder should borrow *directly* from the lending institution and *then* invest in the U.S. company's *shares*. Under these circumstances (where the Canadian borrows funds to invest in shares of a business) the

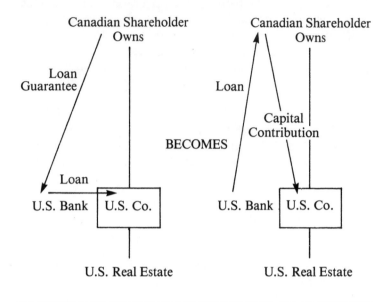

shareholder will get a deduction in Canada—even if no dividends are in fact received from the U.S. subsidiary.

Exposure to U.S. federal and state estate-taxes: Unfortunately, where property is owned by a Canadian individual through a U.S. incorporated company, there is the same potential estate problem which would otherwise arise as a result of direct ownership. When the individual dies, the underlying value of the U.S. incorporated company would be subject to death taxes in the U.S. as well as the deemed disposition provisions in Canada. *Consequently, if for no other reason, direct ownership of the shares of a U.S. company by a Canadian individual is discouraged.*

Use of a U.S. Subsidiary of a Canadian Incorporated Company—Advantages

For most investments in raw land or where there is a purchase of already-developed property, I recommend that ownership be structured through a U.S. subsidiary of a Canadian incorporated parent. The same five tax advantages which are obtained where the property is held directly by a U.S. incorporated company (as described on pages 241–42) will still apply. These are:

1. The requirement to file U.S. returns only,
2. The opportunity to file consolidated tax returns where operations are diversified,
3. Flexibility for generous corporate reorganizations and rollovers in the U.S.,
4. Elimination of timing problems for income recognition, and
5. The availability of favourable U.S. corporate tax rates.

Additional Advantages

Where a U.S. subsidiary is used in conjunction with a Canadian parent, exposure to U.S. death duties is eliminated. This is, again, because of the fact that on the death of an individual, there would be no change in the direct ownership of the U.S. assets. There are also two minor advantages which may be added. These are:

1. The fact that only the subsidiary's assets will be subject to liability for the debts of the U.S. operations, and
2. Only the U.S. subsidiary's operations will be open to U.S. income tax audit.

Disadvantages of Using a U.S. Subsidiary

One would still have to contend with some of the disadvantages of using a U.S. company as described on pages 243–46. These would include:

1. Withholding tax exposure on interest and dividends,
2. Foreign affiliate (FAPI) considerations where the U.S. subsidiary generates passive income,
3. Difficulty of repatriating capital back into Canada, and
4. The pitfall of thin capitalization.

Most of these disadvantages would not apply where the investment consists of raw land holdings. These problems are also not too serious if the idea is to expand one's operations in the U.S. rather than bringing funds back into Canada.

Special Consideration—Loans to Non-Residents Under the Canadian Income Tax Act

In order to avoid the U.S. problem of thin capitalization, a Canadian company might try to make a non-interest-bearing loan to a U.S. company. However, under certain provisions of the Canadian Income Tax Act, where a Canadian company lends money to a non-resident (individual or corporation) and the loan is outstanding for one year or longer without interest being included in the lender's income, interest will be imputed at a prescribed rate, which is presently 12%. This could result in exposure to Canadian tax without an offsetting deduction for U.S. purposes.

These interest provisions do not apply, however, where a loan is made to a *"subsidiary controlled corporation"* and the funds are used by the subsidiary for the purpose of earning income from its business. (A controlled corporation is one where more than 50% of the voting shares are owned by the corporation's parent.) In tax planning for corporate groups you must be very careful. The diagram below shows the pitfall of improper planning.

IMPROPER PLANNING CAN RESULT IN IMPUTED INTEREST

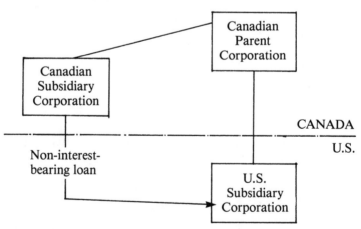

A Canadian corporation makes a non-interest-bearing loan to a U.S. "sister" corporation.

Result: Interest is imputed to the Canadian lender at 12% because the U.S. company is not a "subsidiary controlled corporation".

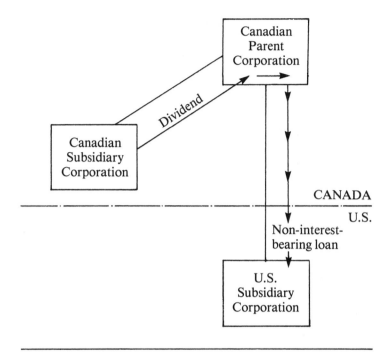

The problem can be avoided by having the Canadian subsidiary corporation pay a dividend to its Canadian parent. Generally, intercorporate Canadian dividends pass tax-free. The Canadian parent would then make a loan on a non-interest-bearing basis to its *own* controlled subsidiary.

Special U.S. Considerations

Sometimes, it is almost as important to know what is irrelevant in tax planning as to know what rules are applicable. You may find yourself caught up in trying to solve tax problems that really don't exist. For example, the U.S. tax provisions for using corporations to earn investment income or service income from fees or commissions are much *stricter* than the corresponding rules in Canada. If a corporation is a U.S. Personal Holding Company, there is a special tax of up to 70% each year on undistributed annual profits.

A U.S. Personal Holding Company is corporation where more than 50% of the shares are owned by not more than five individuals (i.e. the company is extremely closely held) and 60% or more of gross income is from passive sources and/or personal service contracts. However, where *gross* real-estate rentals constitute at least 50% of total gross revenues, the Personal Holding Company classification would *not* apply, as long as other sources of passive income do not exceed 10% of total gross revenues. Thus, Personal Holding Company tax rules are not usually relevant to Canadians in planning for U.S. real-estate activities. It can be assumed that there will be an exemption from the Personal Holding Company classification since the bulk of the income will be derived from rents.

Foreign Personal Holding Companies

The U.S. also has special rules under which a company set up in a foreign jurisdiction may be deemed to be a Foreign Personal Holding Company. Thus, if an American sets up a Canadian corporation, the Foreign Personal Holding Company rules may apply if that company is set up primarily to earn passive income. However, a Canadian company incorporated by Canadians would *not* be a Foreign Personal Holding Company for U.S. purposes. This is because the Foreign Personal Holding Company rules do *not* apply where more than 50% of the shares are owned by *non-resident non-citizens* of the United States.

Subchapter S Corporations

Often, in discussing private business ventures with U.S. advisers, the topic of a "Subchapter S Corporation" may arise. A Subchapter S Corporation is a small business company with twenty-five or fewer shareholders. If an election is made, its profits and losses are deemed to pass through to the individual shareholders. Thus, such corporations are used extensively in the U.S. to allocate losses to individuals in any business operation where there are initial losses. Effectively, each shareholder gets the advantage of deducting these losses personally, as if he were engaged in a partnership, while he still enjoys the limited liability feature of a corporation. However, Subchapter S is not relevant to Canadians. The Subchapter S rules provide that none of the shareholders are permitted to be non-resident aliens of the U.S., and the rules also do not apply where more than 20% of gross revenue is from passive sources, including rents.

Agricultural Foreign Investment Disclosure Act of 1978

In structuring any U.S. real-estate activities, there are reporting requirements which must be adhered to. We have already reviewed the provisions of the new Foreign Investment in Real Property Tax Act (FIRPTA) legislation. There are additional reporting requirements where a foreign person acquires or transfers an interest in U.S. agricultural land after February 2, 1979. These transactions must be reported within ninety days after their occurrence. Agricultural land is defined as U.S. property being used on a current basis for agriculture, or property which has been used within the previous five years for agriculture, forestry or timber production. Disclosure requirements do not apply where land holdings are less than one acre and where less than $1,000 of gross income was received from the property. The definition does, however, include a leasehold interest in excess of ten years and the reporting is not only required by non-resident alien individuals but foreign corporations and foreign governments as well. Failure to file or providing misleading or incomplete reports can result in penalties of up to 25% of the fair market value of the property.

U.S. Partnerships

From time to time, this book has examined the use of a partnership as an arrangement for structuring real-estate acquisitions and development activities. The U.S. rules for partnerships closely approximate the Canadian rules. General, limited, domestic and foreign partnerships are all taxed in essentially the same way. A partner who is a non-resident-alien individual or foreign corporation will be considered to be engaged in a U.S. trade or business if the partnership is so engaged.

However, the concept of a limited partnership is slightly different in the U.S. In Canada, it is usually sufficient to simply draw up the documentation in such a way so as to create a limited partnership. For U.S. purposes, a limited partnership must also meet two specific tests. These are:

1. The presence of associates, and
2. The objective of carrying on business and dividing profits.

Usually, these tests are not difficult. However, to qualify for taxability as a limited partnership, the structure must also *not* meet more than two of the following four characteristics:

1. Continuity of life,
2. Centralized management,
3. Free transferability of interests, and
4. Limited liability.

If more than two of the above characteristics exist, then although the entity may in form be a partnership, for U.S. federal income tax purposes, it will be treated and taxed as a corporation.

Generally, limited liability is required and centralized management is desirable. Therefore, in the U.S. many limited partnerships are structured in such a way that the partners agree to terminate their arrangements at some point in time. In addition, there are often some restrictions on the free transferability of partnership interests. If one is in doubt as to the status of an arrangement, a ruling may be obtained from the Internal Revenue Service.

Adventurous Planning Through the Use of Holding Companies Located in Other Countries

In some cases, especially if U.S. activities are extensive, Canadians may choose to interpose corporations set up under the jurisdictions of other countries between themselves and their U.S. operations. The purpose of such an arrangement is to pass income through the third-country holding companies back into Canada as cheaply as possible without significant withholding taxes. In addition, a proper interplay of other corporations can facilitate intercorporate loans to generate interest and other deductions in the United States, thereby

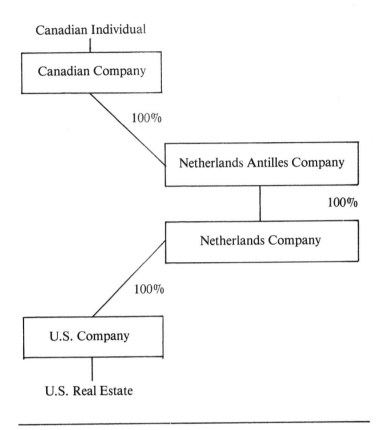

reducing U.S. taxes on real-estate income. One of the favoured methods is to use a Netherlands company and a Netherland Antilles company in an arrangement as described above.

Interest and dividends can then be passed from the U.S. to the Canadian company as follows:

1. The Canadian company advances funds to the U.S. company (within U.S. thin-capitalization limits) *through* the two intermediary corporations.
2. There is no withholding tax on interest paid by the U.S. company to the Netherlands company as long as the rate of interest is reasonable (Article Seven of the

253

U.S.–Netherlands Treaty). Dividends from the U.S. company to the Netherlands are only subject to a 5% withholding tax.

3. The Netherlands company's interest income is offset by interest expense. Usually, there is a spread of one-eighth of a per cent between income and expense. Although Netherlands tax is 48%, this is usually not material. Dividends received by a Netherlands company are not taxable if a "participation exemption" is received under Article Thirteen of the Dutch Corporate Income Tax Act. The Dutch company must be shown to be performing a function which is essential to the overall group of companies. Advance rulings are obtainable.

4. The Netherlands company's interest expense and dividends are not subject to withholding tax when paid to an Antilles company.

5. Interest income received by an Antilles company is only subject to a 3% tax.

6. No withholding tax is eligible under Antilles law on interest and dividends paid to the Canadian company.

It is my understanding, at the present time, that the cost to set up such an arrangement is between $10,000 and $15,000. I also understand that the *annual* cost to maintain this framework is approximately the same. Thus, it is not a suitable structure if your only investment in the U.S. is a single-family condominium dwelling. On the other hand, if U.S. holdings and taxable income are extensive, an arrangement such as the one depicted above may be worthwhile. Needless to say, professional advice is mandatory before going ahead with such a corporate grouping.

U.S. Rules for Principal Residences

The U.S. tax rules for principal residences are not nearly as generous as those in Canada. The United States provides a rollover on the sale of a principal residence as long as proceeds from the sale are reinvested within eighteen months to acquire another principal residence. Only one principal residence may be owned between husband and wife at any given time. There is a one-time exclusion of gains, but this applies only after age fifty-five and where a principal residence had been used as such for at least three years within the preceding five years. The dollar limitation on this exclusion is $100,000 per married couple. By way of contrast, as we saw in Chapter Nine, the Canadian rules provide for an unlimited exclusion of gains and there are no age limitations. Furthermore, in Canada husband and wife are each allowed a principal residence.

Conclusion

Choosing a method for Canadians to hold U.S. real-estate is an extremely complex decision. For summary purposes, the following table suggests some general structures. Unfortunately, given the complexity of both U.S. and Canadian tax laws as well as the introduction of a new Canada–U.S. Income Tax Treaty and the new Foreign Investment in Real Property Tax Act, extreme caution will generally be required.

SUMMARY TABLE FOR U.S. REAL-ESTATE ACTIVITIES OF CANADIAN INVESTORS.

Type of Property	Suggested Structure
Single-family condominium owned for personal purposes or for a combination of personal use and rentals	Direct ownership if value is small. Otherwise, through a Canadian corporation
Real-estate development projects with soft-cost benefits	Ownership by the Canadian taxpayer who requires tax shelter—followed by an eventual rollover to a Canadian corporation if the project is initially owned by an individual
Acquisitions of previously developed property	Ownership by a U.S. subsidiary of a Canadian parent corporation
Raw land held for resale	Ownership by a U.S. subsidiary of a Canadian parent corporation

CHAPTER FOURTEEN

Creative Financing Can Make All the Difference

Throughout this book, I have suggested that you should consider acquiring as much real estate as you can using as little of your own savings as possible. In many cases, you may be able to borrow against your earnings from other sources for your downpayment. This concept is known as leverage. It is the art of using someone else's money. If your venture turns out to be profitable, the less you invest, the more you make.

For example, if you buy property for $100,000 and sell it later on for $120,000 (net of commission and other expenses) your profit is, of course, $20,000. The smaller your cash investment, however, the greater your pre-tax return. Examine the following schedule and you will see what I mean.

PROPERTY IS BOUGHT FOR $100,000 AND IS SOLD FOR $120,000
(NET OF COMMISSION)

Cash Investment	Pre-Tax Return on Cash Investment
$20,000	100%
25,000	80%
30,000	66%
35,000	57%
40,000	50%

While pre-tax returns of between 50% and 100% on cash investments look extremely attractive to the point that our collective mouths water with greed, you should note that the longer it takes to realize your profit, the less attractive your return becomes. Moreover, even if you sell your property shortly after buying it, you will likely be forced to pay taxes on all your profit as opposed to getting the more favourable capital gains treatment.

Also, note that the longer you hold property, the more expensive it is to carry. At today's interest rates, you will probably require a 30%–40% cash investment just to break-even.

Negative Cash Flow

As I have mentioned often in this book, you don't necessarily have to tie up a substantial sum of your own capital—if you are prepared to finance your investment very heavily and accept a negative cash flow. The impact of holding property which does not carry itself may not be overly foreboding when you take into account the tax deductibility of your rental loss. I don't, however, wish to convey an erroneous impression. While a negative cash flow may be acceptable, it is certainly not an ideal to strive for—especially over a long term. Eventually (and perhaps as soon as possible) the owner of property would like to see his investment begin to support itself and the object of the game is to eliminate any cash deficiencies as quickly as possible. Here is where "creative financing" enters the picture. In addition to understanding the real-estate market, or at least forming associations with professionals who have this knowledge, it is important for the investor and prospective investor to understand monetary concepts. You will be amazed to see what you can learn by simply spending a few hours playing with mortgage amortization schedules either alone or together with your accountant or real-estate agent.

Amortization

To amortize a loan is to extinguish it by means of payments over a period of time so that eventually the debt is reduced to zero. The most common amortization programs involve repayment schedules calling for identical monthly payments over the term of the borrowing with each payment consisting of a combination of both principal and interest. Initially, most of the payments are used to pay interest. However, as the principal amount of the debt decreases, more and more of the payments are used to reduce the capital amount.

This is illustrated in the example on page 258 which makes reference to a $10,000 loan at 18% interest compounded semi-annually over twenty-five years.

Initially, each payment is almost all interest. Over the years, however, each instalment will contain less interest and more principal. This is because the borrower only pays interest

25-YEAR $10,000 LOAN AT 18%, WITH INTEREST COMPOUNDED
SEMI-ANNUALLY.
MONTHLY PAYMENT—$146.64

Year	Payments Made $146.64 × 12	Interest	Principal
1	$1,760	$1,730	$ 30
5	$1,760	$1,710	$ 50
10	$1,760	$1,610	$ 150
15	$1,760	$1,420	$ 340
20	$1,760	$1,080	$ 680
25	$1,760 ·	$ 160	$1,600

on the outstanding principal balance of the loan at the time
each payment is made.

With rising interest rates, the only possible way to keep
monthly mortgage payments down is to lengthen the term over
which the loan is amortized. As you will see, there may be
some benefits, but there are also severe pitfalls.

For example, what if the twenty-five-year term on the
above $10,000 loan were extended to thirty, thirty-five, or
forty years? While the monthly payments would decline, the
borrower would find himself faced not only with a much
longer payout but also with a *significant additional debt*. This
is illustrated below.

AMORTIZATION OF $10,000 AT 18% OVER VARIOUS TIME PERIODS

10,000 at 18%	25 Years	30 Years	35 Years	40 Years
Monthly payment	$ 146.64	$ 145.50	$ 145.02	$ 144.82
Annual cost	1,759.68	1,746.00	1,740.24	1,737.84
Total cost	43,992.00	52,380.00	60,908.40	69,513.60
Total interest paid	33,992.00	42,380.00	50,908.40	59,513.60

Monthly payment over 25 years	$ 146.64
Monthly payment over 40 years	144.82
Difference	$ 1.82

Total interest over 40 years	$59,513.60
Total interest over 25 years	33,992.00
Difference	$25,521.60

The results of our analysis are somewhat mind-boggling. By spreading the debt over forty years instead of twenty-five years, there is a monthly saving of only $1.82 in the required mortgage payments. However, the borrower must not only bind himself to payments over an additional fifteen years but he is actually *increasing his debt* by $25,521.60!

Mortgage Acceleration Savings

While extending your debt obligation can, in the long run, be extremely costly, paying down your mortgage from time to time by making extra payments may be one of the best methods available to force yourself to save money. This is especially important planning in conjunction with a principal residence where the interest is non-deductible. Most mortgage contracts today will allow a borrower to repay up to 10% of the original amount of the debt each year as a special principal repayment.

The following schedule shows the principal balance outstanding on a loan of $10,000 at the end of each year for twenty-five years where the interest rate is 18%. At the end of year one, the principal balance outstanding is $9,970, while at the end of year twelve it is $9,060. Therefore, if the borrower were to repay $910 on the first anniversary of the mortgage, he would thus be eliminating *one-half* of the *total* annual

BALANCE OUTSTANDING ON A LOAN OF $10,000 AT 18% (ROUNDED TO NEAREST $10).
MONTHLY PAYMENT $146.64

End of Year	Amount	End of Year	Amount	End of Year	Amount
1	$9,970	9	$9,490	17	$7,580
2	9,940	10	9,370	18	7,100
3	9,910	11	9,230	19	6,530
4	9,860	12	9,060	20	5,850
5	9,810	13	8,860	21	5,050
6	9,750	14	8,610	22	4,090
7	9,680	15	8,330	23	2,960
8	9,600	16	7,990	24	1,600
				25	0

payments which he would otherwise have to make. In other words, if his monthly payments stay the same (which they would) and he makes *no further* special payments against principal, his debt would be completely extinguished only thirteen years later. Given a special payment of $910 at the end of the first year, he would then only owe $8,860 at the end of the year two, $8,610 after year three, and so forth. Of course, if additional principal payments were made at the end of the second year (and subsequently) the debt would be eliminated that much more quickly.

The Mortgage Term

You must always be careful never to confuse the *amortization* of a loan with its *term*. If you are told that a mortgage is to be amortized over twenty-five years, you must not assume that is has a twenty-five-year term. The term of a mortgage is the period of time which is given to a borrower before the lender can demand the principal balance owing on the loan. Until a few years ago, lenders did in fact make loans for long periods of time, such as twenty-five years, at fixed rates of interest. Today, however, mortgage terms rarely exceed five years. Thus, although the amortization schedule may reflect the payments necessary to discharge a debt over twenty-five years, the borrower, in most cases, must still repay the principal balance at the end of five years. Of course, the lender will usually renew the mortgage—at current prevailing rates. (Today, even three-year and one-year term mortgages are becoming more and more common.)

Again, examine the schedule on page 259. If payments of $146.64 are made monthly over twenty-five years, a loan of $10,000 at 18% would be extinguished. However, here is the problem. At the end of five years, the lender will want his money and, on a twenty-five-year loan, you will still owe him $9,810. To repay the loan you would probably have to commit yourself to another mortgage and borrow $9,800 (in round numbers). Assume that the new mortgage is for a further five-year period at the same rate and also with payments calculated to amortize over a twenty-five-year period. This is what your outstanding balance will be over the subsequent five years in round figures:

BALANCE OUTSTANDING ON A LOAN OF $9,800 AT 18%
(25-YEAR AMORTIZATION).

End of
Year	Balance
1	$9,770
2	9,741
3	9,712
4	9,663
5	9,614

At the end of this second five-year period, when you have to repay the loan, you may repeat the process. Each new five-year term will result in smaller monthly payments because the principal amount at the start of each succeeding term will be less. However, instead of amortizing the loan down to zero over twenty-five years, it may take over one hundred years to discharge the loan completely. *The only way a twenty-five year mortgage can be paid off in full over twenty-five years is to arrange to have the principal balance owing amortized each time a mortgage is renewed for a period which is not longer than the remaining number of years in the original amortization.*

I do not, however, wish to scare you. While the compounding effect of interest can be somewhat disconcerting, keep in mind the appreciation factor. Presumably, your property's growth will also be compounding over an extended period of time.

I have already recommended that your financing for a principal residence be paid off as soon as possible. This is because of the non-deductibility of interest. On the other hand, the need to discharge a debt obligation quickly may not be as important when it comes to investment property. This is especially true if your mortgage payments are covered by rentals.

Borrowing Money from Private Sources

With today's high cost of residential housing, more and more young people are finding it difficult to acquire their homes without some sort of family subsidy. Perhaps you may be fortunate to have a "rich relative" who would be willing to lend you money. First of all, your relative would probably be earning slightly less on his capital if it is in term deposits than you would have to pay if you were to approach a lending institution. Perhaps your benefactor might be persuaded to pass this difference on to you. In other words, if he is receiving 15% interest on a term deposit, he may be willing to accept a similar rate on a private loan secured by your residence. Moreover, he may also be willing to allow you to pay interest only until your income increases sufficiently for you to start discharging principal. In many cases, a private lender is quite content with an interest yield on his capital only. He does not necessarily *want* to receive blended payments of capital and interest. For him, there is the satisfaction of keeping his capital intact and not having to worry about reinvesting small payments of principal which he receives from you from time to time.

Sometimes, people will take advantage of the fact that interest income is taxable while the corresponding expense is not deductible when funds are borrowed for personal purposes. For example, if an individual in a 50% bracket is earning interest at 15%, he is only netting 7½% after taxes. That same individual might be willing to lend money to a friend or relative at only 8% or 9% to assist the latter in buying a house, provided his interest is paid to him in *cash*. Often, the borrower won't object to such an arrangement because he will pay a substantially lower rate and he can't deduct his payments anyway. Thus, the borrower pays approximately only half of the prevailing mortgage rate, while the lender ends up keeping more than what he otherwise would have retained, had he received "conventional" taxable interest.

Of course, any practice involving undeclared income is fraudulent and the reader is cautioned to stay away from such an arrangement!

Where Do I Go From Here?

If you are a novice just entering the real-estate market, I cannot caution you strongly enough how important it is to seek professional advice and exercise prudence. Lack of familiarity with a particular type of project or with property situated in a specific area can create a tremendous pitfall.

Last year, a real-estate agent approached me with what he thought was a "super deal". The investment involved an apartment building in Dallas, Texas, which he told me could be acquired for only six times annual rents. On the surface, this appeared to be a tremendous bargain—especially in relation to Calgary real-estate prices, which at the time of writing, appear to be about ten or eleven times gross rents. When I investigated further, however, I found out that the entire apartment complex had only one meter for electricity thereby making the landlord completely responsible for all heating and air-conditioning costs.

Because of these circumstances, it is no wonder that the asking price for the property was so cheap. Look at the exposure. What if each tenant were given a one- or two-year lease at a fixed rent and suddenly the cost of electricity rose dramatically? The landlord would then find himself in the unenviable position of having to absorb the entire increase himself! This is because the common commercial practice of passing on operating cost increases to tenants is still not common in residential real estate. I later found out from other sources that this particular property had been sitting on the market for well over two years with no takers. A lower price does not necessarily mean a good investment.

Special Opportunities

In many parts of the country, apartment builders are looking towards older areas to acquire run-down properties which may then be demolished and rebuilt. In some cases, the inhabitants of such an area are senior citizens who might find it to their advantage to sell. While, on the surface, it may appear that I am suggesting that you exploit the elderly, this is really not the case. In many circumstances, the owners might be better off spending their declining years in a luxurious apartment, with money in the bank, rather than in a run-down home. You must realize that the concept of saving capital for the future eventually ceases to be important and the time comes for each of us to realize the benefits from what we already have accumulated.

Last summer, I was approached for some advice by an elderly couple in their early seventies who were living on an acreage south of Calgary. They owned some sixty acres of land adjacent to their home and had just received an offer of $3,000 per acre for their property. The purchaser was a developer who had already acquired all the surrounding land for the purpose of building a golf course and wanted this particular parcel for future development. It appears that his intention was to eventually subdivide the sixty acres and build luxury homes near the golfing facility. I pointed out to my clients that, five years later, their sixty acres could then consist of ten or fifteen separate parcels worth perhaps $70,000 each to golf enthusiasts who would pay handsomely for the right to live on top of a golf course. I suggested that, from a dollars and cents standpoint, a sale of property for $180,000 is illogical if the value five years later could possibly be between $700,000 and $1,000,000.

My clients pointed out, however, that they weren't getting any younger. They felt that they would rather have some cash to augment their retirement incomes and to allow them to do a little travelling *now* instead of five years later as they each approached age eighty. In their circumstances, these arguments made sense. The developer got a tremendous bargain but my clients' needs were met as well.

Perhaps you can learn something from this story. Sometimes you can take advantage of certain circumstances and obtain a real bonanza. Even if you yourself are not a developer, you might consider acquiring one or two older properties and holding on to them. Eventually, a developer may come to you. If this happens, you can either sell or enter into a joint venture agreement with soft-cost tax benefits such as I described on pages 91 to 95. Everyone can come out ahead.

Farm Land vs. City Land

For many readers, farm land might be one of the most interesting types of acquisitions in today's market. Transactions involving farm land are somewhat anonymous from the point of view that you really don't hear too much about them. However, farm land transactions are happening constantly. Many people are buying farm land for retirement purposes and as long-term investments. Often they get somebody to work the land and, in turn, share in the profits from the sale of crops. Others are acquiring such property in small acreages in the hope that they will be able to subdivide it into residential lots and turn a profit. Corporations are buying whole sections of land and sitting on them for many years in anticipation of expansion and annexation by larger municipalities. There are even maps provided by many municipal districts as to the size of various lands and their owners. Surprisingly, you will see many big developers appearing on the titles who are holding property for future residential, commercial and community expansions.

If you wish to enter this market, however, you must be able to have the staying power to be able to carry your property until your expectations are realized. This is especially difficult since expenses incurred in conjunction with vacant land are not deductible. The major advantage, however, is that even a small investor *can get involved*.

Education vs. Implementation

The main thing, I think, is to get started. It is fine to read books on how to do different things and to expand one's knowledge. But education without implementation is largely a waste. You have all heard friends and relatives, especially older ones, reminisce as to how they "could have" bought this property or that property and how they might have made all kinds of money. But they didn't.

Don't make the same mistake. If you find the idea of real-estate investment attractive, get involved now!